CHAPTERS

FROM THE

BIBLE OF THE AGES

"Slowly the Bible of the race is writ;
Each age, each kindred adds a verse to it,
Texts of despair or hope, of joy or moan.
While swings the sea, while mists the mountains shroud,
While thunder's surges burst on cliffs of cloud,
Still at the prophets' feet the nations sit."
—J. R. Lowell.

"We have but part of our Holy Bible. The time will come when, as in the Middle Ages, all pious books shall be called *Scripturæ Sacra*—Sacred Scriptures."—T. W. Higginson.

Compiled and Edited by

G. B. STEBBINS.

DETROIT, MICHIGAN:

PUBLISHED BY THE EDITOR.

1872.

Entered according to Act of Congress in the year 1872, by
GILES B. STEBBINS,
In the Office of the Librarian of Congress, at Washington.

PRINTED BY
THE DAILY POST COMPANY,
DETROIT, MICH.

WOOD & RAND, Electrotypers, } DETROIT, MICH. { WILLIAM SUCKERT, Binder.

TO THE GROWING MULTITUDE

OF THOUGHTFUL MEN AND WOMEN,

WHO BELIEVE THAT "THE WORD OF GOD IS NOT BOUND" BY ANY LIMITATIONS OF BOOK, OR RACE, OR TIME, OR RELIGIOUS SYSTEMS,

THIS COMPILATION,

FROM THE TEACHINGS AND INSPIRATIONS OF MANY CENTURIES,

AND OF DIFFERENT PEOPLES,

IS RESPECTFULLY DEDICATED.

INDEX.

CHAPTER I.—HINDOSTAN BRAHMINISM.

CHAPTER II.—BUDDHISM.

CHAPTER III.—CHINA.

CHAPTER IV.—PERSIA.

CHAPTER V.—EGYPT.

CHAPTER VI.—HEBREW.

CHAPTER VII.—GREECE.

CHAPTER VIII.—ROME.

CHAPTER IX.—NEW TESTAMENT.

CHAPTER X.—AL KORAN.

CHAPTER XI.—EUROPE.

CHAPTER XII.—GREAT BRITAIN.

CHAPTER XIII.—SYMPATHY OF RELIGIONS.

CHAPTER XIV.—AMERICA.

PREFACE.

THE title of this book bespeaks its aim and scope. For years I have felt the need and importance of such a work, and have waited for abler hands to undertake it on a larger scale; but the people want, and should not wait. After no small labor and care in research and selection, I send this out, to meet in some degree a pressing popular want, and to help, as an incentive, to the more comprehensive work which a fit company of ripe and large-hearted scholars should unite to prepare. Our Bible, as read in the churches and in our homes, is but the record of Hebrew thought and life, and myth; in part fragmentary, inconsistent and imperfect, yet all to be accepted as true and miraculously infallible,—whether Reason, Conscience and Intuition consent or not,—according to a strange theory of theology that God made these supernatural revelations only to this people for a certain time and then ceased.

The Bible of the Ages is the deepest thought, the highest inspiration, the clearest spiritual light and life of the whole human race, constantly being lived and written, and to be read with free and open mind, and the hopeful thought that richer chapters are yet to come, for us and for those who may live after us; since truth and inspiration are the heritage of humanity, correlated, evolved, and developed into higher harmony and perfectness by spiritual laws, which are the Divine Intent, or "the will of God."

Keeping in mind our need of the experiences and aspirations, not only of the Hebrews, but of all humanity, my effort has been to select some of the best thoughts from different races and ages. Full statements of systems of religion or philosophy cannot be given in these narrow limits, yet much of their vital and essential elements will be found, gathered from "Sacred Books," from old philosophers, and from later teachers and seers and reformers. Of course but few are chosen from many equally valuable utterances, and whole nations are, of necessity, passed by, yet enough is offered to show the narrowness and absurdity of our traditional and theological education, that only one book called *the* Bible is divinely inspired, and must therefore be the master of the soul. This education is losing its power, and we want a broader outlook,

> "To seek for Truth, wherever found,
> On Christian, or on Heathen ground."

These rich Chapters are gathered from this broader field, and will show that truth is not partial or limited, but fluent, penetrative and universal, growing, *from within*, with the growth of humanity.

Inspiration—the in-breathing of truth—is for all receptive souls, all golden temperaments, all wise and earnest seekers for light and strength who strive to know and obey the laws by which they may win such rich reward. Hindoo, and Persian and Greek, and American, have spoken words noble as the best of Hebrews, and their sayings are mingled with truth and error even as are those of the Prophets and Apostles of Judea.

From the simple beauty of the Vedas, and the wise and wondrous insight of Buddha, to the noble words of men and women of this generation, we shall find proof enough of this in these chapters, and ample proof too of the unity and fraternity of ideas, the identity of radical elements and underlying principles, constituting that Sympathy of all Religions which bigotry and superstition have hidden from our sight, and which the jar and jangle of theological disputes have well-nigh banished from our thoughts. If read with open mind and firm resolve, while proving all things to hold fast only that which is good, they must help to more impartial judgment, to freedom from arbitrary authority in matters of opinion, and to that hopeful and earnest courage which helps to a better future.

I have aimed to use only the best and most authentic and acknowledged authorities, especially in quoting from the older and more obscure writings.

I am fortunately able to obtain some valuable translations of Talmudic and Rabbinical writings, from Rabbi Lilienthal, of Cincinnati, and Rabbi E. B. M. Browne, of Evansville, Indiana. In an Appendix will be found authorities, dates, and such brief explanations as are indispensable.

While the selections from ancient writings are of signal value and interest, the sweet and noble utterances and aspirations of later days, the great lessons of science, and the teachings in our own time and country, on vital questions and opinions which we must meet and use wisely for our better future, justly claim a good share of space. These later teachings will show that, if there has been an "eclipse of faith" in creeds and dogmas, there is an increase of rational knowledge, of intuition, and of spiritual power and freedom, making true the words of the poet:

"For I doubt not through the Ages
One increasing purpose runs,
And the thoughts of men are widened
With the process of the suns."

GILES B. STEBBINS.

DETROIT, MICHIGAN,
May, 1872.

CHAPTER I.

HINDOSTAN.—BRAHMINISM.

FROM THE RIG VEDA.*

God the Creator.

1. Who is the God to whom we shall offer our sacrifice?

2. He who gives life. He who gives strength; whose command all the bright gods revere; whose shadow is immortality, whose shadow is death. Who is the God to whom we shall offer our sacrifice?

3. He who, through his power, is the one King of the breathing and awakening world. He who governs all, man and beasts. Who is the God to whom we shall offer our sacrifice?

4. He whose greatness these snowy mountains, the sea, and the distant river proclaim. He, whose these regions are, as it were, His two arms. Who is the God to whom we shall offer our sacrifice?

5. He through whom the sky is bright and the earth firm, He through whom the highest heaven was established—He who measures out the light in the air. Who is the God to whom we shall offer our sacrifice?

6. He to whom heaven and earth, standing firm by His will, look up, trembling inwardly—He over whom the rising sun shines forth.

* For date of Vedas, translators' names, and explanations, see Appendix A.

7. Wherever the mighty water-clouds went, where they placed the seed and lit the fire, thence arose He who is the sole light of the bright gods. Who is the God to whom we may offer our sacrifice?

8. He who by His might looked even over the water-clouds, the clouds which gave strength and lit the sacrifices; He alone who is God above all gods.

May He not destroy us. He the creator of the earth; or He the righteous, who created the heavens; He who created the bright and mighty waters.

Hymn to Indra.

1. Keep silence, well! We offer praises to the great Indra, in the house of the sacrificer. Does he find treasure for those who are like sleepers? Mean praise is not valued by the omnipresent.

2. Thou art the giver of horses, Indra, thou art the giver of cows, the giver of corn, the strong Lord of wealth; the old guide of man, disappointing no desires, a friend to friends: to him we address this song.

3. O, powerful Indra, achiever of many works, most brilliant god—all this wealth s known ,o be thine alone; take from it, conqueror, bring it nither! lo not stint the desire of the worshipper who longs for thee!

4. On these days thou art gracious, and on these nights, keeping off the enemy from our cows and rom our stud. Tearing the fiend night after night with the help of Indra, let us rejoice in food, freed from haters.

5. Let us rejoice, Indra, in the treasure and food, in wealth of manifold delight and splendor. Let us rejoice in the blessing of the gods, which gives us the strength of offspring, gives us cows first, and horses.

6. The draughts inspired thee, O Lord of the brave! these were vigor; these libations in battles, when for the sake of the

poet, the sacrificer, thou strikest down irresistibly ten thousand enemies.

7. From battle to battle thou advancest bravely, from town to town thou destroyest all this with might, when thou Indra, with Nami as thy friend, struckest down from afar the deceiver Namuki.

8. Thou hast slain Karnaga and Parnaya with the brightest spear of Atithigon. Without a helper thou didst demolish the hundred cities of Vangrida, which were besieged by Rigisvan.

* * * * * *

11. We who in future, protected by the gods, wish to be thy most blessed friends, we praise thee; blessed by thee with offspring and enjoying henceforth a longer life.

Hymn to Agni.

1. Agni, accept this log which I offer to thee, accept this my service; listen well to these my songs.

2. With this, O Agni, may we worship thee, thou son of strength, conqueror of horses! and with this hymn, thou high-born!

3. May we thy servants serve thee with songs, O granter of riches, who lovest songs and delightest in riches.

4. Thou Lord and giver of wealth, be thou wise and powerful; drive away from us the enemies!

5. He gives us rain from heaven, he gives us inviolable strength, he gives us food a thousand fold.

6. Youngest of the gods, their messenger, their invoker, most deserving of worship, come, at our praise, to him who worships thee and longs for thy help.

7. For thou, O sage, goest wisely between these two creations (heavens and earth, gods and men), like a friendly messenger between two hamlets.

8. Thou art wise, and thou hast been pleased perform, thou intelligent Agni, the sacrifice without interruption. Sit down on this sacred grass!

Hymn to Ushas—The Dawn.

1. She shines upon us like a young wife, rousing every living thing to do his work. When the fire had to be kindled by men, she made the light by striking down the darkness.

2. She rose up, spreading far and wide and moving everywhere. She grew in brightness, wearing her brilliant garment. The mother of the cows, the leader of the days. She shone gold-colored, lovely to behold.

3. She, the fortunate, who brings the eye of the gods, who leads the white and lovely steed (of the sun), The Dawn was seen revealed by her rays, with brilliant treasures following every one.

4. Thou art a blessing where thou art near, drive far away the unfriendly; make the pastures wide, give us safety! Scatter the enemy, bring riches! Raise up wealth to the worshipper, thou mighty Dawn!

5. Shine for us with thy best rays, thou bright Dawn, thou who lengthenest our life, thou the love of all, who givest us food, who givest us wealth in cows, horses and chariots.

Questions on the First Cause.

Nor Aught nor Naught existed; yon bright sky
Was not, nor heaven's broad woof outstretched above.
What covered all? what sheltered? what concealed?
Was it the water's fathomless abyss?
There was not death, yet there was naught immortal,
There was no confine betwixt day and night;
The only One breathed breathless by itself,
Other than It there nothing since has been.
Darkness there was, and all at first was veiled
In gloom profound—an ocean without light.
The germ that still lay covered in the husk
Burst forth, one nature, from the fervent heat.
Then first came love upon it, the new spring
Of mind—yea, poets in their hearts discerned,

Pondering, this bond between created things
And uncreated. Comes this spark from earth,
Piercing and all-pervading, or from heaven?
Then seeds were sown, and mighty power arose—
Nature below, and Power and Will above,—
Who knows the secret? who proclaimed it here,
Whence, whence this manifold creation sprang?
The gods themselves came later into being,—
Who knows from whence this great creation sprang?
He from whom all this great creation came,
Whether his will created, or was mute,
The Most High Seer that is in highest heaven,
He knows it—or perchance even He knows not.

IMMORTALITY AND RESPONSIBILITY.

Extracts from different parts:

He who gives alms goes to the highest place in heaven; he goes to the gods.

The kind mortal is greater than the great in heaven.

Where there is eternal light, in the world where the sun is placed, in that immortal, imperishable world, place me, O Soma!

Where life is free, in the third heaven of heavens, where the worlds are radiant, there make me immortal!

Where wishes and desires are—where the bowl of the bright Soma is, where there is food and rejoicing, there make me immortal!

Where there is happiness and delight, where joy and pleasure reside, where the desires of our desire are attained, there make me immortal!

His path is easy, and without thorns, who does what is right.

Let man fear Him who holds the four dice, before He throws them down (God who holds men's destinies in his hand); let no man delight in evil words.

Prayer For Mercy and Repentance.

1. Let me not yet, O Varuna, enter into the house of clay; have mercy, almighty, have mercy!

2. If we go along trembling, like a cloud driven by the wind, have mercy, almighty, have mercy.

5. Whenever we, O, Varuna, commit an offense against the heavenly host, whenever we break the law through thoughtlessness, punish us not O God, for that offence.

(Or other hymns as follows :)

Was it an old sin, O Varuna, that thou wishest to destroy thy friend who always praises thee?

Tell me, thou unconquerable lord, and I will quickly turn unto thee with praise, freed from sin.

Absolve us from the sins of our fathers, and from those we have committed with our own bodies. Release Vasishtha, O, King, like a thief who has feasted on stolen oxen; release him like a calf from the rope.

It was not our doing, O Varuna! it was necessity (or temptation), an intoxicating draught, passion, dice, thoughtlessness. The old is then to mislead the young; even sleep brings unrighteousness.

Let me without sin, give satisfaction to the angry god, like a slave to his bounteous lord.

The lord god enlighteneth the foolish; he the wisest, leads his worshippers to wealth.

Sun and moon go on in regular succession, that we may see Indra and believe.

Thou Indra never findest a rich man to be thy friend; wine-swillers despise thee. But when thou thunderest, when thou gatherest the clouds, then thou art called like a father.

Hymn to Varuna.

1. However we break thy laws from day to day, men as we are, O Varuna!

2. Do not deliver us unto death, nor to the blows of the furious, nor to the wrath of the spiteful!

3. To propitiate thee we unbend thy mind with songs, as the charioteer a weary steed.

* * * * * * *

7. He who knows the place of the birds, who knows the ships on the waters.

8. He, the upholder of order, who knows the twelve months with the offspring of each. * * He, the wise, sits down among his people to govern. * * He sees what has been, and what will be done.

Yearning for Him, the far-seeing, my thoughts move onward, as kine move to their pastures.

Hymn to Agni.

1. Agni, who art immortal, and cognizant of all begotten things, bring from the dawn to the donor of the oblation wealth of many sorts, with an excellent habitation; bring hither to-day the gods, awaking with the morning.

2. For thou, Agni, art the accepted messenger of the gods, the bearer of oblations, the vehicle of sacrifices.

3. We select to-day, Agni, the messenger, the giver of dwellings, the beloved of many, the smoke-bannered, the light-shedding, the protector of the worship of the worshipper at the break of day.

4. I praise Agni at the break of day, the best and youngest (of the gods), the guest (of man), the universally invoked, who is friendly to the man that offers (oblations), who knows all that are born, that he may go (to bring) the other divinities.

5. Agni, immortal sustainer of the universe, bearer of oblations, deserving of adoration, I will praise thee, who art exempt from death, the preserver, the sacrificer.

HYMN TO SOMA.

Accepting this our sacrifice, and this our praise, approach Soma, and be to us as the augmenter of our rite.

Acquainted with hymns, we elevate thee with praise. Do thou who art benignant approach.

The experienced sage commends the mortal who, through affection, divine Soma, praises thee.

Protect us from calumny; preserve us from sin; pleased with our service, be our friend.

May the milky juices flow around thee; may sacrificial offerings and vigor be concentrated in the destroyer of foes; and, being duly nourished, do thou provide, Soma, excellent viands in heaven for our immortality.

PRAYER IN AFFLICTION.

Where, Agni, is thy benevolence? What new being now possesses it? Heaven and earth be conscious of this (my affliction.)

Gods who are present in the three worlds, who abide in the light of the sun, where now is your truth? Where the ancient invocation (that I have addressed) to you? Heaven and earth be conscious of my affliction.

I am he who formerly recited your praise when the libation was poured out, yet sorrows assail me like a wolf a thirsty deer. The ribs of the well close around me like the rival wives of one husband; cares consume me, as a rat the weaver's thread.

FROM ATHARA VEDA.

Divine Omnipresence.

1. The great Lord of these worlds sees as if he were near. If a man thinks he is walking by stealth, the gods know it all.

2. If a man stands, or walks, or hides, if he goes to lie down or get up; what two people whisper together, King Varuna knows it—he is there as a third.

3. He who should flee far beyond the sky, even he would not be rid of Varuna, the King. His spies proceed from heaven towards this world; with thousand eyes they overlook this earth.

3. Varuna sees all this; what is between heaven and earth, and what is beyond. He has counted the twinkling of the eyes of men. As a player throws the dice he settles all things.

The Divine in Man.

They who know Brahman in man, they know the Highest. He who knows the Highest, and he who knows the lord of all creatures, and they who know the oldest Brahmana, they know the ground.

FROM SAMA VEDA.

Inspiration.

O Indra, do thou, entertaining for us the affection a father does for his son, bring to us wisdom; do thou, the object of worship to adoring multitudes, grant this sacrificial assembly of the gods, that we, the possessors of natural life, may *obtain divine illumination.*

Care and Power of Deity.

Do not, O Indra, cast us off; thou art the only source of our delight, and of that of thousands of immortal beings; thou art our protection, thy favor we must obtain.

O, thunderbolt-wielding Indra, were there an hundred heavens and earths, and a thousand suns, and any other supposable creatures, they could not contain thee; for thou encirclest heaven and earth.

Spirits of our Fathers.

O, Indra and Agni; the footless Morn is advancing, outstripping all the tribes of men, and even the Sun himself, with her silver tongue (bird-songs) and swift pace.

Come close to us, O Indra, bringing with thee aids resulting from sacrifices to the spirits of the departed. Come, O most felicitous divinity, with those happy beings to whom we, in a special manner, offer oblations.

Come, O, Great Father, *along with the spirits of our fathers.*

Indra, who watches over the thousands of human beings, the intelligence of the wise, the all-glorious, the performer of many religious acts, the mighty hero, who knows the dwelling of the Morn, and sends forth the purifying, life-giving, clear, earth-born waters.

Hymn to Agni.

I praise, in this sacrifice, with an enkindling voice, the enkindled Agni. I urge forward him who is himself pure, and the purifier of others, and stable as the pole. I worship with delight-inspiring hymns, the possessor of wisdom, the inviter of the gods, who is extolled by multitudes and without malice; the all-wise god, who is intimately acquainted with every living creature. O, Agni, gods and men have consecrated thee, age after age, as the herald of the gods, the immortal, the offerer of oblations, the preserver, the god who ought to be extolled, and have worshipped thee as the ever-wakeful, the all-pervading, and the lord of men.

O, Agni, who renderest glorious both worlds during the performance of our rites, thou goest backward and forward through the two worlds as the messenger of the gods; since therefore we apply ourselves to the sacred rites and sacred hymns, be thou manifested as the prosperer of the three habitable regions (of earth, air, and heaven.)

Prayer to the Triune Divinity.

May we, who propitiate the gods, arrive at the age laid down by the divinity with undiminished mental and bodily vigor.

May Indra, served with sacrificial viands, grant us prosperity. May the nourishing Sun, who knows all things, grant us prosperity.

May Tarkshya Rishi, the ring of whose chariot-wheel could not be cut, grant us prosperity. (O, triune divinity!) May Vrihuspati grant us prosperity. Triune divinity! grant us prosperity.

Vedas.*

Any place where the mind of man can be undisturbed, is suitable for the worship of the Supreme Being.

The vulgar look for their gods in water; the ignorant think they reside in wood, bricks, and stones; men of more extended knowledge seek them in celestial orbs; but wise men worship the Universal Soul.

There is one living and true God; everlasting, without parts or passion; of infinite power, wisdom, and goodness; the Maker and Preserver of all things.

* From Progress of Religious Ideas, by Mrs. L. M. Childs.

He overspreads all creatures. He is entirely Spirit, without the form either of a minute body, or an extended one, which is liable to impression or organization. He is the ruler of the intellect, self-existent, pure, perfect, omniscient, and omnipresent. He has from all eternity been assigning to all creatures their respective purposes. No vision can approach him, no language describe him, no intellectual power can comprehend him.

As a thousand rays emanate from one flame, thus do all souls emanate from The One Eternal Soul, and return to him.

The Supreme Soul dwells in the form of four-footed animals, and in another place he is full of glory. He lives in the form of the slave, he is smaller than the grain of barley. He is smallest of the small, and the greatest of the great; yet he is neither small nor great.

Without hand nor foot, he runs rapidly and grasps firmly; without eyes, he sees all; without ears, he hears all. He knows whatever can be known; but there is none who knows him. The wise call him the Great, Supreme, Pervading Spirit.

He who considers all beings as existing in the Supreme Spirit, and the Supreme Spirit as pervading all beings, cannot view with contempt any creature whatsoever.

This body, formed of bones, skin, and nerves, filled with fat and flesh, is a great evil, and without reality. It ought to perish. Of what use is it then for the soul to seek corporeal pleasures?

Through strict veracity, universal control of the mind and senses, abstinence from sexual indulgence, and ideas derived from spiritual teachers, man should approach God, who, full of glory and perfection, works in the heart, and to whom only votaries freed from passion and desire can approximate.

May this soul of mine, which is a ray of perfect wisdom, pure intellect, and permanent existence, which is the unextinguishable light fixed within created bodies, without which no good act is performed, be united by devout meditations with the Spirit supremely blest and supremely intelligent.

That All-pervading Spirit, which gives light to the visible sun, even the same in *kind* am I, though infinitely distant in *degree.* Let my soul return to the immortal Spirit of God, and then let my body return to dust.

By one Supreme Ruler is this universe pervaded; even every world in the whole circle of Nature. Enjoy pure delight, O man, by abandoning all thoughts of this perishable world; and covet not the wealth of any creature existing.

God, who is perfect wisdom and perfect happiness, is the final refuge of the man who has liberally bestowed his wealth, who has been firm in virtue, and who knows and adores the Great One.

The way to eternal beatitude is open to him who without omission speaketh truth.

If any one assumes the garb of the religious, without doing their works, he is not religious. Whatever garments he wears, if his works are pure, he belongs to the order of pure men. If he wears the dress of a penitent, and does not lead the life of a penitent, he belongs to the men of the world; but if he is in the world, and practices penitential works, he ought to be regarded as a penitent.

Saints wise and firm, exempt from passion, assured of the soul's divine origin, satisfied solely with the science of God, have seen God everywhere present with them, and after death have been absorbed in him.

To know that God *is*, and that *all* is God, this is the substance of the Vedas. When one attains to this, there is no more need of reading, or of works; they are but the bark, the straw, the envelope. No more need of them when one has the seed, the substance, the Creator. When one knows Him by science, he may abandon science, as the torch which has conducted him to the end.

FROM BHAGVAT GEETA.

IMMORTALITY.

Kreeshna to Arjoun:

I, myself, never *was not*, nor thou, nor all the princes of the earth; nor shall we ever cease *to be*. As the soul in this mortal frame findeth infancy, youth and old age; so, in some future frame will it find the like. One who is confirmed in this belief is not disturbed by anything that may come to pass. The sensibility of the faculties giveth heat and cold, pleasure and pain, which come and go, and are transient and inconstant. Bear them with patience, O Son of Bharat, for the wise man, whom these disturb not, is formed for immortality. * * *

As a man throweth away old garments, and putteth on new, even so the soul, having quitted its old mortal frames, entereth others which are new. The weapon divideth it not, the fire burneth it not, the water corrupteth it not, the wind drieth it not away; for it is indivisible, inconsumable, incorruptible; it is eternal, universal, permanent, immovable; it is invisible, inconceivable and unalterable; therefore, believing it to be thus, thou shouldst not grieve. * * *

Wise men, who have abandoned all thought of the fruit which is produced by their actions, are freed from the chains of birth, and go to the regions of eternal happiness.

INCARNATION.

Although I (Kreeshna) am not, in my nature, subject to birth or decay, and am lord of all created beings; yet having command over my own nature, I am made evident by my own power; and as often as there is a decline of virtue, and an insurrection of vice and injustice, in the world, I make myself evident; and thus I appear from age to age, for the preservation of the just, the destruction of the wicked, and the establishment of virtue.

Of Works, and a Recluse Life.

Arjoun: Thou speakest, O Kreeshna, of the forsaking of works, and again of performing them. Tell me which of the two is best.

Kreeshna: Both the desertion and the practice of works are equally the means of happiness; but of the two, the practice is to be distinguished above the desertion. The perpetual recluse, who neither longeth nor complaineth, is worthy to be known, free from duplicity, and happily freed from the bond of action.

Children only, and not the learned, speak of the speculative and practical doctrines as two. They are but one, for both obtain the self-same end. To be a Sanyássee (or recluse) without application, is to obtain pain and trouble; whilst the Monee, who is employed in the practice of his duty, presently obtaineth Brahm the Almighty. The man who, employed in the practice of works, is of a purified soul, a subdued spirit, and restrained passions, and whose soul is the universal soul, is not affected by so being (employed). * * *

The man who, performing the duties of life, and quitting all interest in them, placeth them upon Brahm, the Supreme, is not tainted by sin; but remaineth like the leaf of the lotus, unaffected by the waters. Practical men, who perform the offices of life but with their bodies, their minds, their understandings and their senses, and forsake the consequences for the purification of their souls, and, although employed, forsake the fruit of action, obtain infinite happiness; whilst the man who is unemployed, being attached to the fruit by the agent (active) desire, is in the bonds of confinement. The man who hath his passions in subjection, and with his mind forsaketh all works, his soul sitteth at rest in the nine-gate city of its abode (in his body), neither acting nor causing to act. *

The duties of a man's own particnlar calling, although not free from faults, are far preferable to the duty of another, let it be ever so well pursued.

A man by following the duties which are appointed by his birth, doeth no wrong. A man's own calling, with all its faults, ought not to be forsaken. Every undertaking is involved in its faults, as the fire in its smoke. * * * A man also being engaged in every work, if he put his trust in me alone shall, by my divine pleasure, obtain the eternal and incorruptible mansions of my abode.

The Brahm.

Those whose understandings are in the Deity, whose souls are in him, whose confidence is in him, are purified by wisdom from all their offenses, and go from whence they shall never return.

The learned behold Deity alike in the revered Brahmin, perfected in knowledge, in the ox, the elephant, the dog, and him who eateth the flesh of dogs. Those whose minds are fixed on this quality, gain eternity, even in this world. They put their trust in Brahm, the Eternal, because he is everywhere without fault.

The man who knoweth, and confideth in, Brahm, and whose steady mind is free from folly, should neither rejoice in prosperity, nor complain in adversity. Such an one, whose soul is fixed upon the study of Brahm, enjoyeth pleasure without decline. The enjoyments which proceed from the feelings are the wombs of future pain. The wise man, acquainted with the beginning and the end (or consequence) of things, delighteth not in these.

He who can bear up against the violence produced from lust and anger in this mortal life, is properly employed, and a happy man. The man happy in his heart, at rest in his mind, and enlightened within, is a Yogee, or one devoted to God, and of a godly spirit; and obtaineth the immaterial nature of Brahm, the Supreme. Such Rishis (Saints) as are purified from their offenses, freed from doubt, of subdued mind, and interested in the good of all mankind, obtain the incorporeal Brahm.

The incorporeal Brahm is prepared from the beginning, for such as are free from lust and anger, of humble minds and subdued spirits, and who are acquainted with their own souls.

BRAHM—THE UNIVERSAL SPIRIT.

I am the sacrifice; I am the worship; I am the spices; I am the invocation; I am the ceremony to the manes (spirits) of the ancestors; I am the provisions; I am the fire, and I am the victim; I am the father and mother of the world, the grandsire and preserver. I am the Holy One, worthy to be known; the mystic figure Aum; the Rig, the San, and Yajoor Veds.

I am the journey of the good; the comforter; the creator; the witness; the resting place; the asylum, and the friend. I am generation and dissolution, the place where all things are reposited, and the inexhaustible seed of all nature. I am sunshine, and I am rain; I now draw in and now let forth. I am death and immortality; I am entity and nonentity. * *

They who serve other gods, with a firm belief, in doing so involuntarily worshlp even me. I am he who partaketh of all worship, and I am their reward. * * *

I am the soul which standeth in the bodies of all beings. I am the beginning, the middle, and the end of all things. * * * I am among worships the silent worship, and amongst immovables the mountain Himmalaya. Of all science, I am the knowledge of the ruling spirit, and of all speaking, I am the oration. I am also never-failing time, the preserver, whose face is turned on all sides. I am all-grasping death, and I am the resurrection of those about to be. Among feminines I am fame, fortune, eloquence, memory, understanding, fortitude, patience. * * * I am the seed of all in nature, not anything animate or inanimate is without me. My divine distinctions are without end. * * * I planted this whole universe with a single portion (motion) and then stood still.

The Good Man—or Devotee.

Kreeshna said: He, my servant, is dear unto me, who is free from enmity, the friend of all nature, merciful, exempt from all pride and selfishness, the same in pain and pleasure, patient of wrong, contented, constantly devout, of subdued passions, and firm resolves, and whose mind and understanding are fixed on me alone. He also is my beloved of whom mankind are not afraid, and who is not afraid of mankind; and who is free from the influence of joy, impatience, and the dread of harm. He, my servant, is dear unto me who is unexpecting, just and pure, impartial, free from distraction of mind, and who hath forsaken every enterprise. He also is worthy of my love, who neither rejoiceth nor findeth fault; who neither lamenteth nor coveteth, and, being my servant, hath forsaken both good and evil fortune. He also is my beloved servant, who is the same in friendship and in hatred, in honor and in dishonor, in cold and heat, in pain and pleasure; who is unsolicitous about the event of things; to whom praise and blame are as one; who is of little speech, and pleased with whatever cometh to pass; who owneth no particular home, and who is of a steady mind.

Divine Destiny—Absorption in the Divine Nature.

Kreeshna said: The man born to divine destiny is endued with the following qualities: exemption from fear, a purity of heart, a constant attention to the discipline of his understanding; charity, self-restraint, religion, study, penance, rectitude, freedom from doing wrong, veracity, freedom from anger, resignation, temperance, freedom from slander, universal compassion, exemption from the desire of slaughter, mildness, modesty, discretion, dignity, patience, fortitude, chastity, unrevengefulness, and freedom from vain-glory: whilst those who come into life under the influence of the evil destiny, are distinguished by pride, hypocrisy, presumption, anger, harshness of speech, and ignorance. The divine destiny is for Moksh, or eternal absorption into the divine nature; and the evil destiny confineth the soul to mortal birth.

FROM CODE AND LAWS OF MENU.

MORAL DUTIES—THE SOUL ITS OWN WITNESS.

To patriarchs, to deities, and to mankind, the scripture is an eye giving constant light. The Veda Shastra could not be made by human faculties, nor can it be measured by human reason.

The birth which man derives from his parents is merely human; that which the Vedas procure for him is the true birth, exempt from age or death.

To a man contaminated by sensuality, neither the Vedas, nor liberality, nor sacrifices, nor strict observances, nor pious austerities, will produce felicity.

A wise man faithfully discharges all moral duties, even though he does not constantly perform the ceremonies of religion. He will fall very low if he performs ceremonies only, and fails to discharge his moral duties.

By honoring his father, mother, and sister, a man effectually does whatever ought to be done. This is the highest duty, and every other is subordinate. All duties are performed by him who completely honors these three; but to him by whom they are dishonored, all other acts are fruitless.

Whatever oblations a man, actuated by strong faith, piously offers, as the sacred laws have directed, become a perpetual, imperishable gratification to his ancestors in the other world.

He whose sins are mostly corporeal, will assume, after death, a vegetable or mineral form; for sins mostly verbal he will assume the form of bird or beast; for sins merely mental he will assume a human form, but in some of its lower conditions. An unauthorized teacher of the Sacred Books will return into a dumb body.

If a wife speak unkindly to her husband, she may be superseded by another, at once. A woman is never fit for independence.

The sacrifice required of Brahmins is to gain knowledge and instruct others; of the Cshatriyas, that they protect others; of the Vaisyas, that they supply the wants of commerce; of the Soodras, that they serve others.

Like a tree carried far from the river which saw its birth, like a bird that flies from the branch on which it rested, man ought to free himself from the body; for thus will he see himself delivered from the devouring monster of this world.

The soul itself is its own witness, and its own refuge. Offend not thy conscious soul, the supreme internal witness of men! Oh, friend to virtue! that Supreme Spirit which thou believest one and the same with thyself, resides in thy bosom perpetually, and is an all-knowing inspector of thy goodness, or wickedness.

The priest, baptising the child, says: "Little babe, thou enterest the world weeping, while all around thee smile. Mayest thou so live that thou mayest depart in smiles, while all around thee weep."

On Creation.

The universe existed in darkness imperceptible, undefinable, undiscoverable, and undiscovered; as if immersed in sleep.

Then the self-existing power, undiscovered himself, but making the world discernible with the five elements and other principles, appeared in undiminished glory dispelling the gloom.

He whom the mind alone can perceive, whose essence eludes the external organs, who has no visible parts, who exists from eternity, even he, *the soul of things*, shows forth in person.

He, having willed to produce various beings from his own divine substance, first created the waters, with a thought, and placed in them a productive seed.

The seed became an egg, bright as gold, blazing like the luminary with a thousand beams, and in that egg he was born himself, in the form of Brahma, the great forefather of all spirits.

The waters are called Nara, because they were the production of Nara, or the Spirit of God; and hence they were his first ayana, or place of motion; he hence is named Narayana, or moving of the waters.

In that egg the great power sat inactive a whole year of the creator, at the end of which, by his thought alone, he caused the egg to divide itself.

And from its two divisions he framed the heavens above, and the earth beneath; in the midst he placed the subtle ether, the eight regions, and the permanent receptacle of the waters.

From the Supreme Soul he drew forth mind, existing substantially, though unperceived by sense, immaterial; and before mind, or the reasoning power, he produced consciousness, the internal monitor, the ruler.

And before them both he produced the great principle of the soul, or first expansion of the divine idea; and all vital forms endued with the three qualities of goodness, passion, and darkness, and the five perceptions of sense, and the five organs of sensation.

That, having at once pervaded with emanations from the Supreme Spirit, the minutest portions of fixed principles immensely operative, consciousness, and the five perceptions, he formed all creatures.

Thence proceed the great elements, endued with peculiar powers, and mind with operations infinitely subtle, the imperishable cause of all apparent forms.

This universe, therefore, is compacted from the minute portions of those seven divine and active principles; the great soul or first emanation, consciousness, and five perceptions; *a mutable universe from immutable ideas.*

Of created things, the most excellent are those who are animated; of the animated, those which subsist by intelligence; of the intelligent, mankind; and of men, the sacerdotal class. Of priests, those eminent in learning; of the learned, those who know their duty; of those who know it, such as virtuously perform it; and of the virtuous, those who seek beatitude from a perfect acquaintance with scriptural doctrines.

* * * * *

Let every Brahman, with fixed attention, consider all nature as existing in the Divine Spirit; all worlds as seated in him; he alone as the whole assemblage of gods; and he as the author of all human actions.

Let him consider the Supreme omnipresent intelligence as the sovereign lord of the universe, by whom alone it exists, an incomprehensible spirit; pervading all beings in five elemental forms, and causing them to pass through birth, growth, and decay, and so revolve like the wheels of a car.

Thus, the man who perceives in his own soul the Supreme Soul present in all creatures, acquires equanimity toward them all, and shall be absolved at last in the highest essence, even that of the Almighty himself.

The only firm friend, who follows men even after death, is Justice; all others are extinct with the body.

Food, eaten constantly with respect, gives muscular force and generative power; but eaten irreverently, destroys them both.

Bodies are cleansed by water; the mind is purified by truth; the vital spirit, by theology and devotion; the understanding, by clear knowledge.

O friend to virtue, that supreme spirit—which thou believest one and the same with thyself—resides in thy bosom perpetually; and is an all-knowing *inspector* of thy goodness or of thy wickedness.

Justice, being destroyed, will destroy; being preserved,

will preserve; it must therefore never be violated. Beware, O judge, lest justice, being overturned, overturn both us and thyself.

Injustice, committed in this world, produces not fruit immediately, but, like the earth, in due season; and advancing by little and little, it eradicates the man who committed it.

Iniquity, once committed, fails not of producing fruit to him who wrought it; if not in his own person, yet in his sons; or, if not in his sons, yet in his grandsons.

He grows rich for a while through unrighteousness; but he perishes at length from his whole root upwards.

THE BRAHMO-SOMAJ—OR CHURCH OF THE TRUE GOD, A. D., 1870.

This modern church and reformation of Hinduism is based on no specifically revealed religion, but on the natural laws of the universe and the natural intuitions of the human soul. The Brahmo-Somaj has its origin, so far as its origin can be traced externally, forty years ago in the life and labors of Rammohun Roy. That great and noble man, convinced that the popular idolatries and superstitions of Hinduism did not belong to the real religion in its original form, established a little church in Calcutta for the simple worship of the Supreme Being, unencumbered by any of the prevalent beliefs and practices. He based this movement on the authority of the old Vedas, claiming, doubtless with truth, that their doctrines were pure theism. Yet he invited "all sorts and descriptions of people, without distinction," to join the movement, and tried to make it so catholic that all persons of monotheistic faith might be at home in it, whether they were Hindus, Mohammedans, Christians, or Jews. Practically, however, the church remained a Hindu Unitarian Church. But about twenty years ago this platform of the specific divine authority of the Vedas was abandoned, and the Brahmo-Somaj took for a basis of faith, "God's revelation in nature and the religious instincts of man." And there is where the the Brahmo-Somaj stands to-day. As its present great representative man, Keshub Chunder Sen, says, "It is an organized theistic church, Indian in its origin, but universal in its scope, which aims to destroy idolatry, superstition, and sectarianism, and propagate the saving truths of absolute religion, and the spiritual worship of the one true God, and likewise to promote the intellectual, moral, and social reformation of individuals and nations, and thus make theism the religion of life."

And since the day that the Bramo-Somaj took this stand on nature and the soul, it has made great advance. Two years ago it counted more than sixty churches in different parts of India, and the number has increased since that faster than before. Its adherents cannot be accurately reckoned in numbers, because they keep no regular record of membership; but it counts many thousands of members, and many Hindus of great influence, which is beginning to be felt in all the civil and social, as well as religious life of India. They have a most devout sense of religious consecration to their work, are self-sacrificing, heroic, and—though in a perfectly peaceful way—aggressive. They believe in actively propagating their faith, and the movement has something of the zealous missionary spirit in which Buddhism began. There is a fervor about them which reminds one of Methodism. Yet their faith is eminently practical, too. They are engaged in all good reforms; they are fighting vigorously against caste, and for civil, social, and religious equality; they are laboring for the education of woman; they are especially bent on removing the oppressive laws and traditions which forbid intermarriage between persons of different castes, and the re-marriage of widows; and generally they are alive to all good works of charity, philanthropy, and advancing civilization.

Now it would not be true to say that no part of this religious reformation is due to the influence of Christianity. The Bramo-Somaj itself confesses its indebtedness to the Christian religion. Its members are well acquainted with the

Hebrew and Christian Scriptures, and highly appreciate the character and teachings of Jesus. But this influence of Christianity has been indirect. The dogmas which the Christian missionaries have generally taught as Christianity, the members of the Brahmo-Somaj utterly reject. They deny that Christianity has any specific authority as a divine revelation above that of other religions, and of course do not call themselves Christians. They accept what is true in the Bible and in the teachings of Jesus, just as they accept what is true in the Vedas and in the prophets of India, because it commends itself to their reason and intuition, and not because any book or prophet has uttered it. In fact the Brahmo-Somaj, the product of many religious and social forces, is an excellent illustration of the historic method by which it seems altogether probable that the various religions of the earth are to affect and modify each other.

It is especially easy to trace in the teachings of the Brahmo-Somaj the influence of the liberal schools of theology in England, and of our own Theodore Parker. That stanch reformer, who struck such vigorous blows here in Boston, and whose body, burned out with the intensity of the life it carried, sank at its noon to rest in the beautiful soil of Italy, is now having his resurrection all round the globe. We hear of him not only through the United States and in England, but in all parts of Europe from Norway to Austria, in South America, in India, and even in such outlying regions of civilization as Australia and Southern Africa. He, at least, is one of the god-fathers of the Brahmo-Somaj.—*W. J. Potter, New Bedford, Mass.*

KESHUB CHUNDER SEN, a leading preacher of the Brahmo-Somaj, writes to his English friends, on his return from England to Hindostan, from Egypt, October, 1870, as follows:

"Indeed the world is moving onward to the consummation of that universal Church which owns no other creed except the Fatherhood of God and the Brotherhood of Man. The history of the past points to it—the present age demands it;

everywhere there are cheering indications of its dawning light. It is God's will that it should come. Let his will be done. Let us all unite to uprear his true Church. Let each nation come with all the elements of truth and goodness in its sacred history, and all that is pure and divine in its national life. No nation, no sect, ought to be excluded, for through each, God has spoken, and in each some form of truth is deposited in the flow of ages. Bring with you English brethren, your noble charities, your industry and earnestness, and your respect for science—that glorious and perpetual revelation of God to man. Come, liberal minded children of America, with your world of modern thought and civilization, and your youthful freshness of mind and soul. Come, all ye nations of the West, with all the riches of truth ye possess. But the circle is not yet complete. Let the nations of the East come, with their ancient civilization, their sublime devotion, fervent faith and deep spirituality; let them come with the precious inheritance of thought and sentiment bequeathed by their venerable ancestors. Let the East come clad in the golden robe of morning light. Then the circle of universal religion will be completed. Thus shall the Scriptures of science in the West, and the Scriptures of inspiration in the East, constitute together the Word of God. Thus shall the "mind and strength" of the one, and the 'heart and soul' of the other, join in the service of God. Thus shall the spirit of charity, which 'went about doing all manner of good,' and the spirit of devotion, which 'went to the mountains to pray,' blend together, and form the unity of divine life in man. Thus shall all sects and races and nations in the world unite to form the catholic church of God, limbs of one body supported by the same vitality, and doing the work of the same Master; a harp of many strings playing harmoniously, and with their blended notes making sweet music in praise of the Great Ruler."

CHAPTER II.

BUDDHISM.*

HINDOSTAN, BURMAH, CHINA, &c.

The Five Buddhist Commandments.

1. Not to destroy life.
2. Not to obtain another's property by unjust means.
3. Not to indulge the passions, so as to invade the legal or natural rights of other men.
4. Not to tell lies.
5. Not to partake of anything intoxicating.

Overcome Evil with Good.

Buddha said: *A man who foolishly does me wrong (or regards me as being or doing wrong), I will return to him the protection of my ungrudging love; the more evil goes from him, the more good shall go from me.* The fragrance of these good actions always redounding to me, the harm of the slanderer's words returning to him.

A foolish man once heard Buddha, in preaching, defend this great principle of returning good for evil, and therefore came and abused him. Buddha was silent, pitying his mad folly. The man having finished his abuse, Buddha said: "Son, when a man forgets the rules of politeness in making a present to another, the custom is to say: 'Keep your present.' Son! you have railed at me! I decline to entertain your abuse! and ask you to keep it, a source of misery to yourself. For, as sound belongs to the drum, and shadow to the sub-

* See Appendix B, for notes.

stance, so in the end misery will certainly overtake the evil doer.'"

Buddha said: A wicked man who reproaches a virtuous one, is like a man who looks up and spits at Heaven; the spittle soils not Heaven, but comes back and defiles his own person.

Again: He is like one who flings dirt at another against the wind—the dirt does but return on him who threw it. The virtuous man cannot be hurt—the misery that the other would inflict comes back on himself.

Who is a Good Man?

Buddha said: Who is the good man? The religious man only is good. And what is goodness? First and foremost, it is the agreement of the will with the conscience (reason). Who is the great man? He who is strongest in the exercise of patience, who patiently endures injury and maintains a blameless life; he is a man indeed! And who is a worshipful man (one deserving reverence, or a Buddha)? A man whose heart has arrived at the highest degree of enlightenment. All dust removed, all wicked actions uprooted, all within calm and pure, without blemish, who is acquainted with all things from first or last, and even with those things that have not yet transpired; who knows and sees and hears all things; such universal wisdom is rightly called "illumination."

Spiritual Culture—Illumination.

Buddha said: A man who cherishes lust and desire, and does not aim after supreme knowledge, is like a vase of dirty water, in which all sorts of beautiful objects are placed—the water being shaken up men can see nothing of the beautiful objects therein placed; so lust and desire, causing confusion and disorder in the heart, are like the mud in the water—they prevent our seeing the beauty of supreme reason (religion). But if a man, by the gradual process of confession and penance, comes near to the acquirement of knowledge, then, the mud in the water being removed, all is clear and pure; remove the pollution, and immediately, of itself, comes forth the substantial form. So the three poisons (covetousness, anger, delusion) which rage within the heart, and the five obscurities (envy, passion, sloth, vacillation, unbelief) which embrace it, effectually prevent one from attaining supreme reason. But once get rid of the pollution of the heart, and then we perceive the spiritual portion of ourselves, which we have had from the first, although involved in the net of life and death. Gladly then we mount to the Paradise of all the Buddhas, where reason and virtue continually abide.

A man who devotes himself to religion is like one who takes a lighted torch to a dark house; the darkness is dissipated! Persevere in the search after wisdom, and obtain knowledge and truth; error and delusion rooted out, what perfect illumination will there be!

In reflection, in life, in conversation, in study, I never for a moment forget the supreme end—Religion.

"Bodhi"—Supreme Reason.

Buddha said: The Shaman who has left his home, banished desire, expelled love, fathomed the bottom of his own heart, penetrated the deep principles of universal mind (Buddha); understood the principle that there is no subjective personal existence, or objective aim in life, or result to be obtained; whose heart is neither hampered by the practice of religion, or fettered by the bonds of life; without anxious thought, without active endeavor, without careful preparation, without successful accomplishment, attaining the highest possible point of true being, without passing through any successive and distinct stages of progress; this is indeed "to be religious" (or to attain or practice Bodhi, i. e., Supreme Reason).

Twenty Difficult Things.

Buddha said: There are twenty difficult things in the world: being poor, to be charitable; being rich and great, to be religious; to escape destiny; to get sight (or understanding) of the Scriptures; to be born when a Buddha is in the world; to repress lust and banish desire; to see an agreeable object and not seek to obtain it; to be strong without being rash (or, having power, not to be proud); to bear insult without anger; to move in the world without setting the heart on it; to investigate a matter to the very bottom; not to contemn the ignorant; thoroughly to extirpate self-esteem; to be good, and at the same time learned and clever (or sagacious); to see the hidden principles in the profession of Religion; to attain one's end without exultation; to show, in the right way, the doctrine of expediency to save men by converting them; to be the same in heart and life; to avoid controversy.

Illumination—Clairvoyance.

At this time Ananda and all the great congregation, gratefully attentive to the words of Buddha Tathagata, as he opened the abstruse points of his argument, their bodies and minds worn out with exertion, they obtained illumination. This great assembly perceived that each one's heart was co-extensive with the universe, seeing clearly the empty character of the universe as plainly as a leaf or trifling thing in the hand, and that all things in the universe are all alike, merely the excellently bright and primeval heart of Bodhi, and that this heart is universally diffused, and comprehends all things within itself.

And still reflecting, they beheld their generated bodies, as so many grains of dust in the wide expanse of the universal void, now safe, now lost; or as a bubble of the sea, sprung from nothing and born to be destroyed. But their perfect and independent soul not to be destroyed, but ever the same; identical with the substance of Buddha; incapable of increase or diminution. And thus, standing before Tathagata, they uttered these verses of commendation, in praise of his august presence :

O ! the mysterious depth, the all-embracing extent, the undisturbed and unmoved Majesty !

O ! that we now might obtain the fruit, and perfect the Royal Treasure (of Nirvana); and yet be the means of converting endless worlds of beings, and causing them to experience this same deep heart of gratitude through endless worlds !

Thus would we return the boundless love of Buddha, and so humbly seek the illuminating energy of the world. Honored, passing through the various worlds, we would rescue the countless beings yet immersed in sin, and in the end with them find rest.

Gathas, or Hymns of Buddhist Priests.

[From the Daily Manual of Shaman, in the Pratimoksha.]

On putting on the clothes :

Assuming this my upper robe,
I pray that every living soul,
Obtaining the most perfect principle,
May reach the other shore of life.

Assuming this my under robe,
I pray that every living soul,
Attaining every virtuous principle,
May perfect himself in true penitence.

On binding on my sash, I pray
That every living soul may closely bind
Each virtuous principle around himself.

On walking so as not to crush an insect, say :

As thus I walk upon my feet,
I pray that every living soul,
Emerging from the sea of life and death,
May soon attain the fulness of the Law.

On washing the face, say:

As thus I wash my face, I pray
That every living soul may gain
Religious knowledge, which admits
Of no defilement through eternity.

On bowing down before Buddha, say:

King of the Law, the most exalted Lord,
Unequalled through the three-fold world,
Teacher and guide of gods and men,
Our loving Father, and of all that breathes,
I bow myself in lowest reverence, and pray.

Sin and Repentance.

Doing what we ought not to do,
Not doing what we ought to do,
The fire of regretful sorrow which burns
In after ages (leads to) ruin and misery.
But if a man is able to repent of his sin,
And to complete his repentance, there is no more grief.
In this way the heart is restored to peace;
But repentance not fulfilled, there is the constant recollection of sin,
Whether of omission or commission,
And this is just the condition of the fool;
Not repenting with all his heart,
Not doing what he is able to do,
He completes the sum of his evil deeds,
And he cannot but do that which he ought not.

THE DHAMMAPADA—OR PATH OF VIRTUE.

By Buddha.

Thought.

All that we are is the result of what we have thought; it is founded on our thoughts, it is made up of our thoughts. If a man speaks or acts with an evil thought, pain follows him, as the wheel follows the foot of him who draws the carriage.

All that we are is the result of what we have thought; it is founded on our thoughts, it is made up of our thoughts. If a man speaks or acts with a pure thought, happiness follows him like a shadow that never leaves him.

As a fetcher makes straight his arrow, a wise man makes straight his trembling and unsteady thought, which is difficult to keep, difficult to turn.

Let the wise man guard his thoughts, for they are difficult to perceive, very artful, and rush wherever they list; thoughts well guarded bring happiness.

Those who bridle their mind, which travels far, moves about alone, is without a body, and hides in the chamber (of the heart), will be free from the bonds of Mara (the tempter).

He who lives looking for pleasure only, his senses uncontrolled, immoderate in his enjoyments, idle and weak, Mara (the tempter) will certainly overcome him, as the wind blows down a weak tree.

He who lives without looking for pleasures, his senses well controlled, his enjoyments moderate, who is faithful and strong, Mara will certainly not overcome him, any more than the wind overthrows a rocky mountain.

As rain breaks through an ill-thatched house, passion will break through an unreflecting mind.

As rain does not break through a well-thatched house, passion will not break through a well-reflecting mind.

The virtuous man delights in this world, and he delights in the next. He delights, he rejoices, when he sees the purity of his own work.

The evil doer suffers in this world, and he suffers in the next. He suffers when he thinks of the evil he has done; he suffers more when going in the evil path.

The thoughtless man, even if he can recite a large portion (of the law), but is not a doer of it, has no share in the priesthood, but is like a cowherd, counting the cows of others.

Hatred Ceases by Love

"He abused me, he beat me, he defeated me, he robbed me,"—hatred in those who harbor such thoughts will never cease.

"He abused me, he beat me, he defeated me, he robbed me,"—hatred in those who do not harbor [such?] thoughts will cease.

For hatred does not cease by hatred at any time—hatred ceases by love; this is an old rule.

On Reflection.

Reflection is the path to immortality, thoughtlessness the path to death. Those who reflect do not die, those who are thoughtless are as if dead already.

Those wise people, meditative, steady, always possessed of strong powers, attain to Nirvana, the highest happiness.

By rousing himself, by reflection, restraint, and control, the wise man makes for himself an island which no flood can overwhelm.

By earnestness did Maghavan (Indra) rise to the lordship of the gods. People praise earnestness; thoughtlessness is always blamed.

Knowing that this body is (fragile) like a jar, and making this thought firm like a fortress, one should attack Mara (the tempter) with the weapons of knowledge, one should watch him when conquered, and should never cease (from the fight).

Flowers.

He who knows that this body is like froth, and has learned that it is unsubstantial as a *mirage*, will break the flower-pointed arrow of Mara (the tempter), and never see the King of Death.

As the bee collects nectar and departs without injuring the flower, or its color or perfume, so let the sage dwell on earth.

Like a beautiful flower, full of color but without perfume, are the fine but fruitless words of him who does not accordingly; but like a beautiful flower, full of color and full of perfume, are the fruitful words of him who acts accordingly.

As on a heap of rubbish cast upon the highway, the lily will grow, full of sweet perfume and delightful, thus the disciple of the truly enlightened Buddha shines forth by his knowledge among those who are like rubbish, among the people that walk in darkness.

The Fool.

If a traveler does not meet with one who is his better or his equal, let him firmly keep his solitary journey; for there is no companionship with a fool.

If a fool be associated with a wise man all his life, he will perceive the truth as little as a spoon perceives the taste of soup; but if an intelligent man be associated with a wise man only for one minute, he will soon perceive the truth, as the tongue perceives the taste of soup.

As long as the evil deed done does not bear fruit, the fool thinks it is honey; but when it ripens the fool suffers grief.

The Venerable.

As a solid rock is not shaken by the wind, wise people falter not amidst praise or blame.

He whose passions are stilled, who is not absorbed in enjoyment, who has perceived the Void, the Unconditioned, the Absolute, his path is difficult to understand, like that of the birds in the ether.

The man who is free from credulity, but knows the Uncreated, who has cut all ties, removed all temptations, renounced all desires, he is the greatest of men. In a hamlet or a forest, in the deep water or on dry land, wherever venerable persons (Arahanta) dwell, that place is delightful.

Self-Conquest.

If one man conquer in battle a thousand times thousand men, and if another conquer himself, he is the greatest of conquerors.

One's own self conquered is better than all other people; not even a god, a Gandharva, not Mara with Brahman, could change into defeat the victory of a man who has vanquished himself and always lives under restraint.

If a man worship Agni (fire) for a hundred years in the forest, and if he pay homage for one moment to a man whose soul is grounded (in true knowledge), better is that homage than sacrifice for a hundred years.

He who lives a hundred years ignorant and unrestrained, a life of one day is better if a man is wise and reflecting; and he who lives a hundred years not seeing the immortal place, a life of one day is better if a man sees the immortal place.

He who lives a hundred years not seeing the highest law, a life of one day is better if a man see the highest law.

Not the failures of others, not their sins of commission or omission, but his own misdeeds and negligences, should the sage take notice of.

By oneself the evil is done, by oneself one suffers, by oneself evil is left undone, by oneself one is purified. Purity and impurity belong to oneself; no one can purify another.

Work out your own Salvation.

You yourself must make the effort. The Tathagatas (Buddhas) are only preachers. The thoughtful who enter the way are freed from the bondage of Mara.

Watching his speech, well restrained in mind, let a man never commit any wrong with his body! Let a man but keep these three roads to action clear, and he will achieve the way which is taught by the wise.

Through zeal knowledge is gotten, through lack of zeal

knowledge is lost; let a man who knows this double path of gain and loss thus place himself that knowledge may grow.

Cut out the love of self like an autumn lotus, with thy hand! Cherish the road to peace.

Reward of Holiness.

Better than sovereignty, better than going to heaven, better than lordship over all worlds, is the reward of the first step in holiness.

Kinsfolk, friends and lovers salute a man who has been long away and returns safe from afar. In like manner his good works receive him who had done good and has gone from this world to another.

He whose evil deeds are covered by good deeds brightens up this world, like the moon freed from clouds.

Good and Evil.

If a man commits a sin, let him not do it again; let him not delight in sin; pain is the outcome of evil.

If a man does what is good let him do it again; let him delight in it; happiness is the outcome of good.

He who has no wound in his hand may touch poison with his hand; poison does not affect him; nor is there evil for one who does not commit evil.

Let no man think lightly of evil, saying in his heart, It will not come near me. Even by the falling of water-drops a water-pot is filled; the fool becomes full of evil, even if he gathers it little by little.

Let no man think lightly of good, saying in his heart, It will not benefit me. Even by the falling of water-drops a water-pot is filled; the wise man becomes full of good, even if he gather it little by little.

Preparation for Death.

Thou art now like a sere leaf, the messengers of death

(Yama) have come near to thee; thou standest at the door of thy departure, and thou hast no provision for thy journey.

Make thyself an island, work hard, be wise! When thy infirmities are blown away, and thou art free from guilt, thou wilt enter into the heavenly world of the elect (Ariya).

Thy life has come to an end, thou art come near to Death (Yama), there is no resting-place for thee on the road, and thou hast no provision for thy journey.

Make thyself an island, work hard, be wise! When thy infirmities are blown away, and thou art free from guilt, thou wilt not enter again into birth and decay.

Let a wise man blow off the infirmities of his soul, as a smith blows off the impurities of silver, one by one, little by little, and from time to time.

Impurity arises from the iron, and having arisen from it, it destroys it: thus do a transgressor's own works lead him to the evil path. * * *

"Here shall I dwell in the rain, here in winter and summer;" thus meditates the fool, and does not think of death.

Death comes and carries off that man, surrounded by children and flocks, his mind distracted, as a flood carries off a sleeping village.

Sons are no help, nor a father, nor relations; there is no help from kinsfolk for one whom death has seized.

A wise man and good man who knows the meaning of this should quickly clear the way that leads to Nirvana.

Overcome Evil with Good.

Let a man overcome anger with love, let him overcome evil by good, let him overcome the greedy by liberality, the liar by truth.

He who holds back rising anger like a rolling chariot, him I call a real driver; other people are but holding the reins.

Practice Before Precept.

Let each man first direct himself to what is proper, then let him teach others; thus a wise man will not suffer.

Let each man make himself as he teaches others to be; he who is well-subdued may subdue (others); one's own self is difficult to subdue.

Temperance.

The man who gives himself to drinking intoxicating liquors, he, even in this world, digs up his own root.

There is no fire like passion, no shark like hatred, no snare like folly, no torrent like greed.

He who by causing pain to others, wishes to obtain pleasure himself, entangled in the bonds of hatred, will never be free from hatred.

The sages who injure nobody, *and who always control their body*, will go to the unchangeable place (Nirvana), where they will suffer no more.

The Awakened.

Not to commit any sin, to do good, and to purify one's mind, that is the teaching of the Awakened.

Not to blame, not to strike, to live restrained under the law, to be moderate in eating, to sleep and eat alone, and to dwell on the highest thoughts; this is the teaching of the Awakened.

There is no satisfying lusts, even by a shower of gold pieces; he who knows that lusts have a short taste and cause pain, he is wise.

He who takes refuge with Buddha, the Law and the Church; he who with clear understanding sees the four holy truths, viz: Pain, the origin of pain, the destruction of pain, and the eightfold holy way that leads to the quieting of pain; that is the safe and best refuge; having gone to that refuge, a man is delivered from all pain.

Health is the greatest of gifts, contentedness the best riches; trust is the best of relatives, Nirvana, the highest happiness.

No Hiding place for Sin.

Not in the sky, not in the midst of the sea, not if we enter into the clefts of the mountains, is there known a spot in the whole world where a man might be freed from an evil deed.

Not nakedness, not platted hair, not dirt, not fasting, or lying on the earth, not rubbing with dust, not sitting motionless, can purify a mortal who has not overcome desires.

If a man has transgressed one law, and speaks lies, and scoffs at another world, there is no evil he will not do.

The Brahmana.

Him I call indeed a Brahmana who does not offend by body, word, or thought, and is controlled on these three points.

He who has cut all fetters, and who never trembles, he who is independent and unshackled, him I call indeed a Brahmana.

He who is tolerant with the intolerant, mild with fault-finders, free from passion among the passionate, him I call indeed a Brahmana.

He from whom anger and hatred, pride and envy, have dropt like a mustard seed from the point of an awl, him I call indeed Brahmana.

He who fosters no desires for this world or for the next, has no inclinations and is unshackled, him I call indeed a Brahmana.

A MODERN BUDDHIST.

Views of Chao Phya Thipakon,

Minister of State for Foreign Affairs, Siam, from 1856 to 1863, on Buddhism and other religions.

Dr. Gutzlaff (a Christian Missionary) declared that 'Samana Khodom only taught the people to reverence himself and his disciples, saying that by such means merit and heaven could be obtained; teaching them to respect the temples and sacred grounds, lest by injuring them they should go to hell—a teaching designed only for the protection of himself and his disciples, and of no advantage to any others." I replied: "In Christianity there is a command to worship God alone, and no other; Mahomet also taught the worship of one only, and promised that he would take into heaven every one who joined his religion, even the murderer of his parents, while those who did not join, however virtuous, should go to hell. * * Is such teaching fit for belief? Buddha did not teach that he alone should be venerated, nor did he, the just one, ever teach that it was right to persecute other religions. As for adoration, so far as I know, men of every religion adore the holy one of their religion. Buddha neither taught it was necessary to adore him alone, nor offered the alternative of hell, as other religions do."

* * * * * * * * *

Dr. Gutzlaff once said to me, "Samana Khodom (or Buddha) having entered Nirvana (the perfect rest), is entirely lost and non-existent; who, then, will give any return for recitations in his praise, benedictions, reverences, observances and merit-making? It is a country without a king, where merit is unrewarded, because there is no one to reward it; but the religion of Jesus Christ has Jehovah and Christ, to receive prayer and praise, to reward merit, and give recompense." I replied, "It is true that the Lord Buddha does not give the reward of merit; but if any do as he has taught, they will find their recompense in the act. Even when on earth Buddha had no power to lead to heaven those who prayed, but did not follow and honor the just way. The holy religion of Buddha is perfect justice springing from a man's own meritorious disposition, which rewards the good and punishes the evil. * * Even though the Lord has entered Nirvana, his grace and benevolence are not exhausted." * * *

Buddha said: "Do not believe merely on the authority of your teachers and masters, or traditions; I tell you all, you must, *of your own selves*, know that 'this is evil and punishable, this is censured by wise men, belief in this will bring no advantage, but will cause sorrow.' And when you know this, eschew it." * * * * *

As to the sin of drinking intoxicating things, consider! By nature there is already an intoxication in man, caused by desire, anger and folly; he is already inclined to excess, and not thoughtful of the impermanence and vanity of things. If we stimulate this by drinking, it will become more daring; and if the natural inclination is to anger, it will become more excessive, and acts of violence and murder will result. So of other inclinations. The drunken man neither thinks of future retribution nor present punishment. Spirituous liquors cause disease and short life; and their use, when a habit, cannot be dispensed with, so that men spend their money unprofitably, and when it is spent become thieves. The evil is both future and immediate. * * *

What is the fate of those who have had no opportunity of learning the religion of Buddha? All men have ideas of right and wrong, and according to their virtues and vices they will accumulate merit and demerit to shape their next existence. *

These sects (of Christians, Catholics, Protestants, &c.) worship the same God and Christ; why then should they blame each other, and charge each other with believing wrongly, and say to each other "you are wrong and will go to hell, we are right and will go to heaven?" It is one religion, yet how can we join it, when each party threatens us with hell if we agree with the other, and there is none to decide between them? I beg comparison of this with the teachings of the Lord Buddha, that whoever endeavors to keep the Commandments, and is charitable, and walks virtuously, must attain heaven. * *

CHAPTER III.

CHINA*

CONFUCIUS—MENCIUS

ANALYCTS OF CONFUCIUS.

THE GOLDEN RULE.

Chung-kung asked about perfect virtue. The Master said: "It is, when you go abroad, to behave to every one as if you were receiving a great guest; to employ the people as if you were asssisting at a great sacrifice; *not to do to others as you would not wish done to yourself;* to have no murmuring against you in the country, and none in the family." Chung-kung said: "Though I am deficient in intelligence and vigor, I will make it my business to practice this lesson."

Tsze-kung asked, saying: "Is there one word which may serve as a rule of practice for all one's life?" The Master said: "Is not RECIPROCITY such a word? What you do not want done to yourself, do not do to others."

UNITY.

The Master said: "A man should say, I am not concerned that I have no place, I am concerned how I may fit myself for one. I am not concerned that I am not known, I seek to be worthy to be known."

The Master said: "Sin, my doctrine is that of an all-pervading unity." The disciple Tsang replied, "Yes."

The Master went out, and the *other* disciples asked, saying: "What do his words mean?" Tsang said: "The doctrine of our master is to be true to the principles of our nature and the benevolent exercise of them to others—this and nothing more."

* See Appendix C, for dates, &c.

The Master said: "The mind of the superior man is conversant with righteousness; the mind of the mean man is conversant with gain."

The Master said: "When we see men of worth, we should think of equaling them; when we see men of a contrary character, we should turn inward and examine ourselves."

The Master said: "Learning without thought is labor lost; thought without learning is perilous."

The Master said: "The study of strange doctrines is injurious indeed!"

The Master said: "Yew, shall I teach you what knowledge is? When you know a thing, to hold that you know it; and when you do not know a thing, to allow that you do not know it; this is knowledge."

The Master said: "If the scholar be not grave, he will not call forth any veneration, and his learning will not be solid."

Hold faithfulness and sincerity as first principles.

Have no friends not equal to yourself.

When you have faults, do not fear to abandon them.

The Master said: "High station filled without indulgent generosity; ceremonies performed without reverence; mourning conducted without sorrow; wherewith should I contemplate such ways?"

Perfect Virtue.

Tsze-chang asked Confucius about perfect virtue. Confucius said: "To be able to practice five things everywhere under heaven constitutes perfect virtue." He begged to ask what they were, and was told: "Gravity, generosity *of soul*, sincerity, earnestness, and kindness. If you are grave, you will not be treated with disrespect. If you are generous, you will win all. If you are sincere, people will repose trust in you. If you are earnest, you will accomplish much. If you are kind, this will enable you to employ the services of others."

Tsze-kung said: "*What I do not wish men to do to me,*

I also wish not to do to men." The Master said: "Tsze, you have not attained to that."

Yen Yuen asked about perfect virtue. The Master said: "To subdue one's-self and return to propriety, is perfect virtue. If a man can for one day subdue himself and return to propriety, all under heaven will ascribe perfect virtue to him. Is the practice of perfect virtue from a man himself, or is it from others?"

Yen Yuen said: "I beg to ask the steps of that process." The Master replied: "Look not at what is contrary to propriety; listen not to what is contrary to propriety; speak not what is contrary to propriety; make no movement which is contrary to propriety."

The Complete Man.

Tsze-loo asked what constituted a *complete* man. The Master said: "Suppose a man with the knowledge of Tsang Woo-chung, the freedom from covetousness of Kung-ch'o, the bravery of Chwang of Peen, and the varied talents of Yen K'ew; add to these the accomplishments of the rules of propriety and music:—such an one might be reckoned a *complete* man."

He then added: "But what is the necessity for a complete man of the present day to have all these things? The man, who in the view of gain thinks of righteousness; who in the view of danger is prepared to give up his life; and who does not forget an old agreement, however far back it extends:—such a man may be reckoned a *complete* man."

Conduct of Life.

The Master said: "At fifteen, I had my mind bent on learning.

"At thirty, I stood firm.

"At forty, I had no doubts.

"At fifty, I knew the decrees of heaven.

"At sixty, my ear was an obedient organ *for the reception of truth.*

"At seventy, I could follow what my heart desired, without transgressing what was right."

THE SUPERIOR MAN.

Sze-ma New asked about the superior man. The Master said: "The superior man has neither anxiety nor fear."

"Being without anxiety or fear," said New, "does this constitute what we call the superior man?"

The Master said: "When internal examination discovers nothing wrong, what is there to be anxious about, what is there to fear?

"Let the superior man never fail reverentially to order his own conduct, and let him be respectful to others and observant of propriety; then all within the four seas will be his brothers."

Tsze-kung asked what constituted the superior man. The Master said: "He acts before he speaks, and afterwards speaks according to his actions.

"The superior man is catholic and no partizan. The mean man is a partizan and not catholic.

"The superior man is modest in his speech, but exceeds in his actions.

"The way of the superior man is threefold, but I am not equal to it. Virtuous, he is free from anxieties; wise, he is free from perplexities; bold, he is free from fear.

"The superior man thinks of virtue; the small man thinks of comfort. The superior man thinks of the sanctions of law; the small man thinks of favors *which he may receive.*

"There are three things of which the superior man stands in awe: He stands in awe of the ordinances of Heaven; he stands in awe of great men; he stands in awe of the words of sages.

"The mean man does not know the ordinances of Heaven, and *consequently* does not stand in awe of them. He is disrespectful to great men. He makes sport of the words of sages.

"There are three things which the superior man guards against. In youth, when the physical powers are not settled, he guards against lust. When he is strong, and the physical powers are full of vigor, he guards against quarrelsomeness. When he is old, and the animal powers are decayed, he guards against covetousness."

Virtue and Simplicity.

The Master said: "Admirable indeed was the virtue of Hwuy! With a single bamboo dish of rice, a single gourd dish of drink, and living in his mean narrow lane, while others could not have endured the distress, he did not allow his joy to be affected by it. Admirable indeed was the virtue of Hwuy!"

Yen K'ew said: "It is not that I do not delight in your doctrines, but my strength is insufficient." The Master said: "Those whose strength is insufficient give over in the middle of the way, but now you limit yourself."

The Master said: "With coarse rice to eat, with water to drink, and my bended arm for a pillow;—I have still joy in the midst of these things. Riches and honors acquired by unrighteousness are to me as a floating cloud."

The Master said: "If the will be set on virtue, there will be no practice of wickedness.

"Riches and honors are what men desire. If they cannot be obtained in he proper way, they should not be held. Poverty and meanness are what men dislike. If it cannot be obtained in the proper way it should not be avoided."

Power of Spirits.

The philosopher Tsang said: "Let there be acareful attention *to perform the funeral rites* to parents, and let them be followed when long gone *with the ceremonies of sacrifice;* then the virtue of the people will resume its proper excellence."

The Master said: "I consider my not being present at the sacrifice, as if I did not sacrifice."

He sacrificed *to the dead*, as if they were present. He sacrificed to the spirits, as if the spirits were present.

He said: "How vast the power of spirits! An ocean of invisible intelligences surround us everywhere. If you look for them you cannot see them. If you listen for them you cannot hear them. Identified with the substance of all things, they cannot be separated from it. They cause men to sanctify and purify their hearts. * * They are everywhere, above us, on the right, and on the left. Their coming cannot be calculated. How important we do not neglect them!"

To Exalt Virtue.

Fan-ch'e rambling with the Master under the trees about the rain-altars, said: "I venture to ask how to exalt virtue, to correct cherished evil, and to discover delusions."

The Master said: "Truly a good question!

"If doing what is to be done be made the first business, and success a secondary consideration;—is not this the way to exalt virtue? To assail one's own wickedness and not assail that of others;—is not this the way to correct cherished evil? For a morning's anger, to disregard one's own life, and involve that of his parents;—is not this a case of delusion?"

Fan-ch'e asked about benevolence. The Master said, "It is to love *all* men." He asked about knowledge. The Master said: "It is to know *all* men.

"To give one's-self earnestly to the duties due to men, and, while respecting spiritual beings, to keep aloof from them, may be called wisdom." He asked about perfect virtue. The Master said: "The man of virtue makes the difficulty *to be overcome* his first business, and success only a subsequent consideration;—this may be called perfect virtue."

The Master said: "Where the solid qualities are in excess of accomplishments, we have rusticity; where the accomplishments are in excess of the solid qualities, we have the manners of a clerk. When the accomplishments and solid qualities are equally blended, we then have the man of complete virtue.

"Man is born for uprightness. If a man lose his uprightness, and yet live, his escape from death is the effect of mere good fortune."

SINCERITY.

They who know the truth are not equal to those who love it, and they who love it are not equal to those who find pleasure in it.

He is the sage who naturally and easily embodies the right way. He who attains to sincerity, is he who chooses what is good, and firmly holds it fast.

To this attainment there are requisite the extensive study of what is good, accurate inquiry about it, careful reflection on it, the clear discrimination of it, and the earnest practice of it.

It is only he who is possessed of the most complete sincerity that can exist under heaven, who can give its full development to his nature. Able to give its full development to his own nature, he can do the same to the nature of other men. Able to give its full development to the nature of other men, he can give their full development to the natures of animals and things. Able to give their full development to the natures of creatures and things, he can assist the transforming and nourishing powers of Heaven and Earth.

Next to the above is he who cultivates to the utmost the shoots of goodness in him. From those he can attain to the possession of sincerity; this sincerity becomes apparent. From being apparent, it becomes manifest; from being manifest, it becomes brilliant; brilliant, it affects others; affecting others, they are changed by it; changed by it, they are transformed. It is only he who is possessed of the most complete sincerity that can exist under heaven, who can transform.

It is characteristic of the most entire sincerity to be able to foreknow. When a nation or family is about to flourish, there are sure to be happy omens; and when it is about to perish, there are sure to be unlucky omens. Such events are seen in the milfoil and tortoise, and affect the movements of the four limbs. When calamity or happiness is about to come, the good shall certainly be foreknown by him, and the evil also. Therefore the individual possessed of the most complete sincerity is like a spirit.

Sincerity is the end and beginning of things; without sincerity there would be nothing. On this account, the superior man regards the attainment of sincerity as the most excellent thing.

The possessor of sincerity does not merely accomplish the self-completion of himself. With this quality he completes other men and things also. The completing himself shows his perfect virtue. The completing other men and things shows his knowledge. Both these are virtues belonging to the nature, and this is the way by which a union is effected of the external and internal. Therefore, whenever he, the entirely sincere man, employs them, that is, these virtues, their action will be right.

Sincerity makes him the coequal of Heaven. So far-reaching and long-continuing, it makes him infinite.

Such being its nature, without any display, it becomes manifested; without any movement, it produces changes; and without any effort, it accomplishes its ends.

The way of Heaven and Earth may be completely declared in one sentence: They are without any doubleness, and so they produce things in a manner that is unfathomable.

The way of Heaven and Earth is large and substantial, high and brilliant, far-reaching and long-enduring.

The heaven now before us is only this bright shining spot; but when viewed in its inexhaustible extent, the sun, moon, stars, and constellations of the zodiac, are suspended in it, and all things are overspread by it. The earth before us is but a handful of soil; but when regarded in its breadth and thickness, it sustains mountains like the Hwa and the Yoh, without feeling their weight, and contains the rivers and seas without their leaking away. The mountain now before us appears only a stone; but when contemplated in all the vastness of its size, we see how the grass and trees are produced on it, and birds and beasts dwell on it, and precious things which men treasure up are found on it. The water now before us appears but a ladleful; yet extending our view to it unfathomable depths, the largest tortoises, iguanas, iguanadons, dragons, fishes and turtles, are produced in them, articles of value and sources of wealth abound in them.

The Doctrine of the Mean.

What Heaven has conferred is called *the nature*; an accordance with this nature is called *the path* of duty; the regulation of this path is called *instruction*.

The path may not be left for an instant. If it could be left, it would not be the path. On this account, the superior man does not wait till he sees things, to be cautious, nor till he hears things, to be apprehensive.

There is nothing more visible than what is secret, and nothing more manifest than what is minute. Therefore the superior man is watchful over himself, when he is alone.

While there are no stirrings of pleasure, anger, sorrow, or joy, the mind may be said to be in the state of *equilibrium*. When those feelings have been stirred, and they act in their due degree, there ensues what may be called the state of *harmony*. This *equilibrium* is the great root *from which grow all the human actings* in the world, and this *harmony* is the universal path *which they all should pursue.*

Let the states of equilibrium and harmony exist in perfection, and a happy order will prevail throughout heaven and earth, and all things will be nourished and flourish.

The superior man cultivates a friendly harmony, without being weak. How firm is he in his energy! He stands erect in the middle, without inclining to either side. How firm is he in his energy! When good principles prevail in the government of his country, he does not change from what he was in retirement. How firm is he in his energy! When bad principles prevail in the country, he maintains his course to death, without changing. How firm is he in his energy!

The Master said: "To live in obscurity, and yet practice wonders, in order to be mentioned with honor in future ages; this is what I do not do.

"The good man tries to proceed according to the right path, but when he has gone halfway, he abandons it; I am not able so to stop.

"The superior man accords with the course of the mean. Though he may be all unknown, unregarded by the world, he feels no regret. It is only the sage who is able for this.

"In a position of wealth and honor, he does what is proper to a position of wealth and honor. In a poor and low position, he does what is proper to a poor and low position. Situated among barbarous tribes, he does what is proper to a situation among barbarous tribes. In a position of sorrow and difficulty, he does what is proper in a position of sorrow and difficulty. The superior man can find himself in no positon in which he is not himself.

"In a high situation, he does not treat with contempt his inferiors. In a low situation, he does not court the favor of his superiors. He rectifies himself, and seeks for nothing from others, so that he has no dissatisfactions. He does not murmur against heaven, nor grumble against men.

"Thus it is that the superior man is quiet and calm, waiting for the appointments of Heaven, while the mean man walks in dangerous paths, looking for lucky occurrences.

"In archery we have something like the way of the superior man. When the archer misses the centre of the target, he turns round and seeks for the cause of his failure in himself."

Sayings of Mencius.

There is a nobility of Heaven, and there is a nobility of man. Benevolence, righteousness, self-consecration and fidelity, with unwearied joy in *these* virtues;—these constitute the nobility of Heaven. To be a kung, a k'ing, or a ta-foo;—this constitutes the nobility of man.

The men of antiquity cultivated their nobility of Heaven, and the nobility of man came to them in its train.

The men of the present day cultivate their nobility of Heaven in order to seek for the nobility of man, and when they have obtained that, they throw away the other:—their delusion is extreme. The end is simply this, that they must lose that nobility of man as well.

To desire to be honored is the common mind of men. And all men have in themselves that which is *truly* honorable. Only they do not think it.

Benevolence subdues its opposite just as water subdues fire. Those, however, who now-a-days practice benevolence, do it as if with one cup of water they could save a whole wagon-load of fuel which was on fire, and when the flames were not extinguished, were to say that water cannot subdue fire. This conduct, moreover, greatly encourages those who are not benevolent.

The final issue will simply be this—the loss of that small amount of benevolence.

Men must be decided on what they will NOT do, and then they are able to act with vigor *in what they ought to do.*

The great man does not think beforehand of his words that they may be sincere, nor of his actions that they may be resolute;—he simply speaks and does what is right.

The great man is he who does not lose his child's heart.

The nourishment of parents when living is not sufficient to be accounted the great thing. It is only in the performing their obsequies when dead, that we have what can be considered the great thing.

Of services which is the greatest? The service of parents is the greatest. Of charges, which is the greatest? The charge of one's-self is the greatest. That those who do not fail to keep themselves are able to serve their parents is what I have heard. But I have never heard of any, who, having failed to keep themselves, were able notwithstanding to serve their parents.

Wherever the superior man passes through, transformation follows; wherever he abides, his influence is of a spiritual nature. It flows abroad, above and beneath, like that of Heaven and Earth.

CHAPTER IV.

PERSIA.*

ZOROASTER.—MODERN PARSEES.

Prayer to the Good Mind.

I raise my hands in adoration and worship: first, all true works of the divine Spirit and the intelligence of the good Mind, that I may be partaker of this blessedness. To those works and the earth-soul do I offer up my prayer.

With pious sense will I approach Thee, thou Wise and Living, with the prayer that thou grant me the earthly and spiritual life. Through truth are these blessings to be attained, which the Self-luminous sends to those who strive therefor.

Long as my strength shall last to worship, so long will I continue in search after truth. * * * *

Thee I conceive as the original First, as the One Supreme, both in nature and in mind, father of the good disposition,—since with clear eye I beheld thee, *as the essential substance of truth.*

Agriculture, Health, Truth.

With the fruits of the field increases the law of Ahura-Mazda (Ormuzd), and with them it is multiplied a hundred fold. The earth rejoices when man builds on it his house, when his flocks abound, when, surrounded by wife and children, he makes the grass and the corn to grow, and plants fruit-trees abundantly.

* See Appendix D.

I invoke and worship health and goodness. I invoke and worship the male and female of animals, houses, the storehouses where corn is kept, water, earth, trees, corn. I adore this earth and sky, the stars, the moon, the sun; light which had no beginning and is increate, and also the works of the holy and celestial being. I invoke and worship the mountains, depositories of the wisdom given by Ahura-Mazda, radiant with purity, perfectly radiant, and the splendor of kings given by Ahura-Mazda, and their unborrowed brightness. I invoke those who are holy, and those who are pure. I invoke and worship the powerful feroners (spirits) of pure men. He who sows the soil with diligence acquires a greater stock of religious merit than he could gain by ten thousand prayers in idleness.

Who purely invokes the truths, he has the essence of the supreme soul; hence is he inspired to the culture of the soil.

Who honors truth in word and deed, O Mazda, *he best serves and worships thee.*

Come to me, ye high realities. Grant me your immortality, your duration of possession forever!

Let me become those things that I have longed for. Grant me the gift of long life. May none of you withhold it, since it is dedicated to the redemption of that world which is thine!

The Beginning.

This will I ask thee, tell me it right, thou Living Wise One: How was the beginning of this best, the actual life? Whereby may we aid that which is now here?

This will I ask thee: Who is the first Father and Progenitor of Truth? Who laid the path for the sun and stars? Who caused the moon to wax and wane, but thou? All this would I know; other things are comprehensible to me.

This will I ask thee: Who made the earth and the sky above it? Who is in the wind and storms that they so swiftly run?

This will I ask thee: Who made the useful light and the

darkness, by their alternation bringing labor and rest? Who the morning, midday, and night, which constantly remind him that knows the divine revealings of his obligations?

This, too, will I ask thee: Who made this high land (Bactria) with its riches? Who forms constantly the fine son from the father, as by the weaver's art?

Oracles of Zoroaster.

The Father hath snatched away himself, neither hath he shut up his own fire in his mental potence.

For the Father perfected all things, and delivered them over to the second mind, which the whole race of men calls the first.

Light, begotten of the Father, for he alone, having plucked the flower of the mind from the Father's vigor—

Neither went he (the Original One) forth, but abode in the parental depth, and in the adytum, according to divinely nourished silence.

He makes similitude of himself, assuming the type of forms.

The parental mind hath sown symbols through the world.

There is something intelligible which it behooves thee to apprehend with the flower of the mind.

Time—the mundane God, eternal, infinite, young, old, of spiral form.

Look not into the fatal name of this nature.

The soul is a bright fire, and by the power of the father remains immortal and is mistress of life.

It is after the model af the mind, but being born, hath something of the body.

The paternal mind hath implanted symbols in souls.

To the slow mortal the gods are swift.

The furies are stranglers of men.

Enlarge not thy destiny.

Right Living and the Future.

Do not be carried away by anger. Angry words and scornful looks are sin. Even the intent to strike another deserves punishment. Opposition to peace is sin. Reply to thine enemy with gentleness. Contend constantly against evil, morally and physically, internally and externally. Strive to diminish the power of Arimanes and destroy his works. If a man has done this he may meet death fearlessly; well assured that radiant Izeds will lead him across the luminous bridge into a paradise of eternal happiness. But though he has been brave in battle, killed wild beasts, and fought with external evil, if he has neglected to combat evil within himself he has reason to fear that Arimanes and his Devs will seize him and carry him to Duzukh (hell), where he will be punished according to his sins; not to satisfy the vengeance of Ormuzd, but because, having connected himself with evil, this is the only means of being purified therefrom, so as to be capable of enjoying happiness in future. Every man pure in thoughts, words and actions will go to the celestial region

Prayer to Ormuzd and his Works.

I address my prayer to Ormuzd, Creator of all things; who always has been, who is, and who will be forever; who is wise and powerful; who made the great arch of heaven, the sun, moon, stars, winds, clouds, water, earth, fire, trees, animals, metals, and men; whom Zoroaster adored. Zoroaster, who brought to the world the knowledge of the law; who knew by natural intelligence and by the ear, what ought to be done, all that has been, that is, or that is to be; the science of sciences, the excellent Word, by which souls pass the luminous and radiant bridge, separate themselves from the evil regions, and go to light and holy dwellings, full of fragrance. O Creator, I obey thy laws. I think, act, speak, according to thy orders. I separate myself from all sin. I do good works according to my power. I adore thee with purity of thought, word and action. I pray to Ormuzd, who recompenses good works, who delivers unto the end those who obey his laws. Grant that I may arrive at Paradise, where all is fragrance, light and happiness. * * * * * *

O, Ormuzd, pardon the repentant sinner. As I, when a man irritates me by his thoughts, words, or actions, carried away or not by his passions, if he humble himself before me, and addresses to me his prayer, I become his friend. * *

I pray to Mithras, who has a thousand ears and ten thousand eyes; who never sleeps, who is always watchful and attentive; who renders barren lands fertile.

Thou fire, son of Ormuzd, brilliant and beneficent, given by Ormuzd, be favorable to me!

I pray to the New Moon, holy, pure and great. I pray to the Full Moon, holy, pure and great. I gaze at the moon on high, and I honor the light of the moon. The moon is a blessed Spirit, created by Ormuzd, to bestow light and glory upon the earth.

I invoke the Source of Waters, holy, pure and great, coming from the throne of Ormuzd, from the high mountains; holy, pure, and great.

I invoke the sweet Earth, I invoke the Mountains, abode of happiness, given by Ormuzd, holy, pure and great.

Hymn to Mithra.

Mithra, whose long arms grasp with Mithra-strength; that which is Eastern India he seizes, and that which is in the Western he smites, and what is on the steppes of Rauha, and what is at the ends of the earth. Thou, O Mithra, dost seize these, reaching out thy arms. The unrighteous destroyed through the just is gloomy of soul. Thus thinks the unrighteous; Mithra, the artless, does not see all these evil deeds, these lies.

But I think in my soul: No earthly man with a hundredfold strength thinks so much evil, as Mithra, with heavenly strength, thinks good. No earthly man, with a hundred-fold strength, speaks and does so much evil, as Mithra, with heavenly strength, speaks and does good. No earthly man hears with the ears as the heavenly Mithra, with a hundred strengths, sees every liar.—*Khordah Avesta.*

Praise to the Creator.

With all strength bring I thanks; to the great among beings, who created and destroyed, and through his own determination of time, wisdom, strength, is higher than the Six Amshaspands (archangels), the circumference of heaven, the shining sun, the brilliant moon, the wind, the water, the fire the earth, the trees, the cattle, the metals, and mankind.

Offering and praise to that Lord, the completer of good works, who made men greater than all earthly beings, and through the gift of speech created them to rule the creatures, as warriors against the Daevas (Devs, evil spirits).

All good do I accept at thy command, O God, and think, speak and do it. I believe in the pure law; by every good work seek I forgiveness for all sin. I keep pure for myself the serviceable work, and abstinence from the unprofitable. I keep pure the six powers—thought, speech, work, memory, mind, and understanding.

I enter on the shining way to Paradise; may the fearful terror of hell not overcome me! May I step over the bridge Chinevat, may I attain Paradise, with much perfume, and all enjoyments and brightness.

Praise to the Overseer, the Lord; who rewards those who accomplish good deeds according to his own wish, purifies at last the obedient, and at last purifies even the wicked ones of hell. All praise to the Creator, to Ormuzd, the all-wise, rich in might; to the Seven Amshaspands; to Ized Bahram, the victorious annihilator of foes.—*Khordah Avesta.*

A Confession.

I repent of all sins. All wicked thoughts, words and works which I have meditated in the world, corporeal, spiritual, earthly and heavenly, I repent of, in your presence, ye believers. O Lord, pardon through the three words.

I confess myself a Zarathustrian, an opponent of the Daevas, devoted to belief in Ahura (Ormuzd), for praise, adoration and satisfaction.

I praise all good thoughts, words, and works, through thought, word and deed. I curse all evil thoughts, words and works, away from thought, word and deed. I lay hold on all good thoughts, words, and works; that is, I perform good acts. I commit no sins.

I give to you, ye who are Amshaspands, offering and praise, with the heart, with the body, with my own vital powers, body and soul.

I praise the best purity, I hunt away the Devs, I am thankful for the good of the Creator, Ormuzd, with the opposition which comes from Gana-mainyo. I am contented, and agreed in the hope of a resurrection. The Zarathustrian law, created by Ormuzd, I take as a plummet. For the sake of this, I repent of all sins.

That which was the wish of Ormuzd the Creator, and I ought to have thought, spoken, or done, and have not. That which was the wish of Abriman, and I ought not to have thought, spoken or done, and yet have; of these sins I repent, with thoughts, words and works.

MODERN PARSEE CATECHISM.

[Translated by Dadabahai Naoroji, Liverpool, 1861.]

A few Questions and Answers to acquaint the Children of the Holy Zarthosti Community with the Mazdiashna Religion, *i. e.*, the worship of God.

Whom do we, of the Zarthosti Community, believe in?

We believe in only one God, and do not believe in any besides Him.

Who is that one God?

The God who created the heavens, the earth, the angels, the stars, the sun, the moon, the fire, the water, or all the four elements, and all things of the two worlds;—that God we believe in. Him we worship, invoke and adore.

Do we not believe in any other God?

Whoever believes in another God is an infidel, and shall suffer the punishment of hell.

What is the form of our God?

Our God has neither face nor form, color nor shape, nor fixed place. There is no other like Him. He is singly such a glory that we cannot praise or describe Him; nor our mind comprehend Him. * * * *

What is our Religion?

Our Religion is, "Worship of God."

Whence did we receive our religion?

God's true prophet, the true Zurthost (Zoroaster) Asphantaman Anoshirwan, brought the religion to us from God. * *

Whose descendants are we?

Of Gayomars. By his progeny was Persia populated.

Was Gayomars the first man?

According to our religion he was so; but the wise men of our community, of the Chinese, the Hindoos, and several other nations, dispute this, and say there was human population on the earth before Gayomars. * * * *

What commands has God sent us through his prophet, the exalted Zurthost?

To know God as one; to know the prophet, the exalted Zurthost, as the true prophet; to believe the religion and the Avosta, brought by him as true beyond all doubt; to believe in the goodness of God; not to disobey any commands of the Mazdiashna religion; to avoid evil deeds; to exert ourself in good deeds; to pray five times in the day; to believe in the reckoning and justice the fourth morning after death; to hope for heaven, and to fear hell; to consider doubtless the day of general destruction and resurrection; to remember always that God has done what he willed, and shall do what he wills; to face some luminous object, while worshiping God. * * *

Some deceivers (the Catechism says—meaning the Christian missionaries), with the view of acquiring exaltation in the world, have set themselves up as prophets, aud going among the ignorant and laboring people, have persuaded them that, "If you commit sin, I shall intercede for you, plead for you, and save you," and thus deceive them; but the wise among the people know the deceit.

If any one commit sin under the belief that he shall be saved by somebody, both the deceiver as well as the deceived shall be damned to the day of Rasta Khez. * * There is no savior. In the other world you shall receive the return according to your actions. * * Your Savior is your deeds, and God himself. He is the pardoner and the giver. If you repent your sins and reform, and if the great Judge considers you worthy of pardon, or would be merciful to you, He alone can and will save you.

CHAPTER V.

EGYPT.*

THE DIVINE PYMANDER, OR SHEPHERD OF MEN.

By Hermes Mercurius Trismegistus.

I, O my Son, write this first book both for humanity's sake and for piety toward God. * * * * *

For never, O Son, shall, or can, that soul, which, while it is in the body, lightens and lifts up itself to know and comprehend that which is Good and True, slide back to the contrary; for it is infinitely enamored thereof, and forgetteth all Evils; and when it hath learned and known its Father and Progenitor, it can no more depart or apostatize from that Good,

And let this, O Son, be the end of Religion and Piety; whereunto thou art once arrived, thou shalt both live well and die blessedly, whilst thy soul is not ignorant whether it must return and fly back again.

For this, O Son, is the way of Truth, which our Progenitors traveled in; and by which, making their journey, they at length attained to the Good. It is a venerable way and plain, but difficult and hard for the soul to go in that is in the body.

* * * * * * *

Of the Soul: that part which is sensible is mortal, but that which is reasonable is immortal.

Every essence is immortal.

Every essence is unchangeable.

Every thing that is, is double.

None of the things that are stand still.

Not all things are moved by a soul, but everything that is, is moved by a soul. * * *

* See Appendix E for Dates, etc.

Heaven is the first element.
Providence is Divine Order.
Necessity is the minister, or servant, of Providence.
What is God? The immutable or unalterable Good.
What is man? An unchangeable Evil.

VISION—ILLUMINATION—ASPIRATION.

For the sleep of my body was the sober watchfulness of my mind; and the shutting of my eyes the true sight, and my silence great with child and full of good; and the pronouncing of my words the blossom and fruit of good things.

And thus came to pass, or happened unto me, which I received from my mind, that is, Pymander, the Lord of the Word; whereby I became inspired by God with the Truth.

For which cause, with my Soul and whole strength, I give praise and blessing unto God the Father.

Holy is God, the Father of all things.

Holy is God, whose will is performed and accomplished by his own powers.

Holy art Thou, that by Thy word hast established all things.

Holy art Thou, of whom all Nature is the image.

Holy art Thou, whom Nature hath not formed.

Holy art Thou, that art stronger than all power.

Holy art Thou, that art greater than all excellency.

Holy art Thou, that art better than all praise.

Accept these reasonable sacrifices from a pure Soul, and a heart stretched out unto Thee.

I beseech Thee, that I may never err from the knowledge of Thee; look mercifully upon me, and enable me, and enlighten with this grace those that are in ignorance, the brothers of my kind, but Thy sons.

Therefore I believe Thee. and bear witness, and go into the Life and Light.

The Beginning.

The glory of all things, God, and that which is Divine, and the Divine Nature, the beginning of things that are.

God, and the Mind, and Nature, and Matter, and Operation or Working, and Necessity, and the End, and Renovation.

For there was in the Chaos an infinite darkness in the abyss, or bottomless depth, and water, and a subtle Spirit, intelligible in power; and there went out the Holy Light, and the elements were coagulated from the land, out of the moist substance.

And all the Gods distinguished the nature full of seeds.

And when all things were interminated and unmade up, the light things were divided on high, and the heavy things were founded on the moist sand, all things being terminated or divided by fire; and being sustained or hung up by the Spirit, they were so carried, and the heaven was seen in seven circles.

And the Gods were seen in their Ideas of the stars, with all their signs, and the stars were numbered with the Gods in them. And the sphere was all lined with air, carried about in a circular motion by the Spirit of God.

And every God, by his internal power, did that which was commanded him; and there were made four-footed things, and creeping things, and such as live in the water, and such as fly, and every fruitful seed, and grass, and the flowers of all greens, all which had sowed in themselves the seeds of regeneration.

As also the generations of men, to the knowledge of the divine works, and a lively or working testimony of nature, and a multitude of men, and the dominion of every thing under heaven, and the knowledge of good things, and to be increased in multitude

And every soul in flesh, by the wonderful working of the Gods in the circles, to the beholding of heaven, the Gods, divine works, and the operations of nature.

The Holy Song.

Let all the nature of the world entertain the hearing of this hymn.

Be opened, O Earth, and let all the treasure of the rain be opened.

Ye trees, tremble not, for I will sing, and praise the Lord of the creation, and the All, the One.

Be opened, ye Heavens, ye winds stand still, and let the immortal circle of God receive these words.

For I will sing and praise Him that created all things, that fixed the earth and hung up the heavens, and commanded the sweet water to come out of the ocean into all the world inhabited, to the use and nourishment of all things, or men.

That commanded the fire to shine for every action, both to God and men.

Let us together give him blessing, which rideth upon the heavens, the Creator of all Nature.

O, all ye powers that are in me, praise the One, the All.

Sing together with my will, all ye powers that are in me.

O holy knowledge, being enlightened by thee, I magnify the Intelligible Light, and rejoice in the Joy of the Mind.

This is God that is better than any name; this is he that is secret; this is he that is most manifest; this is he that is to be seen by the mind; this is he that is visible to the eye; this is he that hath no body; and this is he that hath many bodies, rather there is nothing of any body that is not of him; for he alone is all things.

And for this cause he hath all names, because he is the One Father.

Inscriptions on Egyptian Tombs.

He loved his father, he honored his mother, he loved his brethren, and never went from his home in a bad temper. He never preferred the great man to the low one.—*Tomb in Upper Egypt.*

I honored my father; I esteemed my mother; I loved my brothers; I found graves for the unburied dead; I instructed little children; I took care of orphans as though they were my own. For great misfortunes were on Egypt and this city, in my time.—*Tomb of a Priest at Sais, in reign of Cambyses.*

What I have done I will say. My goodness and kindness were ample. I never oppressed the widow or the fatherless; I did not treat cruelly the fishermen, the shepherds, or the poor laborers. There was nowhere in my time hunger or want, for I cultivated all my fields, far and near, that their inhabitants might have food. I never preferred the great and powerful to the humble and poor, but did equal justice to all. —*Tomb of a Nomad Prince, at Ben Hassan.*

I lived in truth and fed my soul with justice. What I did to men was done in peace, and how I loved God, God and my heart well know. I have given bread to the hungry, water to the thirsty, clothes to the naked, and a shelter to the stranger. I honored the gods with sacrifices and the dead with offerings.—*Tomb of a Pharaoh, at Thebes,*

I never took the child from its mother's bosom, nor the poor man from the side of his wife.—*On a Tomb at Sycopolis.*

Amun to Thothmes.*

I am come; to thee have I given to strike down Syrian princes;
Under thy feet they lie throughout the breadth of their country;
Like the Lord of Light I made them see thy glory,
Blinding their eyes with light, O earthly image of Amun!

I am come; to thee have I given to strike down Asian peoples;
Captive now thou hast led the proud Assyrian chieftains;
Decked in royal robes, I made them see thy glory:
In glittering arms and fighting, high in thy lofty chariot.

* Inscription at Karnak, describing success of Thothmes III, B. C. about 1600, translated by De Ronge. The king's triumphs are ascribed to the god Amun.

I am come; to thee have I given to strike down western
nations;
Cyprus and the Ases have both heard thy name with terror;
Like a strong-horned bull I made them see thy glory;
Strong with piercing horns, so that none can stand before him.

I am come; to thee have I given to strike down Lybian
archers;
All the isles of the Greeks submit to the force of thy spirit;
Like a regal lion, I made them see thy glory;
Couched by the corpse he has made, down in the rocky valley.

I am come; to thee have I given to strike down the ends of
the ocean;
In the grasp of the hand is the circling zone of the waters;
Like the soaring eagle, I have made them see thy glory;
Whose far-seeing eye there is none can hope to escape from.

AMUN.

The spirit of the Supreme moving on the face of the waters.

The Spirit who animates and perpetuates the world by mixing himself with all its parts.

He who brings hidden things to light.

CHAPTER VI.

HEBREW.

JUDAISM, ANCIENT AND MODERN.

TRUE SERVICE AND REWARD.

1. Cry aloud, spare not, lift up thy voice like a trumpet, and show my people their transgressions, and the house of Jacob their sins.

2. Yet they seek me daily, and delight to know my ways, as a nation that did righteousness, and forsook not the ordinances of their God: They ask of me the ordinances of justice: They take delight in approaching to God.

3. Wherefore have we fasted, say they, and thou seest not? Wherefore have we afflicted our soul, and thou takest no knowledge? Behold, in the day of your fast ye find pleasure, and exact all your labors.

4. Behold, ye fast for strife and debate, and to smite with the fist of wickedness: ye shall not fast as ye do this day, to make your voice to be heard on high.

5. Is it such a fast that I have chosen? a day for man to afflict his soul? is it to bow down his head as a bulrush, and to spread sackcloth and ashes under him? wilt thou call this a fast, and an acceptable day to the Lord?

6. Is not this the fast that I have chosen? to loose the bonds of wickedness, to undo the heavy burdens, and to let the oppressed go free, and that ye break every yoke?

7. Is it not to deal thy bread to the hungry, and that thou bring the poor that are cast out to thy house? When thou seest the naked, that thou cover him; and that thou hide not thyself from thine own flesh?

8. Then shall thy light break forth as the morning, and thine health shall spring forth speedily: and thy righteousness shall go before thee; the glory of the Lord shall be thy reward.

9. Then shalt thou call, and the Lord shall answer; thou shalt cry, and he shall say, Here I am. If thou take away from the midst of thee the yoke, the putting forth of the finger, and speaking vanity;

10. If thou draw out thy soul to the hungry, and satisfy the afflicted soul; then shall thy light rise in obscurity, and thy darkness be as the noon-day:

11. And the Lord shall guide thee continually, and satisfy thy soul in drought, and make fat thy bones; and thou shalt be like a watered garden, and like a spring of water, whose waters fail not.

12. And they that shall be of thee shall build the old waste places: thou shalt raise up the foundations of many generations; and thou shalt be called, The repairer of the breach, The restorer of paths to dwell in.—*Isaiah, Old Testament.*

Perfectness of Divine Law.

1. The heavens declare the glory of God; and the firmament sheweth his handy work.

2. Day unto day uttereth speech, and night unto night sheweth knowledge.

3. There is no speech nor language where their voice is not heard.

4. Their line is gone out through all the earth, and their words to the end of the world. In them hath he set a tabernacle for the sun.

5. Which is a bridegroom coming out of his chamber, and rejoiceth as a strong man to run a race.

6. His going forth is from the end of the heaven, and his circuit unto the ends of it: and there is nothing hid from the heat thereof.

7. The law of the Lord is perfect, converting the soul: the testimony of the Lord is sure, making wise the simple.

8. The statutes of the Lord are right, rejoicing the heart: the commandment of the Lord is pure, enlightening the eyes.

9. The fear of the Lord is clean, enduring forever: the judgments of the Lord are true and righteous altogether.

10. More to be desired are they than gold, yea, than much fine gold: sweeter also than honey and the honey-comb.

11. Moreover, by them is thy servant warned: and in keeping of these there is great reward.

12. Who can understand his errors? cleanse thou me from secret faults.

13. Keep back thy servant also from presumptuous sins; let them not have dominion over me: then shall I be upright, and I shall be innocent from the great transgression.

14. Let the words of my mouth and the meditation of my heart, be acceptable in thy sight, O Lord, my strength, and my redeemer.—*Psalms of David.*

Extracts from Talmudical and Rabbinical Literature.

I. Hillel (40 B. C.) said: What is hateful unto thee, thou shalt not do unto others. This rule comprises the whole law; everything else is its mere comment.

2. Rabbi Akiba (A. D. 116) said: Thou shalt love thy fellow-man like thyself is the principal rule of the Bible.

3. The Rabbis (Sanhedrin) said: The good men of all nations and denominations shall participate in the future bliss of heaven.

4. Talmud Peah: Charity and benevolence are of more importance than all the ceremonies together.

5. Talmud Ketuboth: A man who does not practice charity, is not better than the one who worships idols.

6. Yalkut: The Lord said to Moses, do you suppose that I make a difference between Jew and Gentile? I treat them all alike; for every good deed, to each the proper reward.

7. Ethics of the Fathers: Antigonas of Sadro used to say:

Be not like servants who serve their masters for the sake of receiving a reward, but be like servants who serve their master without a view of receiving a reward; and let the fear of God be upon you.

Hillel said: Be of the disciples of Aaron, love peace, pursue peace, love all men, and invite them to a life of virtue and holiness.

Simon, the son of Gamaliel, said: The safety of human society depends on truth, justice and peace.

Rabbi Tarphon said: The day is short, the task is great, the laborers are lazy, the master presses for dispatch. It is not incumbent upon thee to complete the work, but thou art not at liberty to abstain from it.

Rabbi Akiba said: Everything is seen by Providence, though freedom of choice is given to man; the world is judged in paternal kindness; but works of love and charity are man's best and noblest title.

Ben Zoma said: Who is wise? He who is willing to receive instruction from all men. Who is mighty? He who is satisfied with his lot. Who is honorable? He who honors his fellow men.

8. Talmud; Sabbath: The Sabbath is given to you, but you are not given over to the Sabbath.

Make out of your Sabbath day a week day, and secure your independence from the support of men.

9. Talmud, Berachoth: Knowledge is of more importance and consequence than the Temple with all its ceremonies. The verse, "do not touch my Messiah," means, do not disturb the children in their schools.

10. Tulmud, Niddah: Rabbah said: The whole ceremonial law will once be abolished.

11. Aben Esra, (A. D. 1090–1170) said: The mediator between God and man is none but reason and common sense.

12. Maimonides (A. D. 1133–1206) said: In social life we recognize no difference whatsoever between Jew or Gentile. Our Rabbis have commanded us to consider it a

supreme duty to visit the sick of Gentiles, to bury their dead on Jewish burial grounds; to support their poor and needy ones like the Jewish; for the Psalmist has said: "The Lord is good unto all, and his mercy extends over all his works."

13. Jehuda Halevi (A. D. 1120–1150): The creed and denomination of man have nothing to do with his moral worth. God judges man according to his good deeds, and not according to his religion.

13. Isaac Arama (about A. D. 1630): Every true, good and virtuous man is our brother, like any other Jew.

Peace.

Rabbi Yehudah Ben Levy said: Great is the power of peace. It is as indispensable to the welfare of the universe as is the leaven for the fermentation of bread. Were it not for the rule of peace, the sword and wild beasts would long ago have destroyed our world.

Rabbi Ben Gamliel said: The world stands upon three things: justice, truth and peace. Rabbi Munah, explaining this saying, said: Yet all these have only one purpose; that is, peace.

The Rabbis said: Our Lord loves peace above all. Therefore, objects most dear and beloved unto Him, and sacred unto them, they called peace—"Sholom"—likewise; as the Holy City, Jerusalem.

Section "Hasholom," of a book of the Talmud, treats on peace and closes as follows: All those that are toiling for the preservation and restoration of peace, without religious distinction, shall inherit of the Lord peace and happiness, here and hereafter.

PHILO JUDAEUS,

(Born about 20 B. C. in Alexandria, a Pharisee, and learned in Judaism, and in the philosophy of Plato, Pythagoras, &c. His "Fragments" are gathered from incomplete and unpublished works, by Eusebius, John of Damascus, from unpublished MSS. in English and French libraries, and from Questions on Genesis and Exodus, &c.)

OF THOSE WHO OFFER SACRIFICE.

The law chooses that a person who brings a sacrifice shall be pure, both in body and soul: pure in soul from all passions and diseases, and vices, which can be displayed in word or deed; and pure in body from all such things as the body is defiled by. And it has appointed a burning purification for both these things: for the soul, by the means of the animals duly fit for sacrifice, and for the body by ablutions and sprinkling—concerning which we shall speak presently; for it is fit to assign the pre-eminence in honor in every point to the superior and dominant part of the qualities existing in us, namely, the soul. What, then, is the work of purifying the soul?

The law says: "Look, take care that the victim which thou bringest to the altar is perfect, wholly without participation in any kind of blemish, selected from many on account of its excellence, by the uncorrupted judgment of the priests, and by their most acute sight and continued practice exercised in the examination of faultless victims. For if you do not see this with your eyes more than with your reason, you will not wash off all the imperfections and stains which you have imprinted on your whole life, partly in consequence of unexpected events, and partly by deliberate purpose; for you will find that this exceeding accuracy of investigation into the animals, figuratively signifies the amelioration of your own character and conduct; for the law was not established for the sake of irrational animals, but for that of those who have intellect aud reason." So that the real object cared for is not the condition of the victims sacrificed, but that of the sacrificers, that they may not be defiled by any unlawful passion.

Of water and ashes for purifying the body he says: The lawgiver's intention is that those who approach the service of the living God should first of all know themselves and their own essence. For how can a man who does not know himself ever comprehend the supreme and all-excelling power of God? * * For it is somewhere said with great beauty: "He that exhibits proud words or actions offends not man alone, but God also, the maker of equality and of everything excellent." * * For the soul is mistress and queen, superior in everything, as having received a more divine nature. * * God is not pleased even though a man bring hecatombs to his altar; for he possesses all things as his own, and stands in need of nothing. But he delights in minds which love God, and in men who practice holiness, from whom he gladly receives the very cheapest things (in sacrifice) in preference to the most costly. * *

The lawgiver says in effect: "God, O mind of man! demands nothing of you which is either oppressive or difficult, or uncertain, but only such things as are very simple and easy. And these are to love him as a benefactor; and if you fail to do so, at all events to fear him as your Governor and Lord, and to enter zealously upon all the paths which may please him, and to serve him in no careless or superficial manner, but with one's whole soul thoroughly filled with God-loving sentiments, and to cleave to his commandments, and to honor justice." * * But those men are to be pitied, and are altogether miserable, who have never banqueted on the labors of virtue; and they have remained to the end, the most miserable of all men who have been always ignorant of the taste of moral excellence, when it was in their power to have feasted on, and luxuriated among, justice and equality. But these men are uncircumcised in their hearts, as the law expresses it. * *

Of Courage.

I now proceed to speak of courage, not meaning that warlike and frantic delirium, with passion as its counsellor, which the generality of men take for it, but knowledge. * * But then, as some men—who, always remaining in their own houses, while their bodies have been worn away either by long sickness, or old age, still being healthy and vigorous in the better part of their souls, and being full of high thoughts, and inspired with a braver and happier fortitude, never meddling with warlike weapons, even in their dreams,—nevertheless by their exposition and advocacy of wise counsels for the common advantage, have often re-established both the private affairs of individuals, and the prosperity of the country when in danger, putting forth unyielding and inflexible reasonings concerning what has been really expedient. These men are they who practice real courage, being studiers and practicers of wisdom. There is also no small number of other things in life very difficult to endure, such as poverty, want of reputation, and diseases, by which weak-spirited men are broken down, not being able to raise themselves at all through want of courage; but those who are full of high thoughts and noble spirits rise up to struggle against these things with fortitude and exceeding vigor.

The Virtuous alone Free.

My former treatise was intended to prove that every wicked man was a slave, and that proposition I established fully by many natural and unquestionable arguments; and this treatise is akin to that one, in some sort a twin to it, since it will proceed to show that every virtuous man is free.

Now it is said that the most sacred sect of the Pythagoreans, among many other excellent doctrines, taught this one also, that it was not well to proceed by the plain ordinary roads,—not meaning to urge us to walk among precipices, but intimating, by a figurative mode of speech, that we ought not, either in respect to our words or actions, to use only such as are ordinary and unchanged,—and all men who have studied philosophy in a genuine spirit, showing themselves obedient to this injunction, have looked upon it as a sentence, or rather a law, of equal weight with a divine oracle, and, departing from the common opinions of men, they have cut out for themselves a new and hitherto untraveled path, inaccessible to such as have no experience of wise maxims and doctrines, building up systems of ideas which no one who is not pure either can or may handle. When I speak of men not being pure, I mean those who have either been destitute of education, or else have tasted of it obliquely, and not in a straightforward manner, changing the stamp of the beauty of wisdom so as to give an impression of the unsightliness of sophistry.

Slavery is of two kinds—of the soul and of the body. * * * * For in real truth, that man alone is free who has God for his leader; indeed, in my opinion, that man is even the ruler of all others, and has all the affairs of the world committed to him, being, as it were, the viceroy of a great king, the mortal lieutenant of an immortal sovereign. * * * *

If any one examine closely the matter (of freedom) he will see clearly that there is no one thing so nearly related to another as independence of action, on which account there are a great many things which stand in the way of the liberty of a wicked man: coveteousness of money, the desire of glory, the love of pleasure, and so on. But the virtuous man has absolutely no obstacle at all, since he rises up against, and resists, and overthrows, and tramples on, fear and cowardice, and pain, and all things of the kind, as if they were rivals defeated by him in the public games. For he has learned to disregard all the commands which those most unlawful masters of the soul seek to impose upon him; out of his admiration and desire for freedom, of which independence and spontaneousness of action are the most essential and inalienable inheritance; and by some persons the poet (Euripides) is praised who composed the iambic,

> "No man's a slave who does not fear to die,"

as having had an accurate idea of the consequences of such courage.

Fragments from Lost or Unpublished Works.

It is not possible with God that a wicked man should lose his good reward for a single good thing which he may have done among a number of evil actions; nor, on the other hand, that a good man should escape punishment and not suffer it, if, among many good actions, he has done wickedly in anything, for it is infallibly certain that God distributes everything according to a just weight and balance.

—The mind is the witness, to each individual, of the things which they have planned in secret, and conscience is an incorruptible judge, and the most unerring of all judges.

—No wicked man is rich, not even though he be the owner of all the mines in the world; but all foolish men are poor. Every foolish man is straitened, being oppressed by coveteousness, and ambition, and love of pleasure, and things of that sort, which do not permit the mind to dwell at ease or enjoy plenty of room.

—The wise man endeavors to secure quiet and leisure, and periods of rest from work, that he may devote himself peacefully to mediations on divine matters.

—If any one embraces all the virtues with earnestness and sobriety, he is a king, even though he may be in private station.

—Say what is right, and at the time when it is right, and you will not hear what is not right.

—Every wise man is a friend of God.

—There is nothing so opposite to and inconsistent with the most holy power of God as injustice.

—The influx of evils agitates and disturbs the soul, enveloping it in a giddiness which darkens its perceptions, and compels it to suffer that power of sight which by nature was pre-eminent, but which by habit has become blinded, to be obscured.

—All the powers of God are winged, being always eager and striving for the higher path which leads to the Father.

—The man who lives in wickedness, bears about destruction with him, since he has living with him that which is both treacherous, designing, and hostile to him. For the conscience of the wicked is alone a sufficient punishment to him, inflicting cowardice on his soul from its own inmost feelings, as it feared blows.

—Good men are of more value than whole nations, since they support cities and constitutions as buttresses support large houses.

—There is no place on earth more sacred than the mind of a wise man, while all the virtues hover around like so many stars.

—No one may so far yield to unreasonable folly as to boast that he has seen the invisible God.

—As pillars support whole houses, so also do the divine powers support the whole world.

—Justice, above all things, conduces to the safety, both of mankind, and of the parts of the world, earth, and heaven.

—Every soul which piety fertilizes with its own mysteries is necessarily awake to all holy services, and eager for the contemplation of those things which are worth being seen, for this is the feeling of the soul at the great festival, and this is the true season of joy.

—If you have a great deal of wealth, take care and do not be carried away by its overflow; but endeavor to take hold of some dry ground, in order to establish your mind with proper firmness; and this will be the proper exertion of justice and fairness. And if you have abundant supplies of all the things requisite for the indulgence of those passions which lie beneath the belly, be not carried away by such plenty, but oppose to them a saving degree of contentedness, taking in this way dry ground to stand on, instead of an absorbing quicksand.

—The most perfect and greatest of all good things are usually the result of laborious exercise and energetic, vigorous labor. It is absurd for a man who is in pursuit of honors to flee from labors by which honors are acquired.

—The extremity of happiness is to rest unchangeably and immovably on God alone.

—When you are entreated to pardon offenses, pardon willingly those who have offended against you, because indulgence given in requital for indulgence, and reconciliation with our fellow-servants, is a means of diverting the divine anger.

—The virtuous man is a lover of his race, merciful and inclined to pardon, and never bears ill-will toward any man whatever, but thinks it right to surpass in doing good rather than in injuring.

—Let us not fear the diseases which come upon us from without, but those offenses on which account diseases come, diseases of the soul, rather than of the body,

---

MODERN JUDAISM.

Church and State.

Religion is universal; theology is exclusive. Religion is humanitarian; theology is sectarian. Religion unites mankind; theology divides it. Religion is love, broad and all-comprising as God's love; theology preaches love and practices bigotry. Religion looks to the moral worth of man; theology to his creed and denomination. Religion teaches us, as Vice-President Colfax so beautifully expresses it, "The common fatherhood of God, and the common brotherhood of man;" theology teaches predestination, eternal damnation, and that we rather should fear the anger of God, than trust to His paternal love and mercy. Religion, therefore, is light and love, and virtue and peace, unadulterated and immaculate; but theology is the apple of discord, which disunites and estranges us from one another. The sorrowful fact is that we have too much of narrow-minded and narrow-hearted theology, and too little of the spirit of true religion.

The same difference now exists between the *modern* State and Church. The State is humanitarian; the Church sectarian. The State, in conformity with the continuous advancement of the human race, must be progressive; the Church, in accordance with its creed, must be stationary. The State looks after and watches over the interests of all its membere; the Church looks first of all to its own interests and those of its communicants. The State advances and progresses as far as man is able to advance; the Church must discourage any criticism that may sap the foundation of its doctrinal structure.

It is quite an erroneous impression, a complete misrepresentation of facts, that the State is nothing but a national police system for the protection of persons and property. * * This definition is the mediæval one, and reminds us of those times in which the Church assumed the government of all the political and spiritual interests of the world, and the State was nothing but its obedient executive.

But the modern State is quite another organization. * * It says all men are created equal, and hence it breaks down all castes and privileges; erases all titles by "divine right," be they aristocratic or hierarchic, and recognizes but one government, established "by the people and for the people." The modern State says, man is entitled to liberty, and therefore grants freedom of thought, freedom of speech, and freedom of the press. The modern State says, all men are entitled to happiness, and therefore abolishes serfdom and slavery, and grants to every one free exercise of rights and powers, so long as they do not interfere with the rights of his fellow-men. The modern State says, every one has a right to worship his Creator according to his best knowledge, and his conscience, and therefore does not meddle with religious affairs, and leaves them to the care and direction of the individual. Civil and religious liberty, in all their various ramifications, are the children of the modern State. These blessings, which are considered the greatest boon of mankind, and the glory of modern civilization, were bestowed on the present generation by the State and not the Church. * * * The modern State, therefore, is not a national police force, but the noble representative of all those glorious ideas which distinguish our age and civilization from that of past centuries.

The Church treats its votaries as minors, the State wants free and independent men. Sectarian schools educate sectarian pupils; free schools educate freemen—citizens; and hence the State is better fitted to advance the interests of humanity at large than the Church, and every true and marked progress has only been achieved since the State has emancipated itself from the Church, and become separated and divorced from it.

And what State has laid down these humanitarian principles more clearly, more emphatically and unequivocally, than the United States, our God-blessed country?

Where is there a Constitution, and a Declaration of Independence, like that framed by the immortal men of 1776? * *

Do not point to vile politicians and tricky agitators. There are sinners in the State, no less than in the Church. With all their vices and corruptions they cannot detract from the merit and sublimity of the modern, progressive State. They are but excressences of society, only to flourish for awhile; their days are numbered; and when the people arouse, they will be scattered, and vanish like chaff before a whirlwind. * *

We assert, with our old Rabbis, "that the good of all denominations will participate in the future bliss of Heaven." * * And we assert this, because we believe with Moses and Jesus, that the supreme command of all religion is: "Love thy fellow-man as thyself," without distinction of race, or color, or creed. These words comprise all the law and the prophets, and this must be the corner-stone of all future religion. Hence it is our duty to see that justice be meted out to all; that liberty be granted to all; that the inalienable rights with which the Creator has endowed man be enjoyed by all; and that the old golden rule be observed by all: Do unto others as you wish to be done by.

This is the relation which modern Judaism assumes toward the modern State, and especially towards the laws of our beloved country. Hence we have given up all idea of ever returning to Palestine and establishing there an independent nationality. * * Hence we have given up our sectarian schools, and send our children to the free schools; for we wish to educate them as thorough Americans, from their childhood, to fraternize with their future fellow-citizens.—*Rabbi Lilienthal, Cincinnati, Ohio.*

Ethics and Politics.—Reason.

With the universal God and the universal standpoint, universal ethics and politics, as the necessary sequences thereof, must have come; and they did come in the brief words, "Love thy neighbor as thyself," which Confucius, Hillel, and Jesus expounded by the golden rule; and "God is king;" *i. e.*, the absolute wisdom, and justice is the Sole Sovereign of the human race. In principle, nothing can be added thereto, nothing diminished thereof. If man exists only inasmuch as he is in God, in love, wisdom, and justice, and all else is momentary, temporal and perishable, then he truly lives only so far as he loves, thinks, and acts wisely and justly. If all men partake of the same divine nature, then all are of one nature: they are one. Hence the individual is not a unit, the race is. The individual cannot love himself, think and act wisely and justly to himself; he can do all this to the race only of which he is a part. Hence he can live only in love to the human race. Again, if the race is a unit, inasmuch as all partake of the same divine nature, then none but God can be king, because he is the majesty, the centre of all excellencies diffused in the human family. If I must love my neighbor, how shall I tyrannize over him? No man possesses absolute wisdom and justice.

So we have reached the ideals, the final object of historical development, as laid down in the Bible. The people of Israel, in the course of their history, went by all standpoints, from rude fetichism to the highest absolute theism; from the barbarous slaughtering of the Canaanites to the supreme law of humanity; through all forms of religion, ethics, and politics, to the highest and universal standpoint in each. The Bible stories must be understood as phases of development, particular standpoints, temporized and localized, which must be divested of their specialties, to receive their respective positions in history, and their proper place in relation to the universal idea. If Joshua supposed God had commanded him or Moses to accomplish the extinction of the seven nations, he did so from a temporal and local standpoint, formed by the state of civilization and force of circumstances at the period. If the Jew saw in God the mere God of Israel or of Palestine, Paul saw Him in a son of God, and John in the Logos; they temporized and localized the Deity, as those do in ethics who claim justice in heaven and on earth, only for themselves and their friends. All particular standpoints, all phases of development, are represented in Israel's history; and all of them must be passed through by the entire human family, to reach the ideals in religion, ethics, and politics, as set forth in our Bible.

Who shall guide man in this path to perfection? How are we to distinguish the universal from the temporal or local standpoint, God from the gods, justice from compacts of selfishness? History itself as little as the Bible can guide us in this matter, for they contain both the ideal, and the history of development towards it, the universal and all particular standpoints, truth and the various shades of aberrations. If the Bible is to guide, what are we to do with its immoral incidents, the unreasonable tales and myths, the local or temporal presentations of Deity? The religious sentiment called faith cannot guide, for it is evidently uncertain. Whence the various and contradictory views of the Christian sects, all claiming the guidance of faith, if it is reliable? By faith, crusades were organized, inquisitions instituted, *auto da fes* celebrated, tens of thousands were massacred.

The ethical sentiment, conscience, must guide, it may be maintained; but this is also an unsafe guide. Conscience, too, has misguided, and does misguide individuals and nations. The conscience of those parents who drown their new-born daughers because they cannot afford to give them the proper education and outfit; and of those barbarous sons who kill their feeble and aged parents, because they are burdensome to themselves and others; the conscience of fanatics and enraged mobs, of despots and their obedient coadjutors, is human conscience.

Reason, the understanding, is THE guide which God has given us; the highest and last arbiter in all matters, human and divine. Reason is the supreme authority; and there is no appeal from its decisions. By reason we distinguish correctly the true from the false, right from wrong, the universal from the particular. Faith, conscience, history, and Bible must submit to reason This is the touchstone to distinguish gold from brass, the precious metal from the dross. Whatever cannot stand the test of reason is worthless, and to be cast away. This was the case in all ages of history, and will be so forever. With the progress of reason, faith and conscience are purified, humanity is elevated, and the ethical feeling sanctified. Truth is the only Messiah. Reason, says a Jewish authority, is the angel (the mediator) which stands between God and man. Reason has redeemed the human family from barbarism, and will complete the work of redemption. If I speak of reason as the highest authority, I do not mean my reason or your reason; I mean reason itself, universal and eternal, in which and through which the human family is a unit, and God is revealed to man. Reason must distinguish the universal standpoint from the particular ones in the Bible and elsewhere. Truth is the seal of God. Reason is the connecting link of God and man,—like the rays of light that connect the earth with the sun. Therefore, science, the favorite mistress of reason, is the ally of religion and truth. Research, criticism, inquiry, and all other exertions of reason, are divinely appointed means for the progress of humanity to its lofty ideals of God, truth, and happiness.—*Rabbi Isaac M. Wise, Cincinnati, Ohio.*

FRATERNITY — RELIGIOUS LIBERTY — EDUCATION.

Resolutions of Conference of Rabbis, Cleveland, Ohio, July 15, 1870.

These resolves, laid before the Conference by Rabbi Lilienthal, of Cincinnati, and approved by a select committee, were adopted *unanimously*, and engrossed and signed by all present:

At a meeting of the Rabbis of various cities of the Union, held in the city of Cleveland, Ohio, from and after July 13, in consideration of the religious commotion now agitating the public mind in both hemispheres, in accordance with the principles of Judaism, it was unanimously declared:

1. Because, with unshaken faith and firmness we believe in one indivisible and eternal God, we also believe in the common fatherhood of God, and the common brotherhood of men.

2. We glory in the sublime doctrine of our religion, which teaches that the righteous of all nations, without distinction of creed, will enjoy eternal life and everlasting happiness.

3. The divine command, the most sublime passage of the Bible, "Thou shalt love thy fellowman as thyself," extends to the entire human family, without distinction of either race or creed.

4. Civil and religious liberty, and hence the separation of Church and State, are the inalienable rights of men, and we consider them to be the brightest gems in the Constitution of the United States.

5. We love and revere this country as our home and fatherland for us and our children; and therefore consider it our paramount duty to sustain and support the government; to favor by all means the system of free education, leaving religious instruction to the care of the different denominations.

6. We expect the universal elevation and fraternization of the human family to be achieved by the natural means of science, morality, justice, freedom and truth.

Dr. J. Mayer, President, Cleveland, Ohio; Dr. M. Lilienthal, Cincinnati, Ohio; Dr. Ad. Hubsh, New York; Dr. I. M. Wise, Cincinnati, Ohio; Dr. H. S. Sonneshein, St. Louis, Mo.; Dr. L. Kleeberg, Louisville, Ky.; Dr. L. Adler, Chicago, Ill.; Dr. S. Tuska, Memphis, Tenn.; Dr. G. Kalish, New York; Dr. M. Fluegel, Quincy, Ill.; G. M. Cohen, Cleveland, Ohio; A. L. Mayer, Richmond, Va.; Dr. L. Goldhammer, Cincinnati, Ohio.

CHAPTER VII.

GREECE.

ORPHEUS, PYTHAGORAS, PLATO, ETC.

ONE BEING.

There is One Unknown Being, prior to all beings, and exalted above all. He is the author of all things, even of the ethereal sphere, and of all things below it. He is Life, Counsel and Light, which all signify One Power, the same that drew all things visible and invisible, out of nothing. We will sing that eternal, wise, and all-perfect Love, which reduced chaos to order.

The empyrean, the deep Tartarus, the earth, the ocean, the immortal gods and goddesses, all that is, that has been, or that will be, was originally contained in the fruitful bosom of Jupiter. He is the first and the last, the beginning and the end. He is the Primeval Father, the immortal virgin, the life, the cause, the energy of all things. There is One only Power, One only Lord, One Universal King.—*Orpheus, B. C. 1200.*

ONE SOUL,—AND OTHER SAYINGS.

There is One Universal Soul, diffused through all things,—eternal, invisible, unchangeable; in essence like truth, in substance resembling light; not to be represented by any image, to be comprehended only by the mind; not as some conjecture, exterior to the world, but, in himself entire, pervading the universal sphere.

Unity is the principle of all things, and from this unity went forth an infinite duality.

The soul of man being between spirits who always contemplate the Divine Essence, and those incapable of such contemplation, *can raise itself to the one, or sink itself to the* other.

Truth is to be sought with a mind purified from the passions of the body. Having overcome evil things, thou shalt experience the union of the immortal God with the mortal man.

Man is perfected, first by conversing with the gods, which he can only do when he abstains from evil, and strives to resemble the divine nature; second, by doing good to others, which is an imitation of the gods; third, by leaving this mortal body.

A man should never pray for anything for himself, because every one is ignorant of what is really good for him.

Every man ought to speak and act with such integrity that no one would have reason to doubt his simple affirmation.

Do what you believe to be right, whatever people think of you.

It is either requisite to be silent or to say something better than silence.

It is impossible that he can be free who is a slave to his passions.

We should avoid and amputate by every possible artifice, by fire and sword, and all various contrivances; from the body, disease; from the soul, ignorance; from the belly, luxury; from a city, sedition; from a house, discord; and at the same time from all things, immoderation.

It is better to live lying in the grass confiding in divinity and yourself, than to lie in a golden bed with purturbation.—*Pithagoras, B. C. 586.*

ZEUS AND DIVINE LAW.

Greatest of the gods, God with many names, God ever-ruling, and ruling all things!
Zeus, origin of nature, governing the universe by law,
All hail! For it is right for mortals to address thee;

Since we are thy offspring, and we alone of all
That live and creep on the earth have power of imitative speech.
Therefore will I praise thee, and hymn forever thy power.
Thee the wide heaven, which surrounds the earth, obeys;
Following where thou wilt, willingly obeying thy law.
Thou holdest at thy service, in thy mighty hands,
The two-edged, flaming, immortal thunderbolt,
Before whose flash all nature trembles.
Thou rulest in the common reason, which goes through all,
And appears in all things, great and small,
Which, filling all nature, is king of all existences.
Nor without thee, O Deity, does anything happen in the world,
From the ethereal pole to the great ocean,
Except only the evil prepared by the senseless wicked.
But thou also art able to bring to order that which is chaotic,
Giving form to that which is formless, and making the discordant friendly;
So reducing all variety to unity, and even making good out of evil.
Thus through all nature is one great law,
Which only the wicked seek to disobey,—
Poor fools! who long for happiness,
But will not see nor hear the divine commands.

[*Cleanthes, B. C. 260.*

The One Primitive Substance.

The Eternal Living Being, most noble of all beings; distinct from matter, without extension or division, without parts or succession; who understands everything, and, continuing himself immovable, gives motion to all things, and enjoys in himself a perfect happiness, knowing and contemplating himself with infinite pleasure. * * * * *

There are many inferior deities, but One Mover. All that is said of the human shape of those deities is mere fiction, invented to instruct the common people, and secure their observance of good laws. A Spiritual Substance is the cause of the universe, and the source of all order and beauty, all motions, and all the forms we so much admire in it. All must be reduced to this One Primitive Substance, which governs in subordination to the First. * * *

There is one Supreme Intelligence, who acts with order, proportion and design, the source of all that is good and just.

After death, the soul continueth in the ærial body till it is entirely purged from all angry and voluptuous passion; then doth it put off, by a second death, the ærial body, as it did the terrestial body. Wherefore the ancients say there is another heavenly body always joined with the soul, which is immortal, luminous, and star-like.—*Aristotle.*

Prayer of Socrates.

O Beloved Pan, and all ye other Gods of the place, grant me to become beautiful in the inner man, and that whatever outward things I may have may be at peace with those within.

May I deem the wise man rich, and may I have such a portion of gold as none but a prudent man can either bear or employ! Do we need anything else, Phaedrus? For myself I have prayed enough.

PLATO.

Wisdom and Self-knowledge.

I mean that wisdom is the only science which is the science of itself and of the other sciences as well. * * Then the wise or temperate man, and he only, will know himself, and be able to examine what he knows or does not know, and see what others know, and think that they know and do really know; and what they do not know, and fancy that they know, when they do not. No other person will be able to do this. And this is the state and virtue of wisdom, or temperance, and self-knowledge, which is just knowing what a man knows, and what he does not know.

Justice and Reverence in all Men.

Now man, having a share of the divine attributes, was at first the only one of the animals who had any gods, because he alone was of their kindred; and he would raise altars and images of them. He was not long in inventing language and names; and he also constructed houses, and clothes, and shoes and beds, and drew sustenance from the earth. Thus provided, mankind at first lived dispersed, and there were no cities. But the consequence was they were destroyed by wild beasts, for they were utterly weak in comparison of them, and their art was only sufficient to provide them with the means of life, and would not enable them to carry on war against the animals: food they had, but not as yet any art of government, of which the art of war is a part. After awhile the desire of self-preservation gathered them into cities; but when they were gathered together, having no art of government, they evil-entreated one another, and were again in process of dispersion and destruction. Zeus feared that the race would be exterminated, and so he sent Hermes to them, bearing reverence and justice to be the ordering principles of cities and the bonds of friendship and conciliation. Hermes asked Zeus how he should impart justice and reverence among men: should he distribute them as the arts are distributed? that is to say, to a favored few only,—for one skilled individual has enough of medicine, or any other art, for many unskilled ones. Shall this be the manner in which I distribute justice and reverence among men, or shall I give them to all? To all, said Zeus; I should like them all to have a share; for cities cannot exist if a few only share in the virtues, as in the arts.

Death and the After Life.—Socrates to his Friends and Judges.

O my judges—for you I may truly call judges—I should like to tell you of a wonderful circumstance. Hitherto the familiar oracle within me has constantly been in the habit of opposing me, even about trifles, if I was going to make a slip or error about anything; and now, as you see, there has come upon me that which may be thought, and is generally believed to be, the last and worst evil. But the oracle made no sign of opposition, either as I was leaving my house and going out in the morning, or when I was going up into this court, or while I was speaking, at anything which I was going to say; and yet I have often been stopped in the middle of a speech, but now in nothing I either said or did, touching this matter, has the oracle opposed me. What do I take to be the explanation of this? I will tell you. I regard this as a proof that what has happened to me is a good, and that those of us who think that death is an evil are in error. This is a great proof to me of what I am saying, for the customary sign would surely have opposed me had I been going to evil and not to good.

Let us reflect in another way, and we shall see that there is great reason to hope that death is a good, for one or two things: either death is a state of nothingness and utter unconsciousness, or, as men say, there is a change and migration of the soul from this world to another. Now if you suppose that there is no consciousness, but to sleep like the sleep of him who is undisturbed even by the sight of dreams, death will be an unspeakable gain. For if a person were to select the night in which his sleep was undisturbed even by dreams, and were to compare with this the other days and nights of his life, and then were to tell us how many days and nights he had passed in the course of his life better and more pleasantly than this one, I think that any man,—I will not say a private man, but even the great king,—will not find many such days or nights, when compared with the others. Now if death is like this, I say that to die is gain; for eternity is then only a single night. But if death is the journey to another place, and there, as men say, all the dead are, what good, O my friends and judges, can be greater than this? If, indeed, when the pilgrim arrives in the world below, he is delivered from the professors of justice in this world, and finds the true judges who are said to give judgment there, Minos and Rhadamanthus and Æacus and Triptolemus, and other sons of God who were righteous in their own life, that pilgrimage will be worth making. What would not a man give if he might converse with Orpheus and Musaeus and Hesiod and Homer? Nay, if this be true, let me die again and again. I, too, shall have a wonderful interest in a place where I can converse with Palamedes, and Ajax the son of Telamon, and other heroes of old, who have suffered death through an unjust judgment; and there will be no small pleasure, as I think, in comparing my own sufferings with theirs. Above all, I shall be able to continue my search into true and false knowledge; as in this world, so also in that; I shall find out who is wise, and who pretends to be wise, and is not. What would not a man give, O judges, to be able to examine the leader of the great Trojan expedition; or Odysseus or Sisyphus, or numberless others, men and women too! What infinite delight would there be in conversing with them and asking them questions! For in that world, they do not put a man to death for this; certainly not. For besides being happier in that world than this, they will be immortal, if what is said be true.

Wherefore, O judges, be of good cheer about death, and know this of a truth: that no evil can happen to a good man, either in life or after death. He and his are not neglected by the gods; nor has my own approaching end happened by mere chance. But I see clearly that to die and be released was better for me; and therefore the oracle gave no sign. For which reason, also, I am not angry with my accusers or my condemners; they have done me no harm, although neither of hem meant to do me any good; and for this I may gently blame them.

Still I have a favor to ask of them. When my sons are grown up, I would ask you, O my friends, to punish them; and I would have you trouble them, as I have troubled you, if they seem to care about riches, or anything, more than about virtue; or if they pretend to be something when they are really nothing; then reprove them as I have reproved you, for not caring about that for which they ought to care, and thinking they are something when they are really nothing. And if you do this, I and my sons will have received justice at your hands. The hour of departure has arrived, and we go our ways—I to die, and you to live. Which is better, God only knows.

Socrates on the Soul and the Body.

For I am quite ready to acknowledge, Simmias and Cebes, that I ought to be grieved at death, if I were not persuaded that I am going to other gods who are wise and good (of this I am as certain as I can be of anything of the sort), and to men departed (though I am not so certain of this), who are better than those I leave behind; and therefore I do not grieve as I might have done, for I have good hope that there is yet something remaining for the dead, and as has been said of old, some far better thing for the good than for the evil. * * Moreover, if there is time and inclination towards philosophy, yet the body introduces a turmoil and confusion and fear into the course of speculation, and hinders us from seeing the truth; and all experience shows that if we would have pure knowledge of anything, we must be quit of the body, and the soul in herself must behold all things in themselves. Then, I suppose, that we shall attain that which we desire, and of which we say that we are lovers, and that is wisdom; not while we live, but after death, as the argument shows; for if while in company with the body, the soul cannot have pure knowledge, one of two things seems to follow—either knowledge is not to be attained at all, or, if at all, after death. For then, and not till then, the soul will be in herself alone and without the body. In this present life I reckon that we make the nearest approach to knowledge when we have the least possible concern or interest in the body, and are not saturated with the bodily nature, but remain pure until the hour when God himself is pleased to release us. And then the foolishness of the body will be cleared away, and we shall be pure, and hold converse with other pure souls, and know of ourselves the clear light everywhere; and this is surely the light of truth. For no impure thing is allowed to approach the pure. * *

"Then may we not say, Simmias, that if, as we are always repeating, there is an absolute beauty, and goodness, and essence in general, and to this which is now discovered to be a previous condition of our being, we refer all our sensations, and with this compare them—assuming this to have a prior existence, but if not, there would be no force in the argument—there can be no doubt that if these absolute ideas existed before we were born, then our souls must have existed before we were born, and if not the ideas, then not the souls. * * And were we not saying long ago that the soul, when using the body as an instrument of perception, that is to say, when using the sense of sight or hearing, or some other sense (for the meaning of perceiving through the body is perceiving through the senses), were we not saying that the soul too is then dragged by the body into the region of the changeable, and wanders and is confused; the world spins round her, and she is like a drunkard when under their influence?"

"Very true."

"But when returning into herself, she reflects; then she passes into the realm of purity, and eternity, and immortality, and unchangeableness, which are her kindred, and with them she ever lives, when she is by herself and is not let or hindered; then she ceases from her erring ways, and being in communion with the unchanging is unchanging. And this state of the soul is called wisdom?"

"That is well and truly said, Socrates," he replied.

"And to which class is the soul more nearly alike and akin, as far as may be inferred from this argument, as well as from the preceding one?"

"I think, Socrates, that, in the opinion of every one who follows the argument, the soul will be infinitely more like the unchangeable; even the most stupid person will not deny that."

"And the body is more like the changing?"

"Yes."

"Yet once more consider the matter in this light: When the soul and the body are united, then nature orders the soul to rule and govern, and the body to obey and serve; now which of these two functions is akin to the divine? and which to the mortal? Does not the divine appear to you to be that which naturally orders and rules, and the mortal that which is subject and servant?"

"True."

"And which does the soul resemble?"

"The soul resembles the divine, and the body the mortal; there can be no doubt of that, Socrates." * * *

"But then, O my friends," he (Socrates) said, "if the soul is really immortal, what care should be taken of her, not only in respect of the portion of time which is called life, but of eternity! And the danger of neglecting her from this point of view does indeed appear to be awful. If death had only been the end of all, the wicked would have had a good bargain in dying, for they would have been happily quit not only of their body, but of their own evil together with their souls. But now, as the soul plainly appears to be immortal, there is no release or salvation from evil except the attainment of the highest virtue and wisdom. For the soul when on her progress to the world below takes nothing with her but nurture and education; which are indeed said greatly to benefit or greatly to injure the departed, at the very beginning of his pilgrimage in the other world."

No Escape for Evil Doers.

"But, O my friends, you cannot easily convince mankind that they should pursue virtue or avoid vice, not for the reasons which the many give, in order, forsooth, that a man may seem to be good; this is what they are always repeating, and this, in my judgment, is an old wives' fable. Let them hear the truth: In God is no unrighteousness at all, he is altogether righteous; and there is nothing more like him, than he of us who is the most righteous. And the true wisdom of men and their nothingness and cowardice, are nearly concerned with this. For to know this is true wisdom and manhood, and the ignorance of this is too plainly folly and vice. All other kinds of wisdom or cunning, which seem only, such as the wisdom of politicians, or the wisdom of the arts, are coarse and vulgar. The unrighteous man, or the sayer and doer of unholy things, had far better not yield to the illusion that his roguery is cleverness; for men glory in their shame—they fancy that they hear others saying of them, 'these are not mere good-for-nothing persons, burdens on the earth, but such as men should be who mean to dwell safely in a state.' Let us tell them that they are all the more truly what they do not know that they are; for they do not know the penalty of injustice, which above all things they ought to know; nor stripes and death, as they suppose, which evil-doers often escape, but a penalty which cannot be escaped. * * * * * *

There are two patterns set before them in nature: the one blessed and divine, the other godless and wretched; and they do not see in their utter folly and infatuation, that they are growing like the one and unlike the other, by reason of their evil deeds; and the penalty is that they lead a life answering to the pattern which they resemble. And if we tell them that unless they depart from their cunning, the place of innocence will not receive them after death; and that here on earth, they will live ever in the likeness of their own evil selves, and with evil friends: when they hear this, they in their superior cunning will seem to be listening to fools." * * *

The Divine Law.

God, as the old tradition declares, holding in His hand the beginning, middle and end of all that is, moves according to his nature in a straight line towards the accomplishment of His end. Justice always follows Him, and is the punisher of those who fall short of the divine law. To that law, he who would be happy holds fast, and follows it in all humility and order. But he who is lifted up with pride, or money, or honor, or beauty, who has a soul hot with folly, and youth, and insolence, and thinks that he has no need of a guide or ruler, but is able himself to be the guide of others,—he, I say, is left deserted of God; and being thus deserted, he takes to him others who are like himself, and dances about in wild confusion, and many think that he is a great man; but in a short time he pays a penalty which justice cannot but approve, and is utterly destroyed, and his family and city with him. * *

Honor to the Soul.

Of all things which a man has, next to the gods, his soul is the most divine and most truly his own. * * Wherefore I am right in bidding every one next to the gods, who are our masters, and those who in order follow them, to honor his own soul, which every one seems to honor, but no one honors as he ought; for honor is a divine good, and no evil thing is honorable; and he who thinks that he can honor the soul by word or gift, or any sort of compliance, not making her in any way better, seems to honor her, but honors her not at all. For example, every man, in his very boyhood, fancies that he is able to know everything, and thinks that he honors his soul by praising her, and he is very ready to let her do whatever she may like. But I mean to say that in acting thus he only injures his soul, and does not honor her; whereas, in our opinion, he ought to honor her as second only to the gods. Again, when a man thinks that others are to be blamed, and not himself, for the errors which he has committed, and the many and great evils which befel him in consequence, and is always fancying himself to be exempt and innocent, he is under the idea that he is honoring his soul; whereas the very reverse is the fact, for he is really injuring her. * * *

Again, when any one prefers beauty to virtue, what is this but the real and utter dishonor of the soul? For such a preference implies that the body is more honorable than the soul; and this is false, for there is nothing of earthly birth which is more honorable than the heavenly, and he who thinks otherwise of the soul has no idea how greatly he undervalues this wonderful possession. Nor, again, when a person is willing, or not unwilling, to acquire dishonest gains, does he then honor his soul with gifts — far otherwise; he sells her glory and honor for a small piece of gold; but all the gold which is under or upon the earth, is not to be given in exchange for virtue. * * For no one, as I may say, ever considers that which is declared to be the greatest penalty of evil-doing, namely: to grow into the likeness of bad men, and growing like them, to fly from the conversation of the good, and be cut off from them, and cleave to and follow after the company of the bad. And he who is joined to them must do and suffer what such men by nature do and say to one another, which suffering is not justice but retribution; for justice and the just are noble, whereas retribution is the suffering which waits upon injustice; and whether a man escape or endure this, he is miserable: in the former case, because he is not cured; in the latter, because he perishes in order that the rest of the world may be saved.

Divine Justice.

O youth or young man, who fancy that you are neglected by the gods, know that if you become worse you shall go to the worse souls, or if better to the better, and in every succession of life and death you will do and suffer what like may fitly suffer at the hands of like. This is a divine justice, which neither you nor any other unfortunate will ever glory in escaping, and which the ordaining powers have specially ordained; take good heed of them, for a day will come when they will take heed of you. If thou sayest: "I am small and will creep into the depths of the earth," or, "I am high and will fly up to heaven," you are not so small or so high but that you shall pay the fitting penalty, either in the world below, or in some yet more savage place still, to which thou shalt be conveyed.

This is also the explanation of the fate of those whom you saw, who had done unholy and evil deeds, and from small beginnings had become great; and you fancied that from being miserable they had become happy, and in their actions, as in a mirror, you seemed to see the universal neglect of the gods, not knowing how they make all things work together and contribute to the great whole.

Prayer—The Divine Nature—The Just Man.

Prayer is the ardent turning of the soul toward God; not to ask for any particular good, but for good itself; the universal supreme good. We often mistake what is pernicious and dangerous for what is useful and desirable. Therefore remain silent before the gods till they remove the clouds from thy eyes, and enable thee to see by their light, not what appears good to thyself, but what is really good.

Whatever is beautiful is so merely by participation of the Supreme Beauty. All other beauty may increase, decay, change, or perish, but this is the same through all time. By raising our thoughts above all inferior beauties, we at length reach the Supreme Beauty, which is simple, pure and immutable, without form, color, or human qualities. It is the splendor of the Divine image, it is Deity himself. Love of this Supreme Beauty renders a man divine.

God provides for all things, the least as well as the greatest. He is the original life and force of all things, in the ethereal regions, upon the earth, and under the earth. He is the Being, the Unity, the Good; the same in the world of Intelligence that the sun is in the visible world.

God is Truth, and Light is his shadow.

What light and sight are in this visible world, truth and intelligence are in the real unchangeable world.

The end and aim of all things should be to attain to the First Good; of whom the sun is the type, and the material world, with its host of ministering spirits, is but the manifestation and the shadow.

The perfectly just man would be he who should love justice for its own sake, not for the honors or advantages that attend; who would be willing to pass for unjust while he practiced the most exact justice; who would not suffer himself to be moved by disgrace or distress, but would continue steadfast in the love of justice, not because it is pleasant, but because it is right.*

* Plato was born B. C. 429. The new and admirable translation of Professor Jowitt has been followed, except in the last page—the pages and articles not being given, for brevity's sake.

CHAPTER VIII.

ROME.*

THOUGHTS OF MARCUS AURELIUS ANTONINUS.

His Teachers.

From my grandfather Verus I learned good morals and the government of my temper.

From the reputation and remembrance of my father, modesty and a manly character.

From my mother, piety and beneficence, and abstinence, not only from evil deeds, but even from evil thoughts; and further, simplicity in my way of living, far removed from the habits of the rich. * * *

From Diognetus, not to busy myself about trifling things, and not to give credit to what was said by miracle-workers and jugglers about incantations and the driving away of demons and such things.

From Apollonius I learned freedom of will and undeviating steadiness of purpose; and to look to nothing else, not even for a moment, except to reason; and to be always the same, in sharp pains, on the occasion of the loss of a child, and in long illness; and to see clearly in a living example that the same man can be both most resolute and yielding, and not peevish in giving his instruction; and to have had before my eyes a man who clearly considered his experience and his skill in expounding philosophical principles as the smallest of his merits. And from him I learned how to receive from friends what are esteemed favors, without being either humbled by them, or letting them pass unnoticed.

* See Appendix F.

Right Living.

Labor not unwillingly, nor without regard to the common interest, nor without due consideration, nor with distraction; nor let studied ornament set off thy thoughts, and be not either a man of many words, or busy about too many things. And further, let the Deity which is in thee be the guardian of a living being, manly and of ripe age, who has taken his post like a man waiting for the signal which summons him from life, and ready to go, having need neither of oath nor any man's testimony. Be cheerful also, and seek not external help nor the tranquility which others give. *A man must stand erect, not be kept erect by others.*

Never value anything as profitable to thyself which shall compel thee to break thy promise, to lose thy self-respect, to hate any man, to suspect, to curse, to act the hypocrite, to desire anything which needs walls and curtains: for he who has preferred to everything else his own intelligence, and the demon within him and the worship of its excellence, acts no tragic part, does not groan, will not need either solitude or much company, and, what is chief of all, he will live without either pursuing or flying from life; but whether for a longer or a shorter time he shall have the soul inclosed in the body, he cares not at all: for even if he must depart immediately, he will go as readily as if he were going to do anything else which can be done with decency and order; taking care of this only all through life, that his thoughts turn not away from anything which belongs to an intelligent animal and a member of a civil community.

In the mind of one who is chastened and purified thou wilt find no corrupt matter, nor impurity, nor any sore skinned over. Nor is his life incomplete when fate overtakes him, as one may say of an actor who leaves the stage before ending and finishing the play. Besides, there is in him nothing servile, nor affected, nor too closely bound to other things, nor yet detached from other things, nothing worthy of blame, nothing which seeks a hiding-place. * * *

If thou workest at that which is before thee, following right reason seriously, vigorously, calmly, without allowing anything else to distract thee, but keeping thy divine part pure, as if thou shouldst be bound to give it back immediately; if thou holdest to this, expecting nothing, fearing nothing, but satisfied with thy present activity according to nature, and with heroic truth in every word and sound which thou utterest, thou wilt live happy. And there is no man who is able to prevent this.

DISCOURSES OF EPICTETUS.

Kindred to God and its Consequences.

If what philosophers say of the kindred between God and men be true, what has any one to do, but like Socrates, when he is asked what countryman he is, never to say that he is a citizen of Athens, or of Corinth, but of the world? For why do you say that you are of Athens: and not of that corner only, where that paltry body of yours was laid at its birth? Is it not, evidently, from what is principal, and comprehends not only that corner, and your whole house, but the general extent of the country, from which your pedigree is derived down to you, that you call yourself an Athenian, or a Corinthian? Why may not he then, who understands the administration of the world, and has learned that the greatest, and most principal, and comprehensive of all things, is this system, composed of Men and God! and that from him the seeds of being are descended, not only to my father or grandfather, but to all things that are produced and born on earth,—and especially to rational natures, as they alone are qualified to partake of a communication with the Deity, being connected with him by Reason—why may not such a one call himself a citizen of the world? Why not a son of God? And why shall he fear anything that happens among men? Shall kindred to Cæsar, or any other of the great at Rome, enable a man to live secure, above contempt, and void of all fear whatever; and shall not the having God for our Maker and Father, and Guardian, free us from griefs and terrors?

The Essence of Good.

God is beneficial. Good is also beneficial. It should seem, then, that where the Essence of God is, there too is the Essence of Good. What then is the Essence of God? Flesh? By no means. An Estate? Fame?—By no means. Intelligence? Knowledge? Right Reason?—Certainly. Here then, without more ado, seek the Essence of Good. For do you seek it in a plant? No. Or in a brute? No. If then you seek it only in a rational subject, why do you seek it anywhere but in what is distinct from irrationals? Plants have not the use of the appearances of things; and therefore you do not apply the term of Good to them. *Good*, then, requires the use of these appearances. And nothing else? If so, you may say, that good and happiness, and unhappiness, belong to mere animals. But this you do not say, and you are right. * * What then? Are not these likewise the works of the gods? They are: but not Principals, nor Parts of the gods. But you are a Principal. You are a distinct portion of the Essence of God; and contain a certain part of him in yourself. Why then are you ignorant of your noble birth? Why do not you consider whence you came? Why do not you remember when you are eating, who you are who eat; and whom you feed? When you are in the company of women; when you are conversing; when you are exercising; when you are disputing; do not you know that it is a God you feed; a God you exercise? You carry a God about with you, wretch, and know nothing of it. Do you suppose I mean some God without you of gold or silver? It is within yourself you carry him; and profane him, without being sensible of it, by impure thoughts, and unclean actions.

Obedience and Trust in God.

Lastly: to all other pleasures oppose that of being conscious that you are obeying God; and performing not in word, but in deed, the duty of a wise and good man. How great a thing is it to be able to say to yourself, "What others are now solemnly arguing in the schools, and seem to carry beyond probabilty, this I am actually performing. * * Seek not good from without: seek it in yourselves, or you will never find it. For this reason, he now brings me hither, now sends me thither: shows me to mankind, poor, without authority, sick; sends me to Gyaros; leads me to prison: not that he hates me — Heaven forbid! For who hates the best of his servants? Nor that he neglects me: for he doth not neglect any one of the smallest things; but to exercise me, and make use of me as a witness to others. Appointed to such a service, do I still care where I am, or with whom, or what is said of me, instead of being wholly attentive to God, and to his orders and commands?"

Prayer Near Death.

I would be found in the regulation of my own will; how to render it undisturbed, unrestrained, uncompelled, free; that I might be able to say to God,—"Have I transgressed thy commands? Have I perverted the powers, the senses and instincts thou hast given me? Have I ever censured thy dispensations?" I have been sick, because it was thy pleasure, but willingly. I have been poor, because it was thy will, but with joy. I have not been in power, but with joy; and I have never desired power. Hast thou ever seen me saddened because of this? Have I not always approached Thee with cheerful countenance? Is it thy pleasure that I depart from this assembly of living men, I go. I give Thee all thanks that thou hast thought me worthy to have a share in it with Thee; to behold thy works, and join in comprehending thy administration.

MORALS OF SENECA.

On Benefits.

Let us be liberal then, after the example of our great Creator, and give to others with the same consideration that he gives to us. * * *

If there were not an ordering and an overruling Providence, how comes it that the universality of mankind should ever have so unanimously agreed in the madness of worshipping a power that can neither hear nor help us? Some blessings are freely given us; others upon our prayers are granted us; and every day brings forth instances of great and seasonable mercies. There never was yet any man so insensible as not to feel, see, and understand a Deity in the ordinary methods of nature, though many have been so obstinately ungrateful as not to confess it; nor is any man so wretched as not to be a partaker in that divine bounty. * *

All this, says Epicurus, we are to ascribe to Nature. And why not to God, I beseech ye? as if they were not both of them one and the same power, working in the whole, and in every part of it. Or, if you call him the Almighty Jupiter, the Thunderer, the Creator and Preserver of us all, it comes to the same issue; some will express him under the notion of *fate;* which is only a connection of causes, and himself the uppermost and original, upon which all the rest depend. The Stoics represent the several *functions* of the Almighty Power under several appellations. When they speak of him as the father and the fountain of all beings, they call him Bacchus; and under the name of Hercules, they denote him to be indefatigable, and invincible and, in the contemplation of him in the reason, order, proportion, and wisdom of his proceedings, they call him Mercury; so that which way soever they look, and under what name soever they couch their meaning, they never fail of finding him; for he is everywhere and fills his own work.

* * That which God himself does, we are sure is well done; and we are no less sure, that for whatsoever he gives, he neither wants, expects, nor receives, anything in return; so that the end of a benefit ought to be the advantage of the receiver; and that must be our scope without any by-regard to ourselves.

It does not divert the Almighty from being still gracious, though we proceed daily in the abuse of his bounties. How many are there that enjoy the comfort of the light that do not deserve it; that wish they had never been born! And yet Nature goes quietly on with her work, and allows them a being, even in despite of their unthankfulness. Such a knave, we cry, was better used than I: and the same complaint we extend to Providence itself. How many wicked men have good crops when better than themselves have their fruits blasted! Such a man, we say, has treated me very ill. Why, what should we do, but that very thing which is done by God himself? that is to say, give to the ignorant and persevere to the wicked. All our ingratitude, we see, does not turn Providence from pouring down of benefits, even upon those that question whence they come. * * * * *

He who preaches gratitude pleads the cause both of God and man; for without it we can neither be sociable nor religious.

Of a Happy Life.

There is not anything in this world, perhaps, that is more talked of and less understood, than the business of a *happy life.* It is every man's wish and design; and yet not one of a thousand that knows wherein that happiness consists. We live, however, in a blind and eager pursuit of it; and the more haste we make in a wrong way, the farther we are from our journey's end. Let us, therefore, *first* consider, "what it is we should be at;" and, *secondly*, "which is the readiest way to compass it." If we be right, we shall find every day how much we improve; but if we either follow the cry or the track of people that are out of the way, we must expect to be misled, and to continue our days in wanderings and error. Wherefore it highly concerns us to take along with us a skillful guide; for it is not in this, as in other voyages, where the highway brings us to our place of repose; or if a man should happen to be out, where the inhabitants might set him right again; but on the contrary, the beaten road is here the most dangerous, and the people, instead of helping us, misguide us. Let us not, therefore, follow like beasts, but rather govern ourselves by *reason* than by *example.* It fares with us in human life as in a routed army; one stumbles first, and then another falls upon him, and so they follow, one upon the neck of another, until the whole field comes to be but one heap of miscarriages. And the mischief is, "that the number of the multitude carries it against truth and justice;" so that we must leave the crowd, if we would be happy. For the question of a *happy life* is not to be decided by *vote:* nay, so far from it, that plurality of voices is still an argument of the wrong; the common people find it easier to believe than to judge, and content themselves with what is usual, never examining whether it be good or not. By the *common people* is intended *the man of title* as well as the *clouted shoe:* for I do not distinguish them by the eye, but by the mind, which is the proper judge of the man. Worldly felicity, I know, makes the head giddy; but if ever a man comes to himself again, he will confess, that "whatsoever he has done, he wishes undone;" and that "the things he feared were better than those he prayed for."

The true felicity of life is to be free from purturbations; to understand our duties towards God and man; to enjoy the present without any anxious dependence upon the future. Not to amuse ourselves with either hopes or fears, but to rest satisfied with what we have, which is abundantly sufficient; for he that is so, wants nothing. The great blessings of mankind are within us, and within our reach; but we shut our eyes, and like people in the dark, we fall foul upon the very thing we search for without finding it. "Tranquility is a certain equality of mind which no condition of fortune can either exalt or depress." Nothing can make it less: for it is the state of human perfection; it raises us as high as we can go, and makes every man his own supporter; whereas he that is borne up by anything else may fall.

He that judges aright, and perseveres in it, enjoys a perpetual calm; he takes a true prospect of things; he observes an order, measure, a decorum in all his actions; he has a benevolence in his nature; he squares his life according to reason; and draws to himself love and admiration. Without a certain and unchangeable judgment, all the rest is but fluctuation; but "he that always wills and wills the same thing is undoubtedly in the right." Liberty and serenity of mind must necessarily ensue upon the mastering of those things which either allure or affright us; when, instead of those flashy pleasures (which even at the best are both vain and hurtful together), we shall find ourselves possessed of joys transporting and everlasting. It must be a *sound mind* that makes a *happy man;* there must be a constancy in all conditions, a care for the things of this world, but without trouble; and such an indifferency for the bounties of fortune, that either with them or without them we may live contentedly. There must be neither lamentation, nor quarreling, nor sloth, nor fear; for it makes a discord in a man's life. "He that fears, serves." The joy of a wise man stands firm without interruption; in all places, at all times and in all considerations, his thoughts are cheerful and quiet. As it never *came in* to him from *without*, so it will never leave; but it is born within him, and inseparable from him. It is a solicitous life that is egged on with the hope of anything, though never so open and easy, nay, though a man should never suffer any sort of disappointment. I do not speak this either as a bar to the fair enjoyment of lawful pleasures, or to the gentle flatteries of reasonable expectations; but on the contrary, I would have men to be always in good humor, provided that it arises from their own souls, and be cherished in their own breasts. Other delights are trivial; they may smooth the brow, but they do not fill and affect the heart.

"True joy is a serene and sober motion;" and they are miserably out, that take laughing for rejoicing. The seat of it is within, and there is no cheerfulness like the resolution of a brave mind, that has fortune under his feet. He that can look death in the face, and bid it welcome, open his door to poverty, and bridle his appetite, this is the man whom Providence has established in the possession of inviolable delights. The pleasures of the vulgar are ungrounded, thin, and superficial; but the others are solid and eternal. As the body itself is rather a necessary thing, than a great, so the comforts of it are but temporary and vain. Besides that, without extraordinary moderation, their end is only pain and repentance; whereas, a peaceful conscience, honest thoughts, virtuous actions, and an indifference for casual events, are blessings without end, satiety, or measure. This consummated state of felicity is only a submission to the dictates of right nature; the foundation of it is wisdom and virtue—the knowledge of what we ought to do, and the conformity of the will to that knowledge.

Of Virtue.

Virtue is the only immortal thing which belongs to mortality; it is an invincible greatness of mind, not to be elevated or dejected with good or ill fortune. It is sociable and gentle, free, steady and fearless; content within itself; full of inexhaustible delights; and it is valued for itself. One may be a good physician, a good governor, a good grammarian, without being a good man; so that all things from without are only accessories: for the seat of it is a pure and holy mind. * * If one could but see the mind of a good man, as it is illustrated with virtue; the beauty and majesty of it, which is a dignity not so much as to be thought of without love and veneration; would not a man bless himself at the sight of such an object, as at the encounter of some supernatural power? A

8

power so miraculous, that is a kind of charm upon the souls of those that are truly affected with it. There is so wonderful a grace and authority in it, that even the worst of men approve it, and set up for the reputation of being accounted virtuous themselves.

Consolations Against Death.

This life is only a prelude to eternity, where we are to expect another original, and another state of things; we have no prospect of heaven here but at a distance; let us therefore expect our last and decretory hour with courage. The last (I say) to our bodies, but not to our minds: our luggage we leave behind us, and return as naked out of the world as we came into it. The day which we fear as our last is but the birth-day of our eternity; and it is the only way to it. So that what we fear as a rock, proves to be but a port, in many cases to be desired, never to be refused; and he that dies young has only made a quick voyage of it. Some are becalmed, others cut it away before the wind; and we live just as we sail: first, we rub our childhood out of sight; our youth next; and then our middle age; after that follows old age and brings us to the common end of mankind.

To suffer death is but the law of nature; and it is a great comfort that it can be done but once; in the very convulsions of it, we have this consolation, that our pain is near an end, and that it frees us from all the miseries of life. What it is we know not, and it were rash to condemn what we do not understand; but this we presume, either that we shall pass out of this into a better life, where we shall live with tranquility and splendor in diviner mansions, or else return to our first principles, free from the sense of any inconveniences. There is nothing immortal nor many things lasting; but by divers ways everything comes to an end. What an arrogance is it then, when the world itself stands condemned to a dissolution, that man alone should expect to live forever! It is unjust not to allow unto the giver the power of disposing of his own bounty, and a folly only to value the present. Death is as much a debt as money, and life is but a journey towards it: some dispatch it sooner, others later, but we must all have the same period. It is the care of a wise and good man to look to his manners and actions; and rather how well he lives, than how long: for to die sooner or later is not the business; but to die well or ill: for "death brings us to immortality." That death which we so much dread and decline is not the determination, but the intermission of a life which will return again.

CHAPTER IX.

NEW TESTAMENT.

JESUS AND PAUL.

THE SERMON ON THE MOUNT.

And seeing the multitudes he went up into a mountain; and when he was set, his disciples came unto him.

And he opened his mouth, and taught them, saying:

Blessed are the poor in spirit; for theirs is the kingdom of heaven.

Blessed are they that mourn; for they shall be comforted.

Blessed are the meek; for they shall inherit the earth.

Blessed are they which do hunger and thirst after righteousness; for they shall be filled.

Blessed are the merciful; for they shall obtain mercy.

Blessed are the pure in heart; for they shall see God.

Blessed are the peace-makers; for they shall be called the children of God.

Blessed are they which are persecuted for righteousness' sake; for theirs is the kingdom of heaven.

Blessed are ye when men shall revile you, and persecute you, and shall say all manner of evil against you falsely for my sake.

Rejoice, and be exceeding glad; for great is your reward in heaven: for so persecuted they the prophets which were before you. * * *

Let your light so shine before men, that they may see your good works, and glorify your Father which is in heaven.

Ye have that it hath been said, An eye for an eye and a tooth for a tooth.

But I say unto you, That ye resist not evil; but whosoever shall smite thee on thy right cheek, turn to him the other also.

And if a man will sue thee at the law, and take away thy coat, let him have thy cloak also.

And whosoever shall compel thee to go a mile, go with him twain.

Give to him that asketh thee, and from him that would borrow of thee, turn not thou away.

Ye have heard that it hath been said, Thou shalt love thy neighbor and hate thine enemy:

But I say unto you, Love your enemies, bless them that curse you, do good to them that hate you, and pray for them which despitefully use you and persecute you;

That ye may be the children of your Father which art in heaven; for he maketh his sun to rise on the evil and on the good, and sendeth rain on the just and on the unjust.

For if ye love them which love you, what reward have ye? do not even the publicans so?

And if ye salute your brethren only, what do ye more than others? do not even the publicans so?

Be ye therefore perfect, even as your Father which art in heaven is perfect. * *

And when thou prayest thou shalt not be as the hypocrites are: for they love to pray standing in the synagogues, and the corners of the streets, that they may be seen of men. Verily I say unto you, They have their reward.

But thou, when thou prayest, enter into thy closet, and when thou hast shut thy door, pray to thy Father which is in secret; and thy Father, which seeth in secret, shall reward thee openly.

But when ye pray use not vain repetitions as the heathen do; for they think they shall be heard for their much speaking.

Be not ye therefore like unto them; for your Father knoweth what things ye have need of before ye ask him. * *

Therefore, all things whatsoever ye would that men should do to you, do ye even so to them; for this is the law and the prophets.—*Jesus*.

Charity—or Love.

Though I speak with the tongues of men and of angels, and have not charity, I am become as sounding brass, or a tinkling cymbal.

And though I have the gift of prophecy, and understand all mysteries, and all knowledge; and though I have all faith, so that I could remove mountains, and have not charity, I am nothing.

And though I bestow all my goods to feed the poor, and though I give my body to be burned, and have not charity, it profiteth me nothing.

Charity suffereth long, and is kind; charity envieth not; charity vaunteth not itself, is not puffed up.

Doth not behave itself unseemly, seeketh not her own, is not easily provoked, thinketh no evil;

Rejoiceth not in iniquity, but rejoiceth in the truth;

Beareth all things, believeth all things, hopeth all things, endureth all things.

Charity never faileth; but whether there be prophecies they shall fail; whether there be tongues they shall cease; whether there be knowledge it shall vanish away.

For we know in part, and we prophesy in part.

But when that which is perfect is come, then that which is in part shall be done away.

When I was a child, I spake as a child, I understood as a child, I thought as a child: but when I became a man, I put away childish things.

For now we see through a glass darkly; but then face to face: now I know in part; but then shall I know even as also I am known.

And now abideth faith, hope, and charity, these three; but the greatest of these is charity.—*Paul.*

CHAPTER X.

AL KORAN.

PRECEPTS OF MOHAMMED.

EXTRACTS.

The pious is he who believeth in God, and who giveth his money to the needy. Those who perform their covenant with men in adversity (or excessive poverty) and affliction or disease, and do what is right (according to God's law) shall have their reward.

—The service of God is the similitude of a grain that hath produced seven ears—in each ear, a hundred grains.

—A kind speech, and forgiveness, are better than alms which harm or reproach followeth.

—Turn away evil by that which is better (as anger by patience, and ignorance by mildness, and evil conduct by forgiveness), and lo! he between whom and thyself was enmity shall become as though he were a warm friend; but none is endowed with this disposition except those who have been patient, and none except him who hath great good fortune.

—Verily, God commandeth justice and the doing of good, and the giving unto the relation; and he forbiddeth wickedness and iniquity and oppression. He admonisheth you that you may reflect.

—Give the orphans when they come of age their substance, and render them not in exchange bad for good, and devour not their substance by adding it to your own; for this is a great sin.

—Those who do evil ignorantly, and then repent speedily, to them will God be turned, for God is knowing and wise.

—The honest women are obedient, careful in the absence of their husbands, for that God preserveth them by committing them to the care and protection of the men. Seek not an occasion of quarrel against them. Show kindness unto parents, and relations, and orphans, and the poor, and your neighbor. Verily, God will not wrong any one, and if it be a good action, he will recompense it with a great reward.

—Those who believe and do that which is right, we will bring into gardens watered by rivers; therein shall they remain forever.

—And ye also are allowed to marry free women, living chastely with them, neither committing fornication, nor taking them for concubines. Observe justice when ye appear as witnesses, and let not hatred toward any induce you to do wrong, but act justly.

—Show kindness unto your parents, whether the one or both of them attain to old age with thee; speak respectfully unto them, and submit to behave humbly toward them, out of tender affection.

—Give unto him who is of kin to you his due, and also to the poor and the traveler; and waste not thy substance profusely. Let not thy hand be tied up to thy neck; neither open it with an unbounded expansion, lest thou become worthy of reprehension, and be reduced to poverty.

Meddle not with the substance of the orphan, unless it be to improve it. Perform your covenant; and give full measure, when you measure aught, and weigh with a just balance.

Walk not proudly in the land.

He who forgiveth, and is reconciled unto his enemy, shall receive his reward.

—Whosoever resigneth himself unto God, being a worker of righteousness, taketh hold of a strong handle; and unto God belongeth the issue of all things.

—Whosoever desireth excellence; unto God doth all excellence belong; unto him ascendeth the good speech; and the righteous work will he exalt.

—Let not men laugh each other to scorn, who peradventure may be better than themselves; neither let women laugh other women to scorn, who may possibly be better than themselves. Neither defame one another; nor call one another by opprobrious epithets.

—Consume not your wealth among yourselves in vain; nor present it to judges that ye may devour part of men's substance unjustly.

Arabic Inscription.

Sir William Jones, in his voyage to India, found in the island of Johanna, a secluded speck in the Atlantic, off the coast of Africa, this inscription (in Arabic) above the door of a mosque:

"The world was given us for our own edification,
Not for the purpose of raising sumptuous buildings;
Life, for the discharge of moral and religious duties,
Not for pleasurable indulgence;
Wealth, to be liberally bestowed,
Not avariciously hoarded;
And learning, to produce good actions,
Not empty disputes."

I have never seen in any Christian Church a nobler inscription; and we, though the children of Christianity, cannot afford to ignore such teaching.—*Higginson.*

CHAPTER XI.

EUROPE.

SCANDINAVIAN EDDAS.*

Prose Eddas.

The first and oldest of the Aesir is Odin. He governs all things, and although the other gods are powerful, they all serve and obey him, as children do their Father. Frigga is his wife. She foresees the destinies of men, but never reveals what is to come. * * *

Odin is called Alfadir (All-father) because he chooses for his sons all those who fall in combat. * * The mightiest of the other gods is Thor, strongest of Gods and men. * *

Baldur is the second son of Odin, * * the best, and all mankind are loud in his praise. So fair and dazzling is he in form and feature, that rays of light seem to issue from him. * Baldur is the mildest, the wisest, and most eloquent of all the Aesirs, yet such is his nature that the judgment he has pronounced can never be altered. * *

The Alfadir liveth from all ages, governeth all realms, and swayeth all things, great and small. He hath formed heaven and earth, and the air, and all things thereunto belonging.

And what is more, he hath made man, and given him a soul which shall live and never perish, though the body shall have mouldered away, or have been burned to ashes. And all that are righteous shall dwell with him in the place called Gimli, or Vingolf; but the wicked shall go to hell, and thence to Niflhel, which is below, in the ninth world.

* The Eddas are very old as songs and traditions, and the poetic Eddas were first collected in the eleventh century, by Saemund of Iceland, a Christian priest. The prose Eddas were collected by a distinguished man of Iceland, Snorro Sturelcson, about A. D. 1200. They contain the main ideas and traditions of Scandinavian religion which bore sway over Iceland, Sweden and Norway, the homes of the Norsemen.

VOLUSPA—OR WISDOM OF VALA.*

I command the devout attention of all noble souls,
Of all the high and the low—of the race of Heimdall;
I tell the doings of the All-Father,
In the most ancient Sagas which come to my mind.

There was an age in which Ymir lived,
When was no sea, nor shore, nor salt waves;
No earth below, nor heaven above,
No yawning abyss and no grassy land.

Till the sons of Bors lifted the dome of heaven,
Aud created the vast Midgard (earth) below;
Then the sun of the south rose above the mountains,
And green grasses made the ground verdant.

Then the sun of the south, companion of the moon,
Held the horses of heaven with his right hand;
The sun knew not what its course should be,
The moon knew not what her power should be,
The stars knew not where their places were.

Then the councillors went into the hall of judgment,
And the all-holy gods held a council,
They gave names to the night and new moon;
They called to the morning and to midday,
To the afternoon and evening, arranging the time.

* * * *

Then comes the mighty one to the council of the gods,
He with strength from on high who guides all things,
He decides the strife, he puts an end to struggle,
He ordains eternal laws.

HAVAMAL, OR PROVERBS OF "EDDAS."

The guest who enters
Needs water, a towel, and hospitality.
A kind reception secures a return
In word and in deed.

* The Vala was a prophetess of great power, held the same as the Fates, or Nomor, by many.

Do not mock at a stranger
Who comes trusting in your kindness;
For when he has warmed himself at your fire,
He may easily prove a wise man.

No worse companion can a man take on his journey
Than drunkenness;
Not as good as many believe
Is beer to the sons of men.
The more one drinks the less he knows,
And less power has he over himself.

It is better to depart betimes,
And not go too often to the same house;
Love tires and turns to sadness
When one sits too often at another man's table.

One's own house, though small, is better;
At home thou art the master.
Two goats and a thatched roof
Are better than begging.

Two burning sticks placed together
Will burn entirely away.
Man grows bright by the side of man;
Alone, he remains stupid.

The Logos, or Universal Reason.

One article of our faith then is that Christ is the first begotten of God, and we have already proved him to be the very Logos (or universal reason) of which mankind are all partakers; and therefore those who live according to the Logos are Christians, notwithstanding they may pass with you for Atheists: Such among the Greeks were Socrates and Herakleitos and the like; and such among the Barbarians were Abraham and Ananias, and Azarias and Elias, and many others. So, on the other side, those who have lived in former times in defiance of the Logos, or Reason, were evil and enemies to

Christ; but they who have made the Logos, or Reason, the rule of their action, are Christians and men without fear.—*Justin Martyr, A. D. 139.*

THE TRUE RELIGION.

What is called the Christian religion has existed among the ancients, and was not absent from the beginning of the human race until Christ came in the flesh; from which time the true religion which existed already, began to be called Christian.—*St. Augustine, 4th Century.*

TO THE SELF-EXISTENT LIGHT.

Eternal God, Thou self-existent Light, which wast from the beginning, Maker of all creatures, Fountain of Mercy, Ocean of goodness, Thou fathomless Abyss of loving-kindness: suffer now the light of Thy countenance to arise upon us. Shine into our hearts, O Thou true Sun of Righteousness, and fill our souls with Thy beauty. Teach us evermore to think and talk of Thy judgments, and acknowledge Thee at every moment as our Lord and Benefactor. Direct according to Thy will the work of our hands, and lead us in the right way to do that which is pleasing in Thy sight; so that through us, unworthy though we be, Thy holy Name may be glorified, the Name of the Father, the Son, and the Holy Ghost, to whom alone be praise, honor, and glory, for ever and ever. Amen.—*Basil, A. D., 379.*

REST IN GOD.

Thee, O Lord, who fillest the heavens and the earth; Thee who upholdest all things by Thine ever present might; Thee, most merciful God, do I now invoke to descend into my soul, which Thou hast prepared for Thy reception by the desire which Thou hast breathed into it. Enter into it, and renew it in Thy likeness, that Thou mayest possess it and that I may have Thee as a seal upon my heart. Ere ever I cried to Thee, Thou, most Merciful, hadst called and sought me, that I might find Thee, and finding love Thee. Even so I sought and found Thee, Lord, and desire to love Thee. Increase my desire, and grant me what I ask. Bestow Thyself upon me, my God. Yield Thee unto me; see, I love Thee, but too little; strengthen my love; let love to Thee alone inflame my heart, and let the thought of Thee be all my joy. When my spirit aspires to Thee, and meditates on Thine unspeakable goodness, the burden of the flesh becomes less heavy, the tumult of thought is stilled, the weight of mortality is less oppressive. Then fain would my soul find wings, that she might rise in tireless flight ever upwards to Thy glorious throne, and there be filled with the refreshing solace that belongs to the citizens of heaven. Let my soul thus ever seek Thee, and never grow weary of seeking; for he who seeketh Thee not is miserable, and he who refuses to live to Thee is dead. Therefore, O Thou full of compassion, do I commit and commend myself unto Thee, in Whom I am, and live, and know. May my soul be occupied with Thee only. Be Thou the goal of my pilgrimage, and my rest by the way. Let my soul take refuge from the crowding turmoil of worldly thoughts beneath the shadow of Thy wings; let my heart, this sea of restless waves, find peace in Thee, O God. Thou bounteous Giver of all good gifts, give to him who is weary refreshing food; gather our distracted thoughts and powers into harmony again; and set the prisoner free. See, he stands at thy door and knocks; be it opened to him, that he may enter with a free step, and be quickened by Thee. For Thou art the Well-spring of Life, the Light of eternal Brightness, wherein the just live who love Thee. Be it unto me according to Thy word! Amen.—*St. Augustine, A. D. 350.*

Spiritual Life.

The more a man is devoted to internal exercises, and advanced in singleness and simplicity of heart, the more sublime and diffusive will be his knowledge. A spirit pure, simple, and constant, is not like Martha disturbed and troubled with the multiplicity of its employments, however great; because, being inwardly at rest, it seeketh not its own glory in what it does, but "doeth all to the glory of God;" for there is no other cause of perplexity and disquiet, but an unsubdued will and unmortified affections. A holy and spiritual mind, by reducing them to the rule and standard of his own mind, becomes the master of all his outward acts; he does not suffer himself to be led by them to the indulgence of inordinate affections that terminate in self, but subjects them to the unalterable judgment of an illuminated and sanctified spirit.

No conflict is so severe as his who labors to subdue himself; but in this we must be continually engaged, if we would be strengthened in the inner man, and make real progress towards perfection. Indeed, the highest perfection we can attain in the present state is alloyed with much imperfection, and our best knowledge is obscured by the shades of ignorance; we "see through a glass darkly;" an humble knowledge of thyself therefore, is a more certain way of leading thee to God than the most profound investigations of science. Science, however, or a proper knowledge of the things that belong to the present life, is so far from being blamable, considered in itself, that it is good and ordained of God; but purity of conscience, and holiness of life, must ever be preferred before it; and because men are more solicitous to learn much than to live well, they fall into error, and receive little or no benefit from their studies. But if the same diligence was exerted to eradicate vice and implant virtue, as is applied to the discussion of unprofitable questions and the "vain strife of words," so much daring wickedness would not be found among the common ranks of men, nor so much licentiousness disgrace those who are eminent for knowledge. Assuredly in the approaching day of universal judgment it will not be inquired what we have read, but what we have done; not how eloquently we have spoken, but how holily we have lived.

He is truly good who hath great charity; he is truly great

who is little in his own estimation, and rates as nothing, the summit of earthly honor; he is truly wise who "counts all earthly things but as dross, that he may win Christ;" and he is truly learned who hath learned to abandon his own will, and do the will of God.—*Thomas A'Kempis, A. D. 1380.*

For Kindness and Gentleness in Daily Life.

Oh Thou gracious, gentle, and condescending God, Thou God of Peace, Father of mercy, God of all comfort: see, I lament before Thee the evil of my heart; I acknowledge that I am too much disposed to anger, jealousy, and revenge, to ambition and pride, which often give rise to discord and bitter feelings between me and others. Too often have I thus offended and grieved both Thee, O long-suffering Father, and my fellow-men. Oh forgive me this sin, and suffer me to partake of the blessing which Thou hast promised to the peacemakers, who shall be called the children of God.

Bestow on me, O Lord, a genial spirit and unwearied forbearance; a mild, loving, patient heart; kindly looks and gestures; pleasant, cordial speech and manners in the intercourse of daily life; that I may give offense to none, nor mar the peace of my neighbors; but as much as in me lies live in charity with all men. Oh, how excellent a gift is peace! how earnestly and repeatedly did our Saviour entreat His heavenly Father, that we might be one, even as He and the Father are one!

Therefore, O, Thou Supreme Love, unite our hearts in love to Thee. Soften, expand, enkindle all hard and narrow hearts. Enlighten them, that they may learn quickly to forgive and forget all offenses, even as Thou, in Thy great kindness, art ready to forgive and forget, and dost soon lay aside Thy just anger. Let us prize peace more highly than the gratification of our own jealousy or grudges; let us be ready to give way and yield if so we may retain and guard this precious treasure; for woe unto the country and nation, woe to the family or the individual who loses God's gift of peace! O God, resist the adversary who is the source of all discord, that he may not sow the evil seed of anger and disunion among us. Check all disturbers of peace. Scatter the people who delight in war, and bring to naught the counsels that would raise strife, and are pregnant with calamity. Let us seek peace and ensue it, O Thou King of Peace! and may that peace which passeth understanding keep your hearts and minds in Christ Jesus, our Lord.—*J. Arndt, A. D. 1470.*

MARTIN LUTHER.

Christian Wisdom and Moderation.

Christian wisdom does not consist in seeking the company of those who are accounted wise and skillful; and to make mention and talk of them; but to be occupied among the unwise, and those that lack understanding, that they may forsake sin and foolishness, and embrace righteousness and sound understanding. Therefore it appeareth that Christian wisdom doth not consist in lofty looks, and seeing ourselves in things high and wise, as in a glass, but that we look to those things which are below, and mark that which is humble. He that knoweth these things, let him give thanks to God; for by this knowledge he is able to prepare and apply himself to everything that shall take place in the world. But ye shall find many, yea, even among those that preach the gospel, who are not thus far enlightened. * * *

The apostle now declareth, in a few words, how the believers ought to behave themselves toward men; saying, *Let your moderation be known unto all men.* That is, be joyful toward God, always rejoicing in him; but towards men, be of a patient mind, and so conduct yourselves that ye be ready to suffer all things, and yield in everything, as much as possible, without transgressing the commands of God.

We must endeavor to please all men in that which is good; we must interpret aright the sayings of others, and accept the part which is good; that men may see that we are of those who would not disagree with any man for any cause whatever; who are rich with the rich, and poor with the poor, rejoicing with those that rejoice, and weeping with those that weep; in short, that we are all things to all men, that they may acknowledge that we are grievous to none, but agreeable, of a patient mind, and obedient in all things. We must be ready to permit, to take in good part, to obey, to give place, to do, to omit, to suffer all things for the benefit of our neighbor; even though we suffer hindrance, loss of substance, name, and body thereby.

Paul said, "I am made all things to all men, that I might by all means save some." We here see the patient and pliant mind, rightly observing those things which are here commanded. The apostle did sometimes eat and drink and do all things as a Jew; sometimes with the Gentiles, he did all things as free from the law; for only faith in God, and love toward our neighbor, are necessarily required; all other things are free; and we may freely observe them for one man's sake, and omit them for the sake of another.

We read in Matthew and Mark, that Christ suffered his disciples to break the Sabbath, and he himself did also break it, when the case so required; when it was otherwise he kept it, for which he gave this reason: "*The Son of man is lord also of the Sabbath.*" Which is as much as to say, *the Sabbath is free, that thou mayest break it for one man's sake and convenience, and for the sake and convenience of another thou mayest keep it.*

Martin Luther's Table Talk.

—A man must needs be plunged in bitter affliction when in his heart he means good, and yet is not regarded. I can never get rid of these cogitations, wishing I had never begun this business with the pope. So, too, I desire myself rather dead than to hear or see God's Word and His servants contemned; but 'tis the frailty of our nature to be thus discouraged.

—They who condemn the movement of anger against antagonists, are theologians who deal in mere speculations; they play with words, and occupy themselves with subtleties, but when they are aroused, and take a real interest in the matter, they are touched sensibly.

—"In quietness and confidence shall be your strength." This sentence I expounded thus: If thou intendest to vanquish the greatest, the most abominable and wickedest enemy, who is able to do thee mischief both in body and soul, and against whom thou preparest all sorts of weapons, but canst not overcome; then know that there is a sweet and loving physical herb to serve thee, named *Patientia.*

Thou wilt say: How may I attain this physic? Take unto thee faith, which says: no creature can do me mischief without the will of God. In case thou receivest hurt and mischief by thine enemy, this is done by the sweet and gracious will of God, in such sort that the enemy hurts himself a thousand times more than he does thee. Hence flows unto me, a Christian, the love which says: I will, instead of the evil which mine enemy does unto me, do him all the good I can; I will heap coals of fire upon his head. This is the Christian armor and weapon, wherewith to beat and overcome those enemies that seem to be like huge mountains. In a word, love teaches to suffer and endure all things.

—Patience is the most excellent of the virtues, and, in Sacred Writ, highly praised and recommended by the Holy Ghost. The learned heathen philosophers applaud it, but they do not know its genuine basis, being without the assistance of God. Epictetus, the wise and judicious Greek, said very well: "Suffer and abstain."

—It was the custom of old, in burying the dead, to lay their heads towards the sun-rising, by reason of a spiritual mystery and signification therein manifested; but this was not an enforced law. So all laws and ceremonies should be free in the church, and not be done on compulsion, being things which neither justify nor condemn in the sight of God, but are observed merely for the sake of orderly discipline.

—Cursed are all preachers that in the church aim at high and hard things, and, neglecting the saving health of the poor unlearned people, seek their own honor and praise, and therewith to please one or two ambitious persons.

When I preach, I sink myself deep down. I regard neither Doctors nor Magistrates, of whom are here in this church above forty; but I have an eye to the multitude of the young people, children, and servants, of whom are more than two thousand. I preach to those, directing myself to them that have need thereof. Will not the rest hear me? The door stands open unto them; they may begone. I see that the ambition of preachers grows and increases; this will do the utmost mischief in the church, and produce great disquietness and discord; for they will needs teach high things touching matters of state, thereby aiming at praise and honor; they will please the worldly wise, and meantime neglect the simple and common multitude.

An upright, godly, and true preacher should direct his preaching to the poor, simple sort of people, like a mother that stills her child, dandles and plays with it, presenting it with milk from her own breast, and needing neither malmsey nor muscadin for it. In such sort should also preachers carry themselves, teaching and preaching plainly, that the simple and unlearned may conceive and comprehend, and retain what they say. When they come to me, to Melancthon, to Dr. Pomer, &c., let them show their cunning, how learned they be; they shall be well put to their trumps. But to sprinkle out Hebrew, Greek, and Latin in their public sermons, savors merely of show, according with neither time nor place.

Outer and Inner Life—Renunciation.

It is so provided and ordered that in proportion as man thinks and wills from heaven, his internal spiritual man is opened and formed; it is opened into heaven, even unto the Lord, and it is formed according to those things which belong to heaven.

But as man does not think and will from heaven, but from the world, his internal spiritual man is closed and his external man is opened into the world, and is formed according to those things which belong to the world.

For the body does nothing of itself, but is solely actuated by the spirit which is in it. The spirit, after its separation from the body, thinks, wills, speaks and acts as it did in the body.

Of *true* renunciation of the world he says:

To renounce the world is to love God and love the neighbor, and he loves the neighbor when he performs uses. In order therefore that a man receive the life of heaven, it is necessary that he should live in the world and engage in the various affairs of life. A life of abstraction from secular concerns is a life of thought and faith separate from a life of love and charity; and in such a life the principle which prompts man to desire and promote the good of the neighbor must necessarily perish. When this is the case the spiritual life becomes like a house without foundations, which sinks gradually to the ground, or becomes full of clefts and chinks, or totters to its fall.—*Emanuel Swedenborg.*

Intuition.

With the birth of human souls, God imparts to them essential and original knowledge. The soul mirrors the universe, and stands in personal relations to all things. She is illuminated with an inward light. But the tempest of the passions, the multitude of sensual impressions, dissipate and darken this light, its glory diffusing itself only when it bnrns alone, and peace and harmony prevail within us. When liberated from all outward impressions, and desirous only of being guided by this light, then only do we find pure and certain knowledge. In this state of concentration, the soul analyzes all objects upon which its attention rests; unites wholly with them, pierces throngh their substance, and penetrates even to God himself, by feeling His presence in the most important truths.—*Von Helmont.*

Conscience the Divine Law Within.

The Divine Law which tells of what is good and true and right, is written in the human heart. The conscience is a teacher. Let no one endeavor to excuse himself to the world, and still less to himself, or to the Omniscient, with the pretence that he knows not how to distinguish between right and wrong. If thou follow this holy voice within, that leads to good, thou wilt never willingly go astray, or knowingly do evil, and thou wilt ever enjoy internal self-contentment. Conscience is our earnest and just teacher, and only in following its limits and warnings canst thou find true happiness. Do not persuade thyself it is otherwise; seek not by subtle reasoning to find the means of satisfying thy forbidden wishes and vicious tendencies, without violating thy sense of right and decency. Thy reasonings are false. It is an evil deed that thou art tempted to commit, and behind it lurks secret remorse. The conscience admits of no compromise. Thou thinkest thou canst bargain with it; but weak man, thou art only bargaining with thine own shame.—*Zschokke.*

Religion in Life.

Many think it inexpedient to speak of religion, except on most solemn occasions, but none can forbid us to manifest the spirit of religion in a holy life. You may show its essence in every word and deed; even the most ordinary and trivial affairs of life need not be devoid of the expressions of a pious heart. Let the sacred feeling which governs your actions show that even in those common things which a profane mind passes with levity, the music of a lofty sentiment echoes in your heart; let the majestic serenity with which you estimate the great and the small, prove that you refer everything to the Immutable; let the cheerfulness with which you encounter every proof of your transitory nature, reveal to all that you live above time and the world; let your easy and graceful self-denial prove how many of the bonds of egotism you have broken; and let the ever quick and ready spirit from which neither what is rarest nor most common escapes, show with what unwearied ardor you seek for every trace or manifestation of the Godhead. If your whole life, and every movement of your outward and inward being, is thus guided by religion, perhaps the hearts of many will be touched by this mute language, and will open to the reception of that spirit which dwells in you.—*Schleiermacher.*

INTEGRITY.

Be and continue poor, young man, while others around you grow rich by fraud and disloyalty; be without place or power, while others beg their way upward; bear the pain of disappointed hopes, while others gain the accomplishment of theirs by flattery; forego the gracious pressure of the hand, for which others cringe and crawl. Wrap yourself in your virtue, and seek a friend and your daily bread. If you have, in such a course, grown gray with unblemished honor, bless God and die.—*Heinzelman.*

MAN HIGHER THAN HIS DWELLING PLACE.

But man is higher than his dwelling place; he looks up and folds the wings of his soul, and when the sixty minutes we call sixty years have passed, he takes flight, kindling as he rises, and the ashes of his feathers fall back to earth, and the unveiled soul, freed from its covering of clay, and pure as a note of music, ascends on high. Even amidst the dim shadows of life he sees the mountains of the future world gilded with the morning rays of a sun which rises not here below. So the inhabitant of polar regions looks into the long night in which there is no sun-rise; but at midnight he sees a bright light like the first rosy rays of dawn, gleaming on the highest mountain tops, and he thinks of his long summer in which it never sets. —*Jean Paul.*

Maxims.

—Philosophy can bake no bread, but she can procure for us God, Freedom, Immortality. Which then is most practical, Philosophy or Economy?

—To become properly acquainted with a truth, we must first have disbelieved it, and disputed against it.

—Man is the higher sense of our Planet; the star which connects it with the upper world; the eye with which it turns towards heaven.

—What is Nature? An encyclopedical, systematic index, or plan of our Spirit. Why will we content us with a mere catalogue of our Treasures? Let us contemplate them, and in all ways elaborate and use them.

—There is but one temple in the world, and that is the body of man. Nothing is holier than this high form. Bending before men is a reverence done to this revelation in the flesh. We touch heaven when we lay our hand on a human body.

—Plants are children of the earth; we are children of the Æther. Nature is an Eolian harp, whose tones again are keys to higher strings in us.

—Every beloved object is the centre of a Paradise.

—The first man is the first Spirit-Seer; all appears to him as Spirit. What are children but first men? The first gaze of the child is richer in significance than the forecasting of the Seer.

—Man consists in Truth. If he exposes or betrays Truth,

he exposes or betrays himself. We speak not here of Lies, but of acting against conviction.

—Can miracles work conviction? Or is not *real* conviction, this highest function of our soul and personality, the only true God-announcing miracle?

—The Christian religion is especially remarkable, as it so decidedly lays claim to mere good will in man, to his essential temper, and values this independently of culture and manifestation.

—Martyrs are spiritual heroes. Christ was the greatest martyr of our species; through him has martyrdom become infinitely significant and holy.

—Every unpleasant feeling is a sign that I have become untrue to my resolutions; Epictetus was not unhappy. Not chance, but I, am to blame for my sufferings. For virtue's sake I am here; but if a man, for his task, forgets and sacrifices all, why shouldst not thou? Expect injuries, for men are weak, and thou thyself doest such too often. Mollify thy heart by thinking of the sufferings of thy enemy; think of him as one spiritually sick, who deserves sympathy.—*Novalis.*

A Divine Hunger.

We have a divine hunger, and this earth offers us only the food of cattle. The eternal hunger of man, the insatiability of his desires, ask another sort of nutriment. How can a great soul be happy here? Those who have been among mountains and are condemned to live on plains die of an incurable nostalgia. It is because we have issued from above that we sigh for it, and that all music is to us a reminiscence of our home, a *ranz-des-vaches* to the exiled Swiss. An infinite love supposes an infinite object. If all the forests were pleasure parks, and all the isles were Fortunate Isles, and all the fields were Elysian, and all eyes were full of joy, oh! then—But no: then the Infinite Being must have assured us that such felicity would be perpetual. But now that so many houses are houses of mourning, so many fields are fields of battle, so many faces are pale, so many eyes are dulled with tears and closed; when things are thus, how can the tomb be the end of all?—*Jean Paul.*

Immortality.

Man must believe in immortality; his belief corresponds with the wants of his nature. But if the philosopher tries to prove the soul's immortality from a legend, that is very weak, and says little to us. To me, the eternal existence of my soul is proved from my need of activity. If I work incessantly until my death, nature is pledged to give me another form of being, when the present can no longer sustain the spirit.—*Gœthe.*

The Microcosm.

Look within yourself, and you will find everything; and rejoice that without there lies a Nature, that says yea and amen to all you have discovered in yourself.—*Gœthe.*

Gœthe and the Sparrows.

A nest of young hedge-sparrows, with one of the old birds, had lately been brought me. I saw with admiration the bird not only continue to feed the young in my chamber, but, when set free through the window, return to take charge of them. Such parental love, superior to danger and imprisonment, moved me deeply, and I expressed my feelings to Gœthe.

"Simple man!" he replied, with a smile, "if you believed in God you would not wonder.

> "He from within lives through all Nature, rather,
> Nature and spirit fostering each other;
> So that what in Him lives, and moves, and is,
> Still feels His power, and owns itself still His."

"Did not God inspire the bird with this all-powerful love for its young, and did not similar impulses pervade all animate nature, the world could not subsist. But even so is the divine energy everywhere diffused, and divine love everywhere active." —*Eckermann.*

NATURE—THE COSMOS.

In considering the study of physical phenomena, not merely in its bearings on the material wants of life, but in its general influence on the intellectual advancement of mankind, we find its noblest and most important result to be a knowledge of the chain of connection, by which all natural forces are linked together and made mutually dependent upon each other; and it is the perception of these relations that exalts our views and ennobles our enjoyments. Such a result can, however, only be reaped as the fruit of observation and intellect, combined with the spirit of the age, in which are reflected all the varied phases of thought. He who can trace, through by-gone times, the stream of our knowledge to its primitive source, will learn from history how, for thousands of years, man has labored, amid the ever-recurring changes of form, to recognize the invariability of natural laws, and has thus by the force of mind gradually subdued a great portion of the physical world to his dominion. In interrogating the history of the past, we trace the mysterious course of ideas yielding the first glimmering perception of the same image of a Cosmos, or harmoniously ordered whole, which, dimly shadowed forth to the human mind in the primitive ages, is now fully revealed to the maturer intellect of mankind as the result of long and laborious observation. * * * * *

Nature considered *rationally*, that is to say, submitted to the process of thought, is a unity in diversity of phenomena; a harmony, blending together all created things, however dissimilar in form or attributes; one *great whole* animated by the breath of life. * * * * * *

Mere communion with nature, mere contact with the free air, exercise a soothing yet strengthening influence on the wearied spirit, calm the storms of passion, and soften the heart when shaken by sorrow to its inmost depths. Everywhere, in every region of the globe, in every stage of intellectual culture, the same sources of enjoyment are alike vouchsafed to man. The earnest and solemn thoughts awakened by a communion with nature intuitively arise from a presentiment of the order and harmony pervading the whole universe, and from the contrast we draw between the narrow limits of our own existence and the image of infinity revealed on every side, whether we look upward to the starry vault of heaven, scan the far-stretching plain before us, or seek to trace the dim horizon across the vast expanse of the ocean.—*A. Von Humboldt.*

The City of the Gods in Man's Being.

Magnificent! "The City of the Gods"
I fain would see! It actually stands;
But mystical and secret as a dream!
For lo! the head of every little child
Reveals a palace, one divinely built—
Reveals a new original world just made,
Such world as never yet was seen by man,
Such world as never came to human ears.
The child's eye feasts upon the universe,
And whatsoever charms and pleases it,
It draws into the mystic viewless dome;
Like bees the thoughts fly out from it for sweets,
And, heavy-laden, bring their treasures home;
They gather thoughts themselves, which they extract
From stars, and from the clouds, and from the flowers,
And like the blue sky, broad and glistening,
Soon their own heavenly temple rears its arch,
And its own shining sun it hangs therein,
And its own beaming moon; and days and nights,

Spring, summer, autumn, winter, in their pomp,
Move round therein, with new peculiar grace,
Real, and nowhere else to him exist.
A goddess too the master takes to him,
And sends out infant gods before the door!
Of them, each little childish head shines forth
A new, original, and glorious palace,
Full of all treasures, all delight and bliss!
And so, millions of houses come to be
Crowded with suns, and moons, and all things fair,
So a whole city of spirits comes to be!
Does this sound like a fable? But, dear soul,
Not greatly, not admiringly enough
Canst thou e'er think of "being"—of the Master
Who founded this full city of the gods!
What were sublimer, rarer, and more blest
Than all men's daily, homely, common life!
What can be lovelier than to be a man!
What holier than the culture and the love
That open to dim sense its heavenly house.

Leopold Schefer.

Exaltation needed for Sacrifice.

The mount of sacrifice must always be
The mount of vision—he who would renounce
Must rise to the great realms of the pure spirit,
The godlike, the immortal, and the good.

L. Schefer.

Worth of Great Souls.

There are, at all times, but a few great hearts
Who clearly understand the world, and, clearly
Distinguishing the true and good therein,
Clearly reject and hate the bad and false.
Esteeming beauty as a holy thing,

They lift it up before the people's eyes
(As Moses did his magic brazen serpent),
To make them well thereby; their love becomes
The love of many; what they hate influences
The people's hate; forever reprobate
Is that which the great heart hath reprobated.

L. Schefer.

Respect for Woman Tests Man.

So much as one holds woman in esteem,
Purely or basely as he deals with love,
So much is his regard for honor, or
So little; such the honor he receives!
Who not *himself* respects, honors not woman,
Who does not honor woman, knows he love?
Who knows not love can he know honor then?
Who knows not honor what has he beside?

L. Schefer.

Daily Faults.

Never let us be discouraged with ourselves; it is not when we are conscious of our faults that we are the most wicked; on the contrary we are less so. We see by a brighter light, and let us remember for our consolation, that we never perceive our sins till we begin to cure them. We must neither flatter nor be impatient with ourselves, in the correction of our faults. Despondency is not a state of humility; on the contrary it is the vexation and despair of a cowardly pride—nothing is worse; whether we stumble or whether we fall, we must only think of rising again and going on in our course. Our faults may be useful to us, if they cure us of a vain confidence in ourselves, and do not deprive us of our humble and salutary confidence in God. He never makes us feel our weakness but that we may be led to seek strength from him. What is involuntary should not trouble us; but the great thing is, never to act against the light within us, and to desire to follow where God would lead us.—*Fenelon.*

The Law of Nature.

What is the law of Nature?

It is the constant and regular order of facts by which God governs the universe; an order which his wisdom presents to the senses and the reason of men, as an equal and common rule for their actions, to guide them, without distinction of country or sect, towards perfection and happiness.

The definition of law is, "An order or prohibition to act, with the express clause of a penalty attached to the infraction, or of a recompense attached to the observance of the order."

Do such orders exist in Nature? Yes.

What does the word Nature signify? It bears three different senses:

1st. It signifies the universe, the material world; in this sense we say, "the beauty (or richness) of nature," that is, the objects of heaven or earth exposed to our sight.

2d. It signifies the power that animates, that moves the universe, considering it as a distinct being, as the soul is to the body; in this sense we say, "The intentions of nature."

3d. It signifies the partial operation of this power on each being, or each class of beings; as we say, "The nature of man is an enigma."

What are the characters of the laws of nature?

There can be assigned ten principal ones.

What is the first?

To be inherent to the existence of things, and consequently anterior to every other law; so that all others are only imitations.

What is the second?

To be derived immediately from God, and presented by him to each man, whereas all other laws are presented to us by men.

What is the third?

To be common to all times and countries; that is to say, to be one and universal.

Is no other law universal?

No; for no other is applicable to all people,—they originate from persons and places.

What is the fourth character?

To be uniform and invariable.

Is no other law uniform and invariable?

No; for what one and the same law approves at one time or place it condemns in another.

What is the fifth character?

To be evident and palpable, constantly present to the senses, and to demonstration.

What is its sixth character?

To be conformed always to reason as no other laws are.

What is its seventh?

To be wholly just, because the penalties are proportionate to the infractions.

What is its eighth?

To be pacific and tolerant, because in the law of nature all men being brothers, and equal in rights, it recommends only peace, and toleration, even for errors, to them.

What is its ninth?

To be equally beneficent to all, in teaching them the true means of becoming better and happier.

What is its tenth?

That it is alone sufficient to make men happier and better, because it comprises all that is good and useful in other laws, either civil or religious, essentially the moral part of them; so that if other laws were divested of it, they would become chimerical and imaginary opinions, devoid of practical utility. —*C. F. Volney.*

Jesus of Nazereth.

He worked at the trade of his father, which was that of a carpenter. This was no humiliating or unwelcome circumstance. The Jewish customs demanded that the man devoted to intellectual labors should understand some occupation. The most celebrated doctors had trades; thus St. Paul, whose education had been so well cared for, was a tent-maker. Jesus was never married. All his power to love was transferred to what he considered his celestial vocation. The extremely delicate feeling which we notice in him toward women never departed from the exclusive devotion which he had to his idea. He treated as sisters, like Francis d'Assisi and Francis de Sales, those women who were enamored with the same work as he; and he had his St. Claires, his Francoise de Chantal. * * *

What was the progress of the mind of Jesus during this obscure period of his life? Through what meditations did he launch out into the prophetic career? We are ignorant, his history having come to us in isolated stories, and without exact chronology. But the development of living products is everywhere the same, and there can be no doubt that the growth of a personality so mighty as that of Jesus obeyed rigid laws. A lofty idea of Divinity, which he did not owe to Judaism, and which seems to have been entirely the creation of his great soul, was the foundation of all his power.

Here it is that we must, most of all, renounce those ideas with which we are familiar, and those discussions in which small minds wear themselves away. Properly to understand the degree of the piety of Jesus, we must rid ourselves of all that has intruded between the gospel and ourselves. Deism and paganism have become the two poles of theology. The paltry discussion of scholasticisms, the aridity of soul of Descartes, the thorough irreligion of the eighteenth century, by diminishing God, and in some sort limiting him by the exclusion of all that is not him, stifled in the breast of modern rationalism every fruitful feeling of divinity. If God is indeed a determinate being without us, the person who believes that he has private relations with God is a "visionary," and as the physical and physiological sciences have shown us that every supernatural vision is an illusion, the deist who is at all consistent, finds himself beyond the possibility of comprehending the great beliefs of the past. Pantheism, on the other hand, by denying the divine personality, is as far as possible from the living God of the ancient religions.

Were the men who have most loftily comprehended God, Sakya-Mouni, Plato, St. Paul, St. Francis d'Assisi, and St. Augustine, at some moments of their changeful lives, deists or pantheists? Such a question has no meaning. To them the physical and metaphysical proofs of the existence of God would have had no interest. *They felt the divine within themselves.* In the first rank of this grand family of the true sons of God we must place Jesus. He had no visions; God does not speak to him from without; *God is in him;* he feels that he is with God, and he draws from his own heart what he says of his Father. He lives in the bosom of God by uninterrupted communication; he does not see him, but he understands him, without need of thunder and the burning bush like Moses, of a revealing tempest like Job, of an oracle like the old Greek sages, of a familiar genius like Socrates, or of an angel Gabriel like Mahomet. He never, for a moment, enounces the sacrilegious idea that he is God. He believes that he is in direct communication with God; he believes himself the Son of God. The highest consciousness of God which ever existed in the breast of humanity was that of Jesus. * * *

God, conceived immediately as Father, this is the whole theology of Jesus. And that was not with him a theoretical principle, a doctrine more or less proven, and which he sought to inculcate. He used no argument with his disciples; he exacted from them no effort at attention. He did not preach opinions, he preached himself. Often the greatest and most disinterested souls present, associated with a high degree of elevation this peculiarity of perpetual attention to themselves and extreme personal susceptibility. Their persuasion that God is within them, and perpetually caring for them, is so strong that they have no fear of imposing themselves on others; with our reserve, our respect for the opinions of others which is a portion of our weakness, they have nothing to do. This exalted personality is not egotism; for such men, possessed by their idea, gladly give their life to seal their work; it is the identification of *the me* with the object it has embraced, carried to its last extent. It is pride to those who see in it only the personal fantasy of the founder; it is the finger of God to those who see the result. The fool here almost touches the inspired man; only the fool never succeeds.

Hitherto it has never been given to aberration of mind to produce a serious effect upon the progress of humanity.

Jesus undoubtedly did not, at once, reach this lofty affirmation of himself; but it is probable that from the very first he looked to God in the relation of a son to a father. This is his great act of originality; in this he is in no wise with his race. Neither the Jew nor the Moslem have learned this delightful theology of love. The God of Jesus is not the hateful master who kills us when he pleases, damns us when he pleases, saves us when he pleases. He is our Father. We hear him when we listen to a low voice within us which says, "Father."

The God of Jesus is not the partial despot who has chosen Israel for his people, and protects it in the face of all and against all. He is the God of humanity. Jesus will not be a patriot like the Maccabees, or a theocrat like Juda the Gaulonite. Rising boldly above the prejudices of his nation, he will establish the universal fatherhood of God. * * *

Jesus was not sinless; he conquered the same passions which we combat; no angel of God comforted him, save his good conscience; no Satan tempted him, save that which each bears in his heart. As many of the grand aspects of his character are lost to us by the fault of his disciples, it is probable also that many of his faults have been dissembled. But never has any man made the interests of humanity predominate in his life over the littleness of self-love so much as he. Devoted without reserve to his idea, he subordinated everything to it to such a degree, that towards the end of his life the universe no longer existed for him. It was by this flood of heroic will that he conquered heaven.—*Ernest Renan.*

The Spiritual Man Real.

That a man is equally a man after death, although he is not apparent to the eyes, may appear * * * especially from the Lord himself, who showed his disciples that he was a man, by touch, and by eating, and yet became invisible to their eyes. The reason why they saw him was because the eyes of their spirits were then opened; and when these eyes are opened the things in the spiritual world appear as clearly as the things in the natural world.

Since it has pleased the Lord to open the eyes of my spirit, and to keep them open now for nineteen years, it has been given me to see the things which are in the spiritual world, as well as to describe them. I can asseverate that they are not visions, but THINGS SEEN in all wakefulness.

The difference between a man in the natural world and a man in the spiritual world is, that the one is clothed in a natural body, but the other in a spiritual body. * * * What kind of difference this is (between the natural, or material, and spiritual) may be described, but not in a few words.—*Swedenborg.*

The Soul Indestructible.

At the age of seventy-five one must, of course, think frequently of death. But this thought never gives me the least uneasiness, I am so fully convinced that the soul is indestructible, and that its activity will continue through eternity. It is like the sun which seems to our eyes to set in the night, but is really gone to diffuse its light elsewhere. Even while sinking it remains the same sun.—*Gœthe.*

Of Merit.

They who do good with a view of merit are not influenced by the love of God, but by the love of reward; for they who are desirous of merit are also desirous of reward; and have respect to the reward, in which, and not in the good, they place their delight. Such, therefore, are not spiritual men, but natural. To do good which is really such, man must act from the love of good, and thus for the sake of good. * * *

They who do good for the sake of reward, do not act from the Lord, but from themselves; they regard themselves in the first place, inasmuch as they regard their own good. * * * * Genuine charity and faith entirely disclaim all merit; for the delight of charity is good itself, and the delight of faith is truth itself. The Lord Himself plainly teaches that man is not to do good for the sake of reward, where he says: "For if ye love them that love you, what thank have ye? for sinners also love those that love them. But love your enemies, and do good, and lend, hoping for nothing again, and your reward shall be great, and ye shall be the children of the Highest." * * The delight which is inher nt in the love of doing good without any view to reward, is itself an eternal reward; for heaven and eternal happiness are inseminated into that good by the Lord.—*Swedenborg.*

CHAPTER XII.

GREAT BRITAIN.

QUESTIONS.

Ancient Wales.

Knowest thou what thou art,
In the hour of sleep—
A mere body— a mere soul—
Or a secret retreat of light?
Knowest thou where the night awaits
For the passing of the day?
Knowest thou the token
Of every leaf which grows?
What is it which heaves up the mountain
Before the convulsion of the elements?
Or what supports the fabric
Of the habitable earth?
Who is the illuminator of the soul—
Who has seen—who knows him—
What are the properties of the soul,
Of what form are its members?
In what part, and when, it takes up its abode;
By what wind or stream is it supplied?

From Mabgyvrean, or Elements of Instruction, by Taliesin, A. D. 600.

FRANCIS BACON (A. D. 1560).

Of Adversity.

It was a high speech of Seneca (after the manner of the Stoics) that the "good things which belong to prosperity are to be wished, but the good things that belong to adversity are to be admired." (Bona rerum secundarum optabilia, adversarum mirabilia). Certainly, if miracles be the command over nature, they appear most in adversity. It is a yet higher speech of his than the other (much too high for a heathen), "It is true greatness to have in one the frailty of a man, and the security of a God." This would have done better in poesy, where transcendencies are more allowed; and the poets, indeed, have been busy with it—for it is in effect the thing which is figured in that strange fiction of the ancient poets, which seemeth not to be without mystery; nay, and to have some approach to the state of a Christian, "That Hercules, when he went to unbind Prometheus (by whom human nature is represented), sailed the length of the great ocean in an earthen pot or pitcher; lively describing Christian resolution, that saileth in the frail bark of the flesh through the waves of the world." But to speak in a mean, the virtue of prosperity is temperance, the virtue of adversity is fortitude, which in morals is the more heroical virtue. Prosperity is the blessing of the Old Testament, adversity is the blessing of the New, which carrieth the greater benediction, and the clearer revelation of God's favor. Yet even in the Old Testament, if you listen to David's harp, you shall hear as many hearse-like airs as carols; and the pencil of the Holy Ghost hath labored more in describing the afflictions of Job than the felicities of Solomon. Prosperity is not without many fears and distastes; and adversity is not without comfort and hopes. We see in needle-works and embroideries it is more pleasing to have a lively work upon a sad and solemn ground, than to have a dark and melancholy work upon a lightsome ground: judge, therefore, of the pleasure of the heart by the pleasure of the eye. Certainly virtue is like precious odors, most fragant where they are incensed, or crushed; for prosperity doth best discover vice, but adversity doth best discover virtue.

Of Superstition.

It were better to have no opinion of God at all, than such an opinion as is unworthy of him; for the one is unbelief, the other is contumely; and certainly superstition is the reproach of the Deity. Plutarch saith well to that purpose: "Surely," saith he, "I had rather a great deal men should say there was no such a man at all as Plutarch, than that they should say there was one Plutarch that would eat his children as soon as they were born," as the poets speak of Saturn; and as the contumely is greater towards God, so the danger is greater towards men. Atheism leaves a man to sense, to philosophy, to natural piety, to laws, to reputation, all which may be guides to an outward moral virtue, though religion were not; but superstition dismounts all these, and erecteth an absolute monarchy in the minds of men: therefore atheism did never perturb states; for it makes men wary of themselves, as looking no further; and we see the times inclined to atheism, as the time of Augustus Cæsar, were civil times; but superstition hath been the confusion of many states, and bringeth in a new "primum mobile" (first motive cause), that ravisheth all the spheres of government. The master of superstition is the people, and in all superstition wise men follow fools; and arguments are fitted to practice in a reversed order. It was gravely said by some of the prelates in the Council of Trent, where the doctrine of the schoolmen bare great sway, that the schoolmen were like astronomers, which did feign eccentrics and epicycles, and such engines of orbs, to save the phenomena, though they knew there were no such things; and, in like manner, that the schoolmen had framed a number of subtile and intricate axioms and theorems, to save the practice of the church. The causes of superstition are pleasing and sensual rites and ceremonies; excess of outward and physical holiness; over-great reverence of traditions, which cannot but load the church; the strategems of prelates for their own ambition and lucre; the favoring too much of good intentions, which openeth the gate to conceits and novelties; the taking an aim at divine matters by human, which cannot but breed mixture of imaginations; and, lastly, barbarous times, especially joined with calamities and disasters. Superstition, without a veil, is a deformed thing; for as it addeth deformity to an ape to be so like a man, so the similitude of superstition to religion makes it the more deformed; and as wholesome meat corrupteth to little worms, so good forms and orders corrupt into a number of petty observances. There is a superstition in avoiding superstition, when men think to do best if they go furthest from the superstition formerly received; therefore care should be had that (as it fareth in ill purgings) the good be not taken away with the bad, which commonly is done when the people is the reformer.

Plea for a Free Press and Free Thought.

* * * * Good and evil we know in the field of this world grow up together almost inseparably; and the knowledge of good is so involved and interwoven with the knowledge of evil, and in so many cunning resemblances hardly to be discovered, that those confused seeds which were imposed upon Psyche as an incessant labor to cull out and sort asunder, were not more intermixed. It was from out the rind of one apple tasted, that the knowledge of good and evil, as two twins cleaving together, leaped forth into the world. And perhaps this is that doom which Adam fell into, of having good and evil, that is to say, of knowing good by evil. As, therefore, the state of man now is, what knowledge can there be to choose, what continence to forbear, without the knowledge of evil? He that can apprehend and consider vice with all her baits and seeming pleasures, and yet abstain and distinguish, and yet prefer that which is truly better, he is the true wayfaring Christian.

I cannot praise a fugitive and cloistered virtue, unexercised and unbreathed, that never sallies out and sees her adversary, but slinks out of the race, where the immortal garland is to be run for, not without dust and heat. * * * *

That virtue, therefore, which is but a youngling in the contemplation of evil, and knows not the utmost that vice promises to her followers, and rejects it, is but a blank virtue, not a pure; her whiteness is but an excremental whiteness; which was the reason why our sage and serious poet, Spencer, describing true temperance under the person of Guion, brings him in, with his palmer, through the cave of Mammon, and the bower of earthly bliss, that he might see and know, and yet abstain.

Since, therefore, the knowledge and survey of vice is in this world so necessary to the constituting of human virtue and the scanning of error to the confirmation of truth, how can we more safely and with less danger scout into the regions of sin and falsity, than by reading all manner of tractates, and hearing all manner of reason?

* * * * *

Give me the liberty to know, to utter, and to argue freely according to conscience, above all liberties. * * And though all the winds of doctrine were let loose to play upon the earth, so truth be in the field, we do injuriously by licensing and prohibiting to mis-doubt her strength. Let her and falsehood grapple; who ever knew truth put to the worse, in a free and open encounter? He who hears what praying there is for light and clear knowledge to be sent down among us, would think of other matters to be constituted beyond the discipline of Geneva, framed and fabriced already to our hands. Yet when the new light which we beg for shines in upon us, there be those who envy and oppose, if it come not in first at their casement. * * *

For who knows not that truth is strong next to the Almighty; she needs no policies or stratagems to make her victorious; those are but the shifts that error uses against her power. What great purchase is this Christian liberty which Paul so often boasts of? His doctrine is, that he who eats or eats not, regards a day or regards it not, may do either to the Lord. How many other things might be tolerated in peace, and left to conscience, had we but charity, and were it not the chief stronghold of our hypocrisy to be ever judging one another? I fear yet this iron yoke of outward conformity hath left a slavish print upon our necks. * *

And what do they tell us vainly of new opinions, when this very opinion of theirs, that none must be heard but whom they like, is the worst and newest opinion of all others; and is the chief cause why sects and schisms so much abound, and true knowledge is kept at distance from us; besides yet a greater danger which is in it. For when God shakes a kingdom, with strong and healthful commotions, to a general reforming, it is not untrue that many sectaries and false teachers are then busiest in seducing; but yet more true is it, that God raises to his own work men of rare abilities, and more than common industry, not only to look back and revise what hath heretofore been taught, but to gain further, and to go on some new enlightened steps in the discovery of truth.—*John Milton A. D. 1641* .

Thoughts from the Arcadia.

Longer I would not wish to draw breath than I may keep myself unspotted of any heinous crime.

In the clear mind of virtue treason can find no hiding-place.

The hero's soul may be separated from his body, but never alienated from the remembrance of virtue.

Doing good is the only certainly happy action of a man's life.

The journey of high honor lies not in smooth ways.

Remember that in all miseries lamenting becomes fools, and action the wise.

In a brave bosom honor cannot be rocked asleep by affection.

Prefer truth before the maintaining of an opinion.

Joyful is woe for a noble cause, and welcome all its miseries.

A just man hateth the evil, but not the evil-doer.

It is folly to believe that he can faithfully love, who does not love faithfulness.

Everything that is mine, even to my life, is hers I love, *but the secret of my friend is not mine.*

A man of true honor thinks himself greater in being subject to his own word, than in being lord of a principality.

They are never alone that are accompanied with noble thoughts.—*Sir Philip Sidney.*

No Cross, no Crown.

The cross of Christ is a figurative speech borrowed from the outward tree or wooden cross on which Christ submitted to the will of God, in permitting him to suffer death at the hands of evil men. The cross mystical is that divine grace and power which crosses the carnal wills of men, gives a contradiction to their corrupt affections, and constantly opposeth itself to the inordinate and fleshly appetites of their minds; and so may be justly termed the instrument of man's holy dying to the world, and being made conformable to the will of God. * *

Nor is a recluse life, the boasted righteousness of some, much more commendable, or one whit nearer the nature of the true cross; for if it be not unlawful as other things are, it is unnatural, which true religion teaches not. The Christian convent and monastery are within, where the soul is encloistered from sin. And this religious house the true followers of Christ carry about with them, who exempt not themselves from the conversation of the world, though they keep themselves from the evil of the world in their conversation.

That is a lazy, rusty, unprofitable self-denial, burdensome to others to feed their idleness; religious bedlams, where people are kept up, lest they should do mischief abroad; patience *per* force; self-denial against their will, rather ignorant than virtuous; and out of the way of temptation, than constant in it.

No thanks if they commit not what they are not tempted to commit. What the eye views not, the heart craves not, as well as rues not. The cross of Christ is of another nature. It truly overcomes the world, and leads a life of purity in the face of its allurements. They that bear it are not thus chained up, for fear they should bite; nor locked up lest they should be stolen away. They receive power from Christ, their Captain, to resist the evil, and do that which is good in the sight of God; to despise the world, and love its reproach above its praise, and not to offend others, but even to love those who offend them, though not for offending them.

What a world we should have, if everybody, for fear of transgressing, should mew himself up within four walls! No such matter; the perfection of the Christian life extends to every honest labor or traffic used among men.

True godliness does not turn men out of the world, but enables them to live better in it; and excites their endeavors to mend it: "not to hide their candle under a bushel, but to set it upon a table, in a candlestick." Besides, it is a selfish invention; and that can never be the way of taking up the cross, which the true cross is taken up to subject. Again, this humor runs away by itself, and leaves the world behind to be lost. Christians should keep the helm, and guide the vessel to its port; not meanly steal out at the stern of the world, and leave those that are in it without a pilot, to be driven by the fury of evil times upon the rock or sand of ruin. This sort of life, if taken up by young people, is commonly to cover idleness, or to pay portions; to save the lazy from the pain of punishment, or quality from the disgrace of poverty; one will not work, and the other scorns it. If taken up by the aged, a long life of guilt sometimes flies to superstition for refuge; and, after having had its own will in other things, would finish it with a wilful religion to make God amends.

Taking up the cross of Jesus is a more interior exercise.

It is the circumspection and discipline of the soul, in conformity to the divine mind therein revealed. Does not the body follow the soul, and not the soul the body? Consider, that no outward cell can shut up the soul from lust, or the mind from an infinity of unrighteous imaginations! The thoughts of man's heart are evil, and that continually. Evil comes from within, and not from without. How then can an external application remove an internal cause; or a restraint upon the body work a confinement of the mind? Less even than without doors; for where there is least of action, there is most time to think; and if those thoughts are not guided by a higher principle, convents are more mischievous to the world than exchanges. And yet retirement is both an excellent and needful thing: crowds and throngs were not much frequented by the ancient holy pilgrims

Examine, O man, thy foundation, what it is, and who placed thee there; lest in the end it should appear thou hast put an eternal cheat upon thy own soul. The inward steady righteousness of Jesus is another thing, than all the contrived devotion of poor superstitious man; and to stand approved in the sight of God, excels that bodily exercise in religion resulting from the invention of men. The soul that is awakened and preserved by his holy power and spirit, lives to him in the way of his own institution, and worships him in his own spirit, that is, in the holy sense, life, and leadings of it; which indeed is the evangelical worship. Not that I would be thought to slight a true retirement; for I do not only acknowledge, but admire solitude. Christ himself was an example of it: he loved, and chose to frequent, mountains, gardens, sea-sides. It is requisite to the growth of piety, and I reverence the virtue that seeks and uses it, wishing there were more of it in the world: but then it should be free, not constrained.—*William Penn.*

THE TESTIMONIES OF SEVERAL GREAT, LEARNED, AND VIRTUOUS PERSONAGES AMONG THE GENTILES AND CHRISTIANS, URGED IN FAVOR OF SELF-DENIAL, TEMPERANCE, AND PIETY.

PHILIP, king of Macedon, upon three sorts of good news arriving in one day, feared too much success might transport him immoderately; and therefore prayed for some disappointments, to season his prosperity, and caution his mind under the enjoyment of it. He refused to oppress the Greeks with his garrisons, saying, "I had rather retain them by kindness, than fear; and be always beloved, than to be for awhile terrible." One of his minions persuading him to decline hearing a cause, wherein a particular friend was interested; "I had much rather," says he, "thy friend should lose his cause, than I my reputation." Seeing his son Alexander endeavor to gain the hearts of the Macedonians by gifts and rewards, "Canst thou believe," says he, "that a man whom thou hast corrupted to thy interests will ever be true to them?" When his court would have had him quarrel with and correct the Peloponnesians for their ingratitude to him, he said, "By no means; for if they despise and abuse me, after being kind to them, what will they do if I do them harm?"

PHOCION, a famous Athenian, was honest and poor, yea, he contemned riches; for a certain governor making rich presents, he returned them, saying, "I refused Alexander's." And when several persuaded him to accept of such bounty, or else his children would want, he answered, "If my son be virtuous, I shall leave him enough; and if he be vicious, more would be too little." He rebuked the excess of the Athenians, and that openly, saying, "He that eateth more than he ought, maketh more diseases than he can cure." To condemn or flatter him, was to him alike. Demosthenes telling him, "Whenever the people were enraged, they would kill him;" he answered, "And thee also, when they are come to their wits." After all the great services of his life, he was unjustly condemned to die, and going to the place of his execution, lamented of the people, one of his enemies spat in his face; he took it without any disorder of mind, only saying, "Take him away."

HIPPARCHIA, a fair Macedonian virgin, noble of blood, as they term it, but more truly noble of mind, I cannot omit to mention; who entertained so earnest an affection for Crates, the cynical philosopher, as well for his severe life as excellent discourse, that by no means could her relations or suitors, by all their wealth, nobility, and beauty, dissuade her from being his companion. Upon this strange resolution, they all betook themselves to Crates, beseeching him to show himself a true philosopher, by persuading her to desist; which he strongly endeavored by many arguments; but not prevailing, went his way, and brought all the little furniture of his house and showed her. This, saith he, is thy husband; that, the furniture of thy house: consider on it, for thou canst not be mine, unless thou followest the same course of life; for being rich above twenty talents, which is more than fifty thousand pounds, he neglected all, to follow a retired life. All this had so contrary an effect, that she immediately went to him, before them all, and said, "I seek not the pomp and effeminacy of this world, but knowledge and virtue, Crates; and choose a life of temperance, before a life of delicacies: for true satisfaction, thou knowest, is in the mind; and that pleasure is only worth seeking, which lasts forever." Thus she became the constant companion both of his love and life, his friendship and virtues: traveling with hin from place to place, and performing the public exercises of instruction with Crates, wherever they came. She was a most violent enemy to all impiety, but especially to wanton men and women, and those whose garb and conversation showed them devoted to vain pleasures and pastimes: effeminacy rendering the like persons not only unprofitable, but pernicious to the whole world. Which she as well made good by the example of her exceeding industry, temperance, and severity, as those are wont to do by their intemperance and folly: for ruin of health, estates, virtue, and loss of eternal happiness, have ever attended, and ever will attend, such earthly minds.

JUSTIN MARTYR, a philosopher, who received Christianity five and twenty years after the death of Ignatius, plainly tells us, in his relation of his conversion to the Christian faith, that "The power of godliness in a plain, simple Christian, had such influence and operation on his soul that he could not but betake himself to a serious and strict life:" And yet, before, he was a Cynic; a strict sect. And this gave him joy at his martyrdom, having spent his days as a serious teacher, and a good example. And Eusebius relates, "That though he was also a follower of Plato's doctrine, yet, when he saw the Christians' piety and courage, he concluded no people so temperate, less voluptuous, and more set on divine things." Which first induced him to be a Christian.

MICHAEL DE MONTAIGNE, a lord of France, famous with men of letters for his book of Essays, gives these instructions to others, and this character of himself, viz.: "Amidst our banquets, feasts, and pleasures, let us ever have the restraint or object of death before us, that is, the remembrance of our condition. And let no pleasure so much mislead or transport us, as to neglect or forget how many ways our joys or our feastings be subject unto death, and by how many holdfasts she threateneth us and you. So did the Egyptians, who in the midst of their banquetings, and in their greatest cheer, caused the anatomy of a dead man to be brought before them, as a memorandum and warning to their guests. I am now, by means of the mercy of God, in such a taking, that without regret, or grieving at any worldly matter, I am prepared to dislodge, whensoever he shall please to call me. I am everywhere free. My farewell is soon taken of all my friends, except of myself. No man ever prepared himself to quit the world more simply and fully, or did more generally lay aside all thoughts of it, than I am assured I shall do. All the glory that I pretend to in my life, is, that I have lived quietly. Let us not propose so fleeting and so wavering an end to ourselves, as this world's glory. Let us constantly follow truth: and let the vulgar approbation follow us that way, if it please. I care not so much what I am with others, as I respect what I am in myself. I will be rich in myself, and not by borrowing. Strangers see but external appearances and events: Every man can set a good face upon the matter, when within he is full of care, grief and infirmities. They see not my heart, when they look upon my outward countenance. We are nought but ceremony; ceremony doth transport us, and we leave the substance of things. We hold fast by the boughs, and leave the trunk or body, the substance of things, behind us."

SIR WALTER RALEIGH is an eminent instance, being as extraordinary a man as our nation hath produced. In his person, well descended; of health, strength, and masculine beauty; in understanding, quick; in judgment, sound, learned and wise, valiant and skillful; a historian, a philosopher, a general, a statesman, After a long life, full of experience, he drops these excellent sayings a little before his death, to his son, to his wife, and to the world, viz.: "Exceed not in the humor of rags and bravery; for these will soon wear out of fashion; and no man is esteemed for gay garments, but by fools and women. On the other side, seek not riches basely, nor attain them by evil means. Destroy no man for his wealth, nor take anything from the poor; for the cry thereof will pierce the heavens. And it is most detestable before God, and most dishonorable before worthy men, to wrest anything from the needy and laboring soul: God will never prosper thee if thou offendest therein; but use thy poor neighbors and tenants well." A most worthy saying. But he adds, "Have compassion on the poor and afflicted, and God will bless thee for it. Make not the hungry sorrowful; for if he curse thee in the bitterness of his soul, his prayer shall be heard of him that made him. Now, for the world, dear child, I know it too well to persuade thee to dive into the practices of it. Rather stand upon thy guard against all those that tempt thee to it, or may practice upon thee; whether in thy conscience, thy reputation, or thy estate. Resolve that no man is wise or safe, but he that is honest. Serve God; let him be the author of all thy actions. Commend all thy endeavors to him, who must either wither or prosper them. Please him with prayer; lest if he frown, he confound all thy fortune and labor, like the drops of rain upon the sandy ground. Let my experienced advice and fatherly instruction sink deep into thy heart: So God direct thee in all thy ways and fill thy heart with his grace."

His noble and touching letter to his wife, after his condemnation, says: "You shall receive, my dear wife, my last words, in these my last lines. My love I send to you, that you may keep it when I am dead; and my counsel, that you may remember it when I am no more. I would not with my will present you sorrows, dear Bess; let them go to the grave with me, and be buried in the dust; and seeing it is not the will of God that I shall see you any more, bear my destruction patiently, and with a heart like yourself. First, I send you all the thanks which my heart can conceive, or my words express, for your many travails and cares for me; which, though they have not taken effect as you wished, yet my debt to you is not the less; but pay it I never shall in this world. Secondly, I beseech you for the love you bear me living, that you do not hide yourself many days; but by your travails seek to help my miserable fortunes, and the right of your poor child; your mourning cannot avail me, who am but dust. Thirdly, you shall understand that my lands were conveyed (*bona fide*) to my child; the writings were drawn at midsummer was a twelvemonth, as divers can witness; and I trust my blood will quench their malice, who desired my slaughter, that they will not seek to kill you and yours with extreme poverty.

"To what friend to direct you, I know not; for all mine have left me in the true time of trial. Most sorry am I, that being surprised by death, I can leave thee no better estate. God hath prevented all my determinations; that Great God which worketh all in all. If you can live free from want, care for no more; for the rest is but vanity. Love God and begin betimes; in him shall you find true, everlasting and endless comfort. When you have wearied yourself with all sorts of worldly cogitations, you shall sit down by sorrow in the end. Teach your son also to serve and fear God, whilst he is young, that the fear of God may grow up in him; then God will be a husband to you, and a father to him; a husband and a father that can never be taken from you.

"Dear wife, I beseech you, for my soul's sake, pay all poor men. When I am dead, no doubt you will be much sought unto, for the world thinks I was very rich; have a care of the fair pretences of men; for no greater misery can befall you in this life, than to become a prey to the world, and after to be despised. As for me, I am no more yours, nor you mine. Death hath cut us asunder; and God hath divided me from the world, and you from me. Remember your poor child for his father's sake, who loved you in his happiest estate. I sued for my life, but God knows it was for you and yours that I desired it. For know it, my dear wife, your child is the child of a true man, who in his own respect despiseth death, and his mis-shapen and ugly forms. I cannot write much; God knows how hardly I steal this time, when all are asleep: And it is also time to separate my thoughts from the world. Beg my dead body, which living was denied you; and either lay it in Sherburne, or in Exeter Church, by my father and mother. I can say no more; time and death call me away. The everlasting God Almighty, who is goodness itself, the true light and life, keep you and yours, and have mercy upon me, and forgive my persecutors and false accusers; and send us to meet in His glorious kingdom. My dear wife, farewell; bless my boy; pray for me; and let my true God hold you both in His arms.

"Yours that was, but not now my own,

"WALTER RALEIGH."

Behold wisdom, resolution, nature and grace! how strong in argument, wise in council, firm, affectionate and devout. O that your heroes and politicians would make their example in his death, as well as magnify the great actions of his life. I doubt not, had he been to live over his days again, with his experience, he had made less noise, and yet done more good to the world and himself.—*William Penn.*

EXTRACT FROM A NOBLE ADDRESS TO KING CHARLES II., ON HIS RESTORATION.

To Charles II., King, &c.:

Robert Barclay, a servant of Jesus Christ, called of God to the dispensation of the Gospel, wishes health and salvation. As it is inconsistent with the truth I bear, so it is far from me to use this epistle as an engine to flatter thee. * * * To God alone I owe what I have, and that more immediately in matters spiritual; and therefore to Him alone, and to the service of His truth, I dedicate whatever work He brings forth in me.

Thou hast tasted of prosperity and adversity; thou knowest what it is to be banished thy native country, to be overruled as well as to rule and sit upon the throne; and being oppressed, thou hast reason to know how hateful the oppression is both to God and man.

God hath done great things for thee; He hath sufficiently shown thee that it is by Him princes rule, and that He can pull down and set up at His pleasure. He hath often faithfully warned thee by His servants, since He restored thee to the royal dignity, that thy heart might not wax wanton against Him to forget His mercies and providence towards thee; whereby He might permit thee to be soothed up and lulled asleep in thy sins by the flattering of court parasites, who by their fawning are the ruin of many princes.

God Almighty, who hath so signally hitherto visited thee with His love, so touch and reach thy heart, ere the day of thy visitation be expired, that thou mayest effectually turn to Him so as to improve thy place and station for His name. So wisheth, so prayeth,

Thy faithful friend and subject,

ROBERT BARCLAY, *a Friend, or Quaker.*

DIVINE SAGACITY, OR INTUITION.

I shall commend to them that would successfully philosophize the belief and endeavor after a certain principle more noble and inward than reason itself, and without which, reason will falter, or at least reach but to mean and frivolous ends. I have a sense of something in me while I thus speak, which, I must confess, is of so recluse a nature that I have no name for it, unless I should adventure to call it divine sagacity, which is the first rise of a successful reason.—*Dr. Henry More.*

COURAGE.

Certainly the purging of our natural spirits and raising our soul to her due height of piety, and weaning her from the love of the body, and too tender a sympathy with the frail flesh, begets that courage and majesty of mind in a man, that both inward and outward fiends shall tremble at his presence, and fly before him as darkness at light's approach. For the soul hath then ascended her fiery vehicle, and it is noon to her midnight, be she awake herself.—*Dr. H. More.*

SPIRITUAL INTERCOURSE.

I believe there is a supernatural and a spiritual world, in which human spirits both good and bad live in a state of consciousness.

I believe that any of these spirits may, according to the order of God, in the laws of their place of residence, have intercourse with this world, and become visible unto mortals.

I believe Samuel did actually appear unto Saul, and that

he was sent by the especial mercy of God, to warn the infatuated King of his approaching death.—*Adam Clarke.*

Future Growth of the Soul.

Among excellent arguments for the immortality of the soul there is one, drawn from its perpetual progress to its perfection, without a possibility of ever arriving at it; which is a hint that I do not remember to have seen opened and improved on by others, though it seems to me to carry great weight. How can it enter into the thoughts of man, that the soul, which is capable of such immense perfections and of receiving new improvements to all eternity, shall fall away into nothing almost as soon as it is created? * * *

Would an infinitely wise Being make such glorious beings for so mean and brief a purpose? Would he give us talents not to be exerted, capacities never to be gratified? How can we find that wisdom that shines in all his works, in the formation of man, without looking on this world as only a nursery for the next, and believing that the several generations which rise and disappear in quick succession are only to receive their first rudiments of existence here, and to be transplanted into a more friendly climate, where they may spread and flourish to all eternity? There is not a more pleasing consideration in religion than this of the perpetual progress which the soul makes toward the perfection of its nature, without ever arriving at a period in it. To look upon the soul as going on from strength to strength, to consider that she is to shine forever with new accessions of glory, that she will still be adding virtue to virtue, and knowledge to knowledge, carries in it something wonderfully agreeable to that ambition which is natural to the mind of man.

Methinks this one consideration of the progress of a finite spirit to perfection, will be sufficient to extinguish all envy in inferior natures, and all contempt in superior. The cherub that now appears as a god to a human soul, knows that a time will come when that soul shall be as perfect as he now is; nay, when she shall look down on that degree of perfection. It is true the higher nature still advances, and preserves his superiority, but he knows that how high soever the station may be of which he stands prepossessed, the inferior nature will mount up to it, and shine in the same degree of glory.

With what astonishment and veneration may we look into our own souls, where there are such hidden stores of virtue and knowledge! Such inexhaustible sources of perfection!—*Addison.*

God's Angels.

How many times have we been strangely and unaccountably preserved in sudden and dangerous falls? And it is well if we did not impute that preservation to chance, or to our own wisdom or strength. Not so: God, perhaps, gave his angels charge over us, and in their hands they bore us up. Indeed, men of the world will always impute such deliverances to accident or second causes.

When a violent disease, supposed incurable, is totally and suddenly removed, it is by no means improbable that this is effected by the ministry of an angel. And perhaps it is to the same cause that a remedy is unaccountably suggested either to the sick person, or some one attending upon him, by which he is entirely cured.

It seems what are usually called divine dreams may be frequently ascribed to angels. We have a remarkable instance of this kind related by one who will hardly be called an enthusiast, for he was a heathen, a philosopher, and an emperor: I mean Marcus Antoninus. "In his meditations, he solemnly thanks God for revealing to him when he was at Cajeta, in a dream, what totally cured the bloody flux, which none of his physicians were able to heal." And why may we not suppose that God gave him this notice by the ministry of an angel?—*John Wesley.*

Presence of Spirits.

It appears to me no way contrary to reason to believe that the happy departed spirits see and know all they would wish, and are divinely permitted to know. In this, Mr. Wesley (the founder of Methodism) is of the same mind,—and that they *are* concerned for the dear fellow pilgrims whom they have left behind. I cannot but believe they are. Nor doth it seem contrary to reason to suppose a spirit in glory can turn its eye with as much ease, and look on any object below, as a mother can look through a window, and see the actions of her children in the court beneath it. If bodies have a language by which they can convey their thoughts to each other, though sometimes at a distance, have spirits no language, think you, by which they can converse with our spirits, and by impressions on the mind, speak to us as easily as before they did by the tongue? And what can interrupt either the presence, communication, or sight of a spirit?

> "Walls within walls no more its passage bar
> Than unopposing space of liquid air."

Though it is allowed we may have communion with angels, various are the objections raised against the belief of our communion with that other part of the heavenly family,—*the disembodied spirits of the just.* If there is joy throughout all the realms above, yea, "more joy over one sinner that repenteth than over the ninety and nine which went not astray," how evident it is to an impartial eye that the state of both the one and the other must be known there, together, with the progress of each individual! Have not spirits faculties suited to spirits, by which we may suppose they can as easily discern our soul as we could discern their body when they were in the same state as ourself? If "he maketh his angels spirits, and his ministers a flame of fire," cannot a spirit be with me in a moment, as easily as a stroke from an electrical machine can convey the fire for many miles in one moment, through thousands of bodies, if properly linked together?—*Mrs. Mary Fletcher* (*an early English Methodist*).

Love of Truth.

He who begins by loving Christianity better than Truth, will proceed by loving his own sect or church better than Christianity, and by loving himself better than all.—*S. T. Coleridge.*

The true Priest—Reformer—and one Army for Right.

We have repeatedly endeavored to explain that all sorts of Heroes are intrinsically of the same material; that, given a great soul, open to the Divine Significance of Life, then there is given a man fit to sing of this, to fight and work for this, in a great, victorious, and enduring manner; there is given a Hero—the outward shape of whom will depend on the time and the environment he finds himself in. The Priest too, as I understand it, is a kind of Prophet; in him there is required to be a light of inspiration, as we name it. He is the Uniter of the people with the Unseen Holy. He is the Spiritual Captain of the people; as the true Prophet is their spiritual King, with many captains; he guides them heavenward, by wise guidance through this earth and its work. The ideal of him is, that he too be what we can call a voice from the unseen heaven,—the "open Secret of the Universe," which so few have an eye for! He is the Prophet shorn of his more awful splendor; burning with mild equable radiance, as the enlightener of daily life. This is the ideal of a Priest in old times, in these, n all times. One knows very well that, in reducing ideals to practice, great latitude of toleration is needed. But a Priest who is not this at all, who does not any longer aim or try to be this, is a character of—whom we had rather not speak. * * Nay, I may ask, is not every true Reformer, by the nature of him, a *Priest* first of all? He appeals to Heaven's invisible justice against Earth's visible force; knows that it, the invisible, is strong and alone strong. He is a believer in the divine truth of things; a *Seer*, seeing through the shews of things; a worshipper, in one way or the other, of the divine truth of things. * * * Every man is not only a learner but a doer; he learns with the mind given him, what has been; but with the same mind he discovers farther, he invents and devises somewhat of his own. No man believes or can believe exactly what his grandfather believed; he enlarges somewhat, by fresh discovery, his view of the Universe, and consequently his Theorem of the Universe, which is an *infinite* Universe, and can never be embraced wholly or finally in any conceivable enlargement. * * He finds somewhat that was credible to his grandfather, incredible to him, false and inconsistent with some new thing he had discovered or observed. * * * So with all beliefs whatsoever in this world, all Systems of Belief, and Systems of Practice that spring from these. * * Surely it were mournful enough to look only at this face of the matter, and find in all human opinions and arrangements merely the fact that they were uncertain, temporary, subject to the law of death! At bottom it is not so; all death, here too we find, is but of the body, not of the essence of the soul; all destruction, by violent revolution or however, is but a new creation on a wider scale. Odinism was *Valor;* Christianity was *Humility*, a nobler kind of valor. No thought that ever dwelt honestly as true in the heart of man, but *was* an honest insight into God's truth on man's part, and *has* an essential truth in it which endures through all changes, an everlasting possession for us all.

And on the other hand, what a melancholy notion is that which has to represent all men, in all countries and times except our own, as having spent their lives in blind condemnable error, mere lost pagans, Scandinavians, Mahometans, only that we might have the true ultimate knowledge! All generations of men were lost and wrong, only that this present little section of a generation might be saved and right! They all marched forward there, all generations since the beginning of the world, like the Russian soldiers into the ditch of Schweidnitz Fort, only to fill up the ditch with their dead bodies that we might march over and take the place! It is an incredible hypothesis.

Such incredible hypothesis we have seen maintained with fierce emphasis, and this or the other man, with his sect, marching as over the dead bodies of all men, towards sure victory; but when he too, with his hypothesis and ultimate infallible creeds, sank into the ditch and became a dead body, what was to be said? Withal it is an important fact in the nature of man that he tends to reckon his own insight as final, and goes upon it as such. He will always do it, I suppose, in one or the other way; but it must be in some wider and wiser way than this. Are not all *true men* that live or that ever lived, soldiers of the same army; enlisted under Heaven's captaincy to do battle against the same enemy, the empire of Darkness and Wrong? Why should we misknow each other, fight not against the enemy, but against ourselves, from mere difference of uniform? All uniforms shall be good, so they hold in them true and valiant men. All fashions of arms, the Arab turban and swift scimetar, Thor's strong hammer, smiting down Jotuns, shall be welcome. Luther's battle-voice, Dante's march-melody, all genuine things are with us, not against us. We are all under one Captain, soldiers of the same host.—*Thomas Carlyle.*

What Religious Teachers Should Do.

We no longer look on the different creeds of the world, as did the martyrs of old, as being absolutely true or absolutely false, the service of God himself or of the Devil himself.

We see them to be only steps upward in an infinite ascent; only the substitution for a lower of a higher but still all-imperfect ideal of the Holy One. Doubtless we are nearer the true judgment. Doubtless also it was well that of old, in the days of the stake and the rack, men should have seen these things differently; for few indeed could have borne to die, clearly seeing their persecutors to be only partially mistaken in their own creed—the creed for which they were enduring torture and agony—only one of the thousand "little systems" of earth,—

"Which have their day and cease to be,"

a "broken light" from the inaccessible Sun of Truth. * *

But we, in our day, have reached a different pass. We seem to have quitted the region of light and darkness, truth and falsehood, and have come to a land—

"Where it is always afternoon."

There is among the highest order of minds a disposition to accept finally a condition which may be designated as one of reverential skepticism. * * * A sort of direful fashion has set in to praise whatever seems vaguest in doctrine, and weakest in faith, as if *therefore* it were necessarily wisest and most philosophic. We look distrustfully on any one who has not dissolved away in some mental crucible all solid belief in a personal God, and a conscious immortality into certain fluid and gaseous ideas of eternities and immensities. We assume it contentedly as proven that the "limitations of rel gious thought" make it as hopeless for us to find a faith which will keep alive our souls, as an *elixir vitæ* to keep alive our bodies. We wander to and fro hopelessly through the wilderness of doubt; and if any come to tell us of a land flowing with milk and honey, the glory of all lands, which they have found beyond, we dismiss them with a complacent sigh, even if they bring back noblest fruits from their Canaan.

There is surely great error in this state of feeling. Though infallible knowledge is not for men—though we have neither faculties to receive it nor language to convey it—yet it is far indeed from established that our powers fall short of attaining such a share of knowledge of divine things as may suffice for the primary wants of our souls. We need such knowledge for the higher part of our nature, as much as we need bread and clothing for the lower. It is the greatest want of the greatest creature; and if indeed it have no supply, then is the analogy of the universe broken off. There is a presumption of incalculable force that these cravings which arise in the profoundest depths of our souls, which we can never put away, and on which our moral health depends, are not to be forever denied their natural satisfaction, while the ravens are fed and the grass of the field drinks in the dew. We have indeed asked too much hitherto. We have cried like children for the moon of an unattainable infallibility. We have called for systems of theology dissecting the mysteries of our Maker's nature and attributes. But because these things are denied us, are we therefore to despair of knowing those fundamental truths which we must either gain, or else morally and spiritually die? * * *

It is a simple induction from the order of the universe that the soul of man is not the only thing left without its food, its light, its guide, its soul-sufficing end and aim. * *

We must not, dare not, doubt that it will be to a larger, higher, purer truth the human race is being led onward, and that that truth is *safer* than all the well-tried errors of the past. The old Ragnarok, the "Twilight of the Gods," in which our heathen forefathers believed, may be coming now; but there will be a glorious sunrise afterward. The "ages of faith" are not behind us, but before us.

The task then of the religious teacher of our time is to prepare and strengthen men for the future; to give them such faith in God and reverence for his law, *independently* of traditional creeds, as shall avail them when these are overwhelmed. —*Frances Power Cobbe.*

LEIGH HUNT.

The Religion of the Heart.

God,—which is the name for the great First Cause of the Universe, for the power which has set it in motion, which adorns it with beauty, and which, in this our portion of it, and through the mystery of time and trouble, incites us to attain to the welfare and the joy which are therefore to be considered the purpose of final existence, here or hereafter,—God has written his religion in the heart, for growing wisdom to read perfectly, and time to make triumphant.

Without this First Divine Writing, and this power to outgrow barbarous misconceptions of it, no writing claiming to be divine, could be estimated, or understood. The human being would have no language to correspond with its meaning, no faculties to recognize whatever divineness it contained, or to reject what was mixed with it of unworthy. Decline its arbitration, when ascertained by the only *final* evidence of its correctness,—that of a thorough harmony with itself,—and there is no folly, cruelty, or impiety of belief, which the mind, however unwillingly, and to its ultimate confusion, shall not be led to take for religion. Admit the arbitration so ascertained, and such mistakes become impossible. Doctrines revolting to the heart are not made to endure, however mixed up they may be with lessons the most divine. They contain the seeds of their dissolution. They cannot even be thoroughly well taught. Something inconsistent, something quarrelsome, something dissatisfied with itself, or uncharitable to others, something uneasy, unlovely, or unpersuasive, will sooner or later disclose the incongruity, and leave the gentle and coherent wisdom to be found the only guide.

With a like necessity for relief from the otherwise imperfect conclusions of the understanding, mankind have been so constituted, that for the most part they cannot without uneasiness dissociate the ideas of order and design, of means taken and ends contemplated, of progressive humanity and a divine intention. They are conscious of a difference between mind and body, between the greatness of their intellectual aspirations and the smallness of their knowledge; and most of all, between their capacity for happiness and the amount of it which they realize: and for all these reasons they desire a Giver and a Comforter, whom they thank in joy, and turn for support to in affliction, and feel to be the only fulfiller and security of that triumph over the visible and the mortal, which their nature has been made to desire.

Impressed more and more with a sense of the Great Beneficence, in proportion as we become intimate with his works, the holders of the Religion of the Heart believe, that part of his divine occupation is to work ends befitting his goodness, out of different forms of matter, and out of transient, qualified, and unmalignant evils; probably to the endless multiplication of heavens.

They believe, that in the world which they inhabit, its human beings are among the instruments with which the Great Beneficence visibly operates, to purposes of this nature; that is to say, with manifest change and advancement: and they are of opinion, that wherever a so-called divinely-inspired man has appeared, the inspiration has been justly attributed to his unusual participation of the beneficent impulse, in proportion as the lessons which he has taught have been effective, reasonable and lasting.

They are of opinion, that enough of these lessons have been given mankind to furnish them with right principles of conduct, mental and bodily; but that the particulars of conduct into which those principles should be carried out, are too commonly lost sight of in the supposed sufficiency of general precepts, perfect in spirit, but incessantly violated for want of reduction to such particulars. It is therefore their opinion, that this want ought to be zealously and constantly supplied; that health of mind and health of body are to be professedly cultivated in unison, as the only sure means of completing the rational and cheerful creature, which the human organization, in empowering him, requires him to become; that some of what are called minor morals, or those affecting temper and manners, deserve, on that account, to be known for what they are,—the particulars of great ones,—the everyday moments of which life is made, household moments especially, being deeply concerned in the recognition; that any further insistment on the necessity of such points of faith as have divided and scandalized the world, and maintained the worst notions of the divinest things, is not only worse than useless to man, but impious (however unwillingly so) towards God; and that the great business of Faith is to believe in the goodness of the Creator and all his works; of Hope, to look for the thorough manifestation of it in time or eternity; and of Charity, to do and think everything meanwhile in the spirit of kindness.

For they believe that the Divine Being is a wholly good and beneficent being; wholly and truly the Great Beneficence; not to be thought of in any other light; free and distinct, in essence, and to all final purpose, from admixture of the least evil through which he works, as the light itself is from the substance which it penetrates. And though they hold it to be as impossible for his human creatures entirely to comprehend him, as it is for their arms to embrace infinitude, yet inasmuch as they are his work, and gifted by him with affections, they may feel conscious of him with their hearts on the side at which his infinitude touches humanity, and without presuming to conceive any portion of him in human likeness, consider the Author of their Being as including a Divine Paternity.

Nor do the holders of these opinions the less hope for a heaven elsewhere, or for an endless succsssion of heavens, or for an equal measure of happiness for all who have lived and suffered in past times, let earth be rendered never so heavenly. For what marvel, deeply considered, is more marvellous than another? And who shall limit the possibilities of adjustment, during the endlessness of space and time, in the hands of the maker of the stars?

On all these accounts, it is their persuasion that every human being, for his own sake, and (not to speak it presumptuously) for God's, is bound to maintain all his faculties, mental and bodily, in their healthiest, hopefullest, most active, and most affectionate condition.

Aspiration in the Morning.

In the name of the Great Beneficence, to whom be all reverence, with a filial trust.

My first duty this day is to delay, or slur over, nothing which I am bound in conscience to perform.

The hour has come, at which it is therefore time for me to rise.

Thou, O my heart, biddest me rise, for the sake of others as well as myself.

Because on thee the Divine Spirit has written the laws, which love teaches knowledge to read:

And because they tell me, that duty must be done, and that affection must be earned by good offices.

May I discharge, throughout the day, every other such duty as conscience enjoins me:

Beginning the day with a kind voice to others;

And ending it with no reproach to myself.

Of the Great Benefactors of the World.

Let us be grateful, without idolatry, without worship of any sort, to the memories of those divine men who from time to time have advanced the human species in knowledge and goodness. They partook of our infirmities; but the divine particle was stronger within them; they may have been misrepresented in some instances by their followers; their history may have been mingled with unworthy fables; they themselves, the best of them, from excessive sensibility, and their very impatience with what was wrong, may have failed in becoming patterns of humanity. But it is our duty to separate what is good and likely in their history, from that which is of doubtful character. They who loved us, and we who love and honor them, have equally a right to the benefit of the separation.

Let us reverence and love all who have acted or suffered in the great cause of beneficence.

Let us reverence the bright names in dark periods, the remote philosophers of Europe and Asia; Confucius in particalar, the first great light of rational piety and benignant intercourse.

Let us reverence our latest benefactors, the exposers of intolerance, the overthrowers of cruel substitutions of force for argument, the furtherers of the love of reason.

Let us reverence the great teachers of experiment, the liberators of the hands of knowledge; and their disciples, the movers of the earth.

Let us reverence and love those extraordinary men of action, the Alfreds, Epaminondases and their like, who have been busiest in the thick of the world, and yet it polluted them not; thus enabling us, for ever, to refute the sophistries of the worldly.

Let us reverence and love Socrates, who next to the great philosopher of China shewed the way to this union of the active and contemplative; who was the first among Europeans to teach us, that philosophy does not require lofty occasions on which to exert itself, but may become a part of the daily business of life.

Let us reverence and love Epictetus and Antoninus, who, though the one was a slave and the other an emperor, alike told us to bear and forbear; being self-denying to themselves, and indulgent to others; and teaching beneficence, not only towards friends, and men in general, but towards enemies and those who ill treat us.

Let us reverence and love above all, their martyred brother

Jesus; not because he was in all respects their superior, or to be looked upon as that "perfect man," which, with an injurious want of sincerity, he has been pronounced; for his temperament was less under his control, and sometimes contradicted his doctrines; but because he was the man who felt most for the wants of his fellow-creatures, and who saw deepest into their remedy; the man fullest of love for the loving, of forgiveness for the ignorant, of pity for the unfortunate and the outcast; the identifier of one's neighbor with every human being; the freer of spirit from letter; the proclaimer of the rights of the poor. May he never be deprived of the love and honor that are his due, by having had the claims for them stretched beyond the limits of conscience and common sense.

We should consider it incumbent upon us, that no evil endured for the sake of mankind by any such men as these, at any time, or in any country, should lose its good effects, as far as our efforts can realize them. But faith in their names, without imitation of their virtues, is often worse than nothing.

The Great Means and Ends of Endeavor.

The great means and ends of all Social Endeavor are these:—

The Means,—Unbounded Inquiry; Unchallenged Rights of Conscience; Universal Education (including Knowledge of the Bodily Frame); Universal Extinction of the Doctrine of Fear by that of Love; Universal and Reasonable Employment; Universal Leisure.

The Ends,—Universal Healthy Enjoyment of all the Faculties, Bodily and Mental; Universal Love of the Beautiful; Universal Brotherhood; Universal Hope of Immortality; Universal Trust in the Goodness and All-Reconciling Futurities of God.

Rules of Life and Manners.

1. To reverence God and his purposes with a filial trust.

2. To study, as far as in us lies, his creation, and be sensible of its beauties.

3. To consider duty our first object, and the highest warrant of our pleasures.

4. To delay, or slur over, nothing which it is incumbent on us to perform.

5. To keep our bodies clean, things about us in order, and our appearance decent and unaffected.

6. To keep our blood pure with exercise and fresh air, and to be as conversant always with the air as befits creatures that exist only by means of it.

7. To avoid oppressing, exciting, or drowsing ourselves with over-eating, or drinking, or with narcotics.

8. To consider kind manners, and a willingness to please and be pleased, not superficial, but substantial duties.

9. To hold censorious talk dishonorable to the motives, and in a creation so full of interest, disgraceful to the understanding.

10. To set examples, in word and deed, of the truthfulness that we demand from others; not indeed saying all that we think at all times (which would be inhuman), but never saying anything we do not think, or doing anything with duplicity.

11. To cultivate large-heartedness; endeavoring to think and to do on all occasions the reverse of what is petty and self-seeking, even at the hazard of misconstruction.

12. To consider, nevertheless, indifference to misconstruction as a presumption and of bad example.

13. To inflict no pain on any creature for the sake of a pleasure.

14. To shrink from no pain to ourselves, which in wholesomeness or in kindness ought to be met.

15. To visit the sick, and others who need comfort.

16. To encourage unbounded inquiry, particularly into the

causes of social evils; and to do what we can towards their alleviation and extinction.

17. To consider the healthy, and therefore, as far as mortality permits, happy exercise of all the faculties with which we have been gifted, as the self-evident final purpose of our being, so far as existence in this world is concerned; and as constituting therefore the right of every individual human creature, and the main earthly object of all social endeavor.

18. To reflect at the same time, that man's hope of immortality is also the gift of his Creator; that the certainty of it in his life, might in some way or other be inconsistent with the very perfection of its happiness when attained; and that in the meantime, the hope of that happiness for all is a heavenlier thing, and more suitable to a good heart, than assumptions of certainty barbarized with unhappiness to any.

19. To bear in mind, that Morals mean Habits; that good as well as bad habits are acquirable; and that satisfaction, instead of regret, increases with their advancement.

20. Never to forget, that as the habits of childhood commence with its existence, they are the most acquirable of any, and are of all the most important.

Of Religion.

Religion (*religio—religare*, to rebind) is the rebinding of conscience, with a belief in its divine origin.

Religion is as natural to man as his sight of the stars, and his sense of a power greater than his own.

But systems of religion vary with successive generations; and though it becomes all men to entertain a certain reverence for the past, and to regard its sufferings, and perhaps its mistakes, as having been good for the future, yet it is not in the nature of the feelings which God has given us, that any good heart, in proportion as it reflects on the subject, should be content with any system of religion inferior to its notions of what is best.

With no religion at all, men are in danger or falling into a mechanical dullness, or into preposterous self-worship, or into heart-hardening abandonment to the senses.

With a religion that is unworthy of them, they make God himself unworthy, and fill their belief with cruelty and melancholy, with dispute and scandal.

With a religion satisfactory to the heart, men love and do honor to God, make brothers of their fellow-creatures, are animated in their endeavors, comforted in their sufferings, and encouraged to hope everything from the future.

Religion is reverence without terror, and humility without meanness. It is a sense of the unknown world, without disparagement to the known; an admiration of the material beauties of the universe, without forgetfulness of the spiritual; an enhancement in both instances, of each by each.

Religion doubles every sense of duty, great and small; from that to the whole human race, down to manners towards individuals, and even to appearance in ourselves; from purity of heart to cleanliness of person.

But it does all without gloom or oppressiveness. It does not desire us to reflect in any painful manner or to any painful extent, unless some necessity for the good of others demands it; and then it would terminate the pain with the necessity.

The very uncertainties of a right religion are diviner than the supposed certainties of a wrong one; for its hopes for all are unmixed with terrible beliefs for any.

Religion, earthwards, begins with reverence to offspring before they are born; and heavenwards, it sees no more end to its hopes than to the number of the stars.

The Reconciliation Between Conservatism and Radicalism.

These admissions will perhaps be held to imply, that the current theology should be passively accepted; or, at any rate, should not be actively opposed. Why, it may be asked, if all creeds have an average fitness to their times and places, should we not rest content with that to which we are born? If the established belief contains an essential truth—if the forms under which it presents this truth, though intrinsically bad, are extrinsically good—if the abolition of these forms would be at present detrimental to the great majority—nay, if there are scarcely any to whom the ultimate and most abstract belief can furnish an adequate rule of life, surely it is wrong for the present at least, to propagate this ultimate and most abstract belief.

The reply is, though existing religious ideas and institutions have an average adaptation to the characters of the people who live under them, yet as these characters are ever changing, the adaptation is ever becoming imperfect, and the ideas and institutions need remodeling with a frequency proportionate to the rapidity of the change. Hence, while it is requisite that free play should be given to conservative thought and action, progressive thought and action must also have free play. Without the agency of both, there cannot be those continual readaptations which orderly progress demands.

Whoever hesitates to utter that which he thinks the highest truth, lest it should be too much in advance of the time, may reassure himself by looking at his acts from an impersonal point of view. Let him duly realize the fact that opinion is the agency through which character adapts external arrangements to itself—that his opinion rightly forms part of this agency—is a unit of force, constituting, with other such units, the general power which works our social changes; and he will perceive that he may properly give full utterance to his innermost convictions, leaving it to produce what effect it may. It is not for nothing that he has in him these sympathies with some principles and repugnance to others. He, with all his capacities and aspirations and beliefs, is not an accident, but a product of the time. He must remember that while he is a descendant of the past, he is a parent of the future; and that his thoughts are as children born to him, which he may not carelessly let die.

Not as adventitious, therefore, will the wise man regard the faith which is in him. The highest truth he sees he will fearlessly utter; knowing that, let what may come of it, he is thus playing his right part in the world—knowing that if he can effect the change he aims at—well; if not—well also; though not so well.—*Herbert Spencer.*

A Man Conquered by Vice.

If we wish to know who is the most degraded, and most wretched of human beings; if it be any object to gauge the dimensions of wretchedness, and to see how deep the miseries of man can reach; look for the man who has practiced a vice so long that he curses it and clings to it; that he pursues it because he feels a great law of his nature driving him on towards it; but, reaching it, knows that it will gnaw his heart, and tear his vitals, and make him roll himself in the dust in anguish.—*Sydney Smith.*

Religion Pervading Nature.

It is a meek and blessed influence, stealing in, as it were, unawares upon the heart; it comes quietly and without excitement; it has no terror, no gloom as it approaches; it does not rouse up the passions; it is untrammeled by the creeds, and unshadowed by the superstitions of man; it is fresh from the hands of the Author, glowing from the immediate presence of the Great Spirit, which pervades and quickens it. It is written on the arched sky; it looks out from every star; it is on the sailing cloud, and in the invisible wind; it is among the hills and valleys of the earth, where the shrubless mountain-top pierces the thin atmosphere of eternal winter, or where the mighty forest, with its dark waves of green foliage, fluctuates before the strong wind. It is spread out like a legible language, upon the broad face of the unsleeping ocean; it is the poetry of nature. It is this which uplifts the spirit within us, until it is strong enough to overlook the shadow of our place of probation; which breaks, link after link, the chain that binds us to materiality; aud which opens to our imagination a world of spiritual beauty and holiness.—*Ruskin.*

Heart Power.

A man's force in the world, other things being equal, is just in the ratio of the force and strength of his heart. A full-hearted man is always a powerful man; if he be erroneous, then he is powerful for error; if the thing is in his very heart, he is sure to make it notorious, even though it be a downright falsehood. Let a man be never so ignorant, if his heart be full of love to a cause he becomes a powerful man for that object, because he has heart-power. A man may be deficient in education, in many niceties so much looked upon in society; but once give him a good strong heart and there is no mistake about his power. Let him have a heart full to the brim with an object, and that man will do the thing, or else he will die gloriously defeated, and will glory in his defeat. Heart is Power.—*Spurgeon.*

Varnished Evils.

If the devil comes to my door with his horns visible, I will never let him in; bnt ıf he comes with his hat on, as a respectable gentleman, he is at once admitted. This may be quaint, but it is true. Many a man has taken in an evil thing, because it has been varnished and glossed over, and not apparently an evil; and he has thought in his heart there is not much harm in it; so he has let in the little thing, and it has been like the breaking forth of water—the first drop has brought a torrent after it—the beginning of a fearful end.—*Spurgeon.*

Death of the Young a Light to Heaven.

When Death strikes down the innocent and the young, for every fragile form from which he lets the panting spirit free, a hundred virtues rise, in shapes of mercy, charity, and love, to walk the world and bless it. Of every tear that sorrowing mortals shed on such green graves, some good is born, some gentler nature comes. In the destroyer's steps there spring up bright creations that defy his power, and his dark path becomes a way of light to Heaven.—*Charles Dickens.*

Rational Faith.

Faith is the free exercise of the mind, *resting only on the discernment of the truth;* just as sight is the free exercise of the eye, resting only on the discernment of the light; and no man can possibly believe, in submission to authority, that which he does not discern to be true, any more than he can behold the sun at midnight in obedience to a positive command. A man may indeed be taught to keep his eyes shut, and by discipline and training, may be brought not only to say, but even to fancy, that he sees whatever he is told ought to be seen, distrusting his own natural perceptions. A man may also be trained to look only and always through lenses of a prescribed color and form, and to disuse and supersede his unassisted vision. So also may men, yea, nations and generations of men, be kept in more or less ignorance, distrust, and neglect of their own faculty of discerning what is true, and thus be made to surrender, or never to know, the right of private judgment; so that even those things which are most thoroughly believed by such men, are believed, not because they are conscious of their truth, but because they have the sanction of authority.—*John Robertson.*

The Future that Awaits Us.

We must also understand, that the words dark and light, which in this world of appearance we use metaphorically to express good and evil, must be understood literally when speaking of that other world where everything will be seen as it is. Goodness is truth, and truth is light; and wickedness is falsehood, and falsehood is darkness, and so it will be seen to be. Those who have not the light of truth to guide them will wander darkly through this valley of the shadow of death; those in whom the light of goodness shines will dwell in the light, which is inherent in themselves. The former will be in the kingdom of darkness, the latter in the kingdom of light. All the records existing of the blessed spirits that have appeared, ancient or modern, exhibit them as robed in light, whilst their anger or sorrow is symbolized by their darkness. Now there appears to me nothing incomprehensible in this view of the future; on the contrary, it is the only one which I ever found myself capable of conceiving or reconciling with the justice and mercy of our Creator. He does not punish us, we punish ourselves; we have built up a heaven or a hell to our own liking, and we carry it with us. The fire that forever burns without consuming is the fiery evil in which we have chosen our part; and the heaven in which we shall dwell will be the heavenly peace which will dwell in us. We are our own judges and our own chastisers.

But this self-pronounced sentence we are led to hope is not final, nor does it seem consistent with the love and mercy of God that it should be so. There must be few, indeed, who leave this earth fit for heaven; for although the immediate frame of mind in which dissolution takes place is probably very important, it is surely a pernicious error, encouraged by jail chaplains and philanthropists, that a late repentance and a few parting prayers can purify a soul sullied by years of wickedness. Would we at once receive such an one into our intimate communion and love? Should we not require time for the stains of vice to be washed away, and habits of virtue to be formed? Assuredly we should! And how can we imagine that the purity of heaven is to be sullied by that approximation that the purity of earth would forbid? It would be cruel to say, irrational to think, that this late repentence is of no avail; it is doubtless so far of avail that the straining upwards and the heavenly aspirations of the parting soul are carried with it, so that when it is free, instead of choosing the darkness, it will flee to as much light as is in itself; and be ready, through the mercy of God and the ministering of brighter spirits, to receive more. * * *

The question that will now naturally arise, and which I am bound to answer, is, how have these views been formed? and what is the authority for them? And the answer I have to make will startle many minds, when I say they have been gathered from two sources; first, and chiefly, from the state in which those spirits appear to be, and sometimes avow themselves to be, who, after quitting the earth, return to it and make themselves visible to the living; and secondly, from the revelations of numerous somnambules of the highest order, which entirely conform in all cases, not only with the revelations of the dead, but with each other. I do not mean to imply, when I say this, that I consider the question finally settled, as to whether somnambules are really clear-seers or only visionaries; nor that I have by any means established the fact that the dead do actually sometimes return; but I am obliged to beg the question for the moment, since whether these sources be pure or impure, it is from them the information has been collected. It is true, that these views are extremely conformable with those entertained by Plato and his school of philosophers; and also with those of the mystics of a later age; but the latter certainly, and the former probably, built up their systems on the same foundation: and I am very far from using the term *mystics* in the opprobrious, or at least contemptuous tone, in which it has of late years been uttered in this country; for although abounding in errors, as regarded the concrete, and although their want of an inductive methodology led them constantly astray in the region of the real, they were sublime teachers in that of the ideal; and they seem to have been endowed with a wonderful insight into this veiled department of our nature.—*Catharine Crowe.*

The Reign of Law.

The Reign of Law—is this, then, the reign under which we live? Yes, in a sense it is. There is no denying it. The whole world around us, and the whole world within us, are ruled by Law. Our very spirits are subject to it—those spirits which yet seem so spiritual, so subtle, so free. How often in the darkness do they feel the restraining bounds within which they move, conditions out of which they cannot think! The perception of this is growing in the consciousness of men. It grows with the growth of knowledge; it is the delight, the reward, the goal of Science. From Science it passes into every domain of thought, and invades, amongst others, the Theology of the Church. And so we see the men of Theology coming out to a parley with the men of Science,—a white flag in their hands, and saying, "If you will let us alone, we will do the same by you. Keep to your own province, do not enter ours. The Reign of Law which you proclaim, we admit—outside these walls, but not within them:—let there be peace between us." But this will never do. There can be no such treaty dividing the domain of Truth. Every one Truth is connected with every other Truth in this great universe of God. The connection may be one of infinite subtlety, and apparent distance, running, as it were, underground for a long way, but always asserting itself at last, somewhere and at some time. No bargaining, no fencing off the ground, no form of process, will avail to bar this right of way. Blessed right, enforced by blessed power! Every truth, which is truth indeed, is charged with its own consequences, its own analogies, its own suggestions. These will not be kept outside any artificial boundary; they will range over the whole field of thought, nor is there any corner of it from which they can be warned away.

And therefore we must cast a sharp eye indeed on every form of words which professes to represent a scientific truth. If it be really true in one department of thought, the chances are that it will have its bearing on every other. And if it be not true, but erroneous, its effect will be of a corresponding character; for there is a brotherhood of Error as close as the brotherhood of Truth. Therefore, to accept as a truth that which is not a truth, or to fail in distinguishing the sense in which a proposition may be true, from other senses in which it is not true, is an evil having consequences which are indeed incalculable. There are subjects on which one mistake of this kind will poison all the wells of truth, and affect with fatal error the whole circle of our thoughts.

It is against this danger that some men would erect a feeble barrier, by defending the position that Science and Religion may be, and ought to be, kept entirely separate: that they belong to wholly different spheres of thought, and that the ideas which prevail in the one province have no relation to those which prevail in the other. This is a doctrine offering many temptations to many minds. It is grateful to religious men who are afraid of being thought to be afraid of Science. To these, and to all who are troubled to reconcile what they have been taught to believe with what they have come to know, the doctrine affords a natural and convenient escape. There is but one objection to it—but that is the fatal objection—that it is not true. The spiritual world and the intellectual world are not separated after this fashion; and the notion that they are so separated does but encourage men to accept in each, ideas which will at last be found to be false in both. The truth is that there is no branch of human inquiry, however purely physical, which is no more than the word branch implies; none which is not connected through endless ramifications with every other, and especially that which is the root and centre of them all. If He who formed the mind be one with Him who is the Orderer of all things concerning which that mind is occupied, there can be no end to the points of contact between our different conceptions of them, of Him and of ourselves.

The instinct which impels us to seek for harmony in the truths of Science and the truths of Religion, is a higher instinct and a truer one than the disposition which leads us to evade the difficulty by pretending that there is no relation between them. For after all it is a pretence and nothing more. No man who thoroughly accepts a principle in the philosophy of nature which he feels to be inconsistent with a doctrine of Religion, can help having his belief in that doctrine shaken and undermined. We may believe and we must believe, both in Nature and Religion, many things we cannot understand; but we cannot really believe two propositions which are felt to be contradictory. It helps us nothing in such a difficulty to say that the one proposition belongs to Reason and the other to Faith. The endeavor to reconcile them is a necessity of the mind. We are right in thinking that, if they are both indeed true, they can be reconciled, and if they really are fundamentally opposed, they cannot both be true. That is to say, there must be some error in our manner of conception in one or in the other, or in both. At the very best, each can represent only some partial and imperfect aspect of the truth. The error may lie in our Theology, or it may lie in what we are pleased to call our Science. It may be that some dogma, derived by tradition from our fathers, is having its hollowness betrayed by that light which sometimes shines upon the ways of God out of a better knowledge of His works. It may be that some proud and rash generalization of the schools is having its falsehood proved by the violence it does to the deepest instincts of our spiritual nature.—*Duke of Argyle.*

FRANCIS W. NEWMAN.

[*Professor in University College, London.*]

SAYINGS AND FORETELLINGS.

Virtue is man's highest good,
Justice the chief virtue between man and man,
Truth makes sure the instincts of virtue;
Free thought is needed for the search of Truth.

Man has a mind for virtue and truth,
As truly as limbs for useful labor,
And labor and virtue are close akin.
Labor of head or labor of hand
Are needful to health of mind and body.
Either labor is noble and right;
No rightful labor ought to be debasing.

Women are weakest and most need defense,
Yet in Christian cities they are trampled under foot,
Through the league between Mammon and a spurious policy.

When woman is duly honored and homes are purified,
And fiery drink is withheld from the weak in mind,
And the traffickers in Sin are pursued as felons,
And Truth is open-mouthed, and Thought is free—
God will soon bless the land with blessings undreamed of.

Woman's Duty, and the World's Need.

Yet I speak not for women only, but also for men; that is, for our common country. All who have read history, even superficially, are aware that it is usual to moralize over the fall of great States after they become rich and powerful, and to impute it to luxury. Luxury is not the correct word. Historians ought to say impurity; fostered by wealth, by venal Art, by vicious trade and vicious philosophy. The very profligates of old Rome saw and avowed how much these causes conduced to fatal degeneracy. Paris is discovering that despotism and immorality are firm allies, and that the State-patronage of Vice is fatal to freedom. For myself, I have learned in a few months, more than in fifty years before, how deep are the corruptions of England, and how vehement her downward career. With minds preoccupied by materialism and fatalism, our publicists and officials are quietly accepting our abominable state as the natural order of things, which ought to be organized and made comfortable by Law and Art; thus smoothing our path downwards into a hell of sensuality. The public men who will arrest this seem to be a small minority, and hitherto feeble: their adversaries have a permanent hold of official posts, where they are practically irresponsible and most difficult to dislodge. I see not how anything can purify English society, and destroy the legal incentives and facilities of manifold corruption, quickly enough and decisively enough to save our future, without a greater intensity in the political influence of women.

Because this is a crisis, at which our nation is called to choose between moral life and death, I am bold to address women themselves, and especially educated ladies. If you, ladies, are happy, remember that others are unhappy. If you have kind and just husbands, remember that thousands of women have selfish or wicked husbands. If you have enough of this world's goods, remember that scores of thousands of women and girls can scarcely get bread and shelter even by an excess of toil. If you have been tenderly watched over from childhood, learn that thousands of your sisters are untaught and untrained, and many hundreds wickedly sold by parents or kinsfolk to the shambles of the voluptuous rich. It is a grievous fact, that men possessed of political power, and fully aware of things concerning which we fear to speak very plainly, have enacted in a course of many centuries just enough law against these horrors to salve their own consciences, but never have so enforced any enactment as to make the law a reality; much less have they enacted all that the case demands. I boldly say, that History and the voice of God sounding through its miserable pages, call upon pure hearted and happier women to succor their unhappy sisters, whom the ruder and less virtuous sex tramples down. You cannot succor them without some power to mould the law and incite its enforcement. To claim a purely *domestic* status, disables you for contest against odious enormities, pregnant with fraud, cruelty and social decay. Such modesty is not womanly sensitiveness; it is rather to be called womanish selfishness. I implore you, ladies, in the cause of the wretched and injured, and to quell that licentiousness which is the ruin of great nations,—arise and claim your rightful position in the State!

Justice.

Between man and man, or between man and brute, Justice is Righteousness.

So between nations, or orders of men, Justice is the law of duty.

Justice is the cement of mankind. A Nation or Empire which neglects to be internally just, falls asunder by discord or decay.

To be first just and then loving, is to advance towards fullness of virtue.

To refuse Justice and bestow Love, is an affectation of Mercy and a reality of Insult.

Without Chastity in man, there is no Justice to woman.

Peace, without Justice, is not peace, but a truce of war.

Policy which shuts its eyes to Justice is pernicious folly.

Without entire Virtue there is no entireness of Justice; for all Vice disables soul or body for some active service.

Sacred Books.

Books pre-eminently honored by the voluntary selection of piety, are reasonably held to be sacred, in a high and peculiar sense; and such books may fulfil a high function in moral history, as have the sacred books of India, Persia, Judea and Christendom.

Their benefit nevertheless has been grievously lessened by the strong tendency of mankind to idolize and lift into ideal perfection whatever has engaged their sacred feelings.

Hebrew and Christian books for which the writers advanced no high pretensions have thus been gratuitously and hurtfully exalted into a miraculous greatness. Even the Confessions of

Faith put forth by Protestant Reformers have been in most countries pushed into unnatural and absurd eminence.

Such events generally impose upon others the disagreeable duty of appearing as depreciators of books once valuable.

Hymn Books have been, to the Protestant Churches, the chief representative of new sacred writings. No Bibliolatry has been paid to them, and none have more effectually promoted spiritual life.

All Sacred Books, however valuable, must be pervaded by the errors of their age, and become unfit for practical use to generations which have unlearned those errors.

Education.

Education consists in training the Faculties to full self-possession, the Habits to industry and refinement, the Sentiment to rightfulness and warmth.

We may passively receive a stock of knowledge, without having the faculties active and well subordinated.

Men ought not to be called educated when they have merely learned to obey; but much rather, when they have attained Self-guidance.

To use power aright is a great test of sound education. The uneducated either uses it badly, or, as if terrified by its possession, drops it from his grasp.

Leisure is a great power, and to use it aright is also a mark of the educated.

Without some leisure, none but a narrow and accidental cultivation of the mind is possible.

The millions of England have one-seventh part of time as leisure; but they do not employ this for any real or valuable education, chiefly because they are not educated enough to estimate the advantage; partly also, because those who ought to assist it impede it.

Where trades are apt to be ruined and superseded from public causes beyond the control of the laborer, public justice, as well as expediency, demands that the State busy itself to secure versatile powers of industry in the working classes.

The primary education of the multitude has two principal roots, Industrial Art and Poetical Recitation. Industrial Art furnishes the laborer with the power of physical support, and in its higher forms rises into Science. Poetic Recitation teaches moral sentiment, musical rhythm, refinement, imaginative beauty, pride in nationality, patriotism. It culminates into religion.

In the present condition of trade and complex constitutions, some instruction in politics and political economy is necessary. Religious institutions might be and ought to be the most efficient educators of the Sentiments; but unhappily, a great change must pass over existing churches, before they can regain the lead which they have lost.

Sectarianism hinders all national religion and sound national education.

Theism is the only cure. When it has once fair play, it will educate nations and unite the world in harmony as yet unimagined.

Aspiring Virtue—The Hero-Saint.

Those who abound in leisure, with wealth or knowledge,
Are open to new virtue, and to much new vice.
How to bestow free time, is a problem for each to answer,
According to his means, and capacity and bent;
And therein Selfishness has wide room to lead astray.
Those who have grown strong, are bound to higher tasks,
And, when the Good has become easy, to pursue the Better,
And to find *what is* their task, and perform it manfully.
High duties require labor, or at least permit not ease;

* * * * *

The purer a man's conscience the higher is his thought of Duty.
Duty is a taskmaster who prescribes endless work,
And the higher virtue rises, the more she aspires.

* * * * * * *

Who shall speak fitly of that virtue, sublime though imperfect,
The virtue of the hero-saint, hidden, yet visible to the open eye,
For the good of others resolute and surrendering its all,
Large-hearted to imagine, vigilant to act, unwearied to persevere?
It is sorrowful, yet always rejoices; humble yet very confiding;
Aware of human ignorance, yet bold to track divine mysteries.
It exists not, save in the deep of soul and patient of thought.
It thrives with man's whole nature—intellect, fancy, conscience,—
And dwindles with the cramping of genius or narrowing of knowledge.
Therefore its diffusion is for future ages or future worlds,
When mutual love and prudence shall better conspire,
And the lack of one shall be supplied by the riches of many.

On the Study of Physics

I do not think that it is the mission of this age, or of any other particular age, to lay down a system of education which shall hold good for all ages. The basis of human nature is, perhaps, permanent, but not so the forms under which the spirit of humanity manifests itself. It is sometimes peaceful, sometimes warlike, sometimes religious, sometimes skeptical, aud history is simply the record of its mutations.

> "The eternal Pan
> Who layeth the world's incessant plan
> Halteth never in one shape,
> But forever doth escape
> Into new forms."

This appears to be the law of things throughout the universe, and it is therefore no proof of fickleness or destructiveness, properly so called, if the implements of human culture change with the times, and the requirements of the present age be found different from those of the preceding. Unless you are prepared to say that the past world, or some portion of it, has been the final expression of human competency; that the wisdom of man has already reached its climax; that the intellect of to-day possesses feebler powers, or a narrower scope, than the intellect of earlier times—you cannot, with reason, demand an unconditional acceptance of the systems of the past, nor are you justified in divorcing me from the world and times in which I live, and conforming my conversation to the times gone by. Who can blame me if I cherish the belief that the world is still young; that there are great possibilities in store for it; that the Englishman of to-day is made of as good stuff, and has as high and independent a vocation to fulfill, as had the ancient Greek or Roman.

While thankfully accepting what antiquity has to offer, let us never forget that the present century has just as good a right to its forms of thought and methods of culture as any former centuries had to theirs, and that the same sources of power are open to us to-day as were ever open to humanity in any age of the world.

In the earliest religious writings we find man described as a mixture of the earthly and the divine. The existence of the latter implies, in his case, that of the former; and hence the holiest and most self-denying saint must, to a certain extent, protect himself against hunger and cold. But every attempt to restrict man to the dominion of the senses has failed and will continue to fail. He is the repository of forces which push him beyond the world of sense. He has intellect as well as a palate, and the demands of the latter being satisfied, the former inevitably puts in its claim. We cannot quench these desires of the intellect. They are stimulated by the phenomena which surrounds us, as the body is by oxygen; and in the presence of these phenomena we thirst for knowledge as an Arab longs for water when he smells the Nile. The Chaldean shepherds could not rest content with their bread and milk, but found that they had other wants to satisfy. The stars shed their light upon the shepherd and his flock, but in both cases with different results. The quadruped cropped the green herbage and slept contented; but that power which had already made man the lord of the quadruped was appealed to night after night, and thus the intellectual germ which lay in the nature of these Chaldeans was stimulated and developed. Surely, it might be urged, if man be not made, and stars scattered by guess-work, there is strong reason for assuming that it was intended that mental power should be developed in this way. But if this be granted, it must be admitted that we have the very highest sanction for the prosecution of physical research. Sanction, indeed, is a term too weak to express the inference suggested by a comparison of man's powers with his position upon earth; it points to an imperative command to search and to examine, rather than to a mere toleration of physical inquiry.—*John Tyndall.*

Experience of the Poet Tasso.

Whether grave or gay, this spirit often came to him, and he often held long discourses with it. Manso endeavored to persuade him that it was a fancy; but Tasso maintained that it was as real as themselves, a Christian spirit, and which Manso admits gave him great comfort and consolation. Tasso, to convince Manso of the reality of this spirit, begged him to be present at an interview. Manso says that he saw Tasso address himself to some invisible object, listen in return, and then reply to what it appeared to have said. He says that the discourses of Tasso "were so lofty and marvelous, both by the sublimity of their topics and a certain unwonted manner of talking, that, exalted above myself into a certain kind of ecstacy, I did not dare to interrupt them." Tasso was disappointed, however, that Manso did not see or hear the spirit—which he ought not to have been after what he himself tells us, that to see spirits the human eye must be purified, or the spirits must array themselves in matter. This is the present acknowledged law in such cases of apparitions. They who see them must be mediums—that is, have their spiritual eyes open—or the spirits must envelop themselves in matter obvious to the outer eye. Tasso did not recollect that Manso might not be in the clairvoyant condition in which he himself was; and Manso, wholly ignorant of these psychological laws, could only suppose Tasso dealing with a subjective idea. Yet Manso evidently *felt* the presence of the spirit, for he was raised by it "into a kind of ecstacy," and he confesses that Tasso's spiritual interviews were more likely to affect his own mind than that he should dissipate Tasso's true or imaginary opinion.—*William Howitt.*

THE SCIENCE OF RELIGION.

The difficulties which trouble us, have troubled the hearts and minds of men as far back as we can trace the beginnings of the religious life. The great problems touching the relation of the Finite to the Infinite, of the human mind as the recipient, and the Divine Spirit as the source of truth, are old problems indeed; and while watching their appearance in different countries, and their treatment under varying circumstances, we shall be able, I believe, to profit ourselves, both by the errors which others have committed before us, and by the truth which they have discovered. We shall know the rocks that threaten every religion in this changing and shifting world of ours, and having watched many a storm of religious controversy, and many a shipwreck in distant seas, we shall face with greater calmness and prudence the troubled waters at home.

Whenever we can trace back a religion to its first beginnings, we find it free from many of the blemishes that offend us in its later phases. The founders of the ancient religions of the world, as far as we can judge, were minds of high stamp, full of noble aspirations, yearning for truth, devoted to the welfare of their neighbors, examples of purity and unselfishness. What they desired to found upon earth was but seldom realized, and their sayings, if preserved in their original form, offer often a strange contrast to the practice of those who profess to be their disciples. * * * * Even those who lived with Buddha misunderstood his words; and at the Great Council which had to settle the Buddhist canon, Asoka, the Indian Constantine, had to remind the assembled priests that "what had been said by Buddha, that alone was well said;" and that certain works ascribed to Buddha, as for instance, the instruction given to his son Rahula, were apochryphal, if not heretical. * * * *

To those, no doubt, who value the tenets of their religion as the miser values his pearls and precious stones, thinking their value lessened if pearls and stones of the same kind are found in other parts of the world, the Science of Religion will bring many a rude shock; but to the true believer, truth, wherever it appears, is welcome, nor will any doctrine seem the less true or the less precious, because it was seen, not only by Moses or Christ, but likewise by Buddha or Lao-tse. Nor should it be forgotten, that while a comparison of ancient religions will certainly show that some of the most vital articles of faith are the common property of the whole of mankind,—at least of all who seek the Lord, if haply they might feel after Him,—and find Him, the same comparison alone can possibly teach us what is peculiar to Christianity, and what has secured to it that pre-eminent position which now it holds in spite of all obloquy. The gain will be greater than the loss, if loss there be, which I, at least, shall never admit.—*Max Muller.*

The Functions of Unbelief.

To skepticism we owe that spirit of inquiry which during the last two centuries has gradually encroached on every possible subject; has reformed every department of practical and speculative knowledge, has weakened the authority of the privileged classes, and thus placed liberty on a surer foundation; has restrained the arrogance of the nobles, has chastised the despotism of princes, and has even diminished the prejudices of the clergy. * * *

No single fact has so extensively affected the different nations as the duration, the amount, and above all the diffusion of their skepticism. In Spain, the church, aided by the Inquisition, has always been strong enough to punish skeptical writers, and prevent, not indeed the existence, but the promulgation of skeptical opinions. But in England and France, which are the countries where skepticism first openly appeared and where it has been most diffused, the results are altogether different, and the love of inquiry being encouraged, there has arisen that constantly progressive knowledge to which these two great nations owe their prosperity.—*Buckle.*

Human Interest in History.—Its Moral Elements.

One lesson, and only one, history may be said to repeat with distinctness: that the world is built somehow on moral foundations; that in the long run, it is well with the good; in the long run, it is ill with the wicked. But this is no science; it is no more than the old doctrine taught long ago by the Hebrew prophets. The theories of M. Comte and his disciples advance us, after all, not a step beyond the trodden and familiar ground. If men are not entirely animals, they are at least half animals, and are subject in this aspect of them to the conditions of animals. So far as those parts of man's doings are concerned, which neither have, nor need have anything moral about them, so far the laws of him are calculable. There are laws for his digestiou, and laws of the means by which his digestive organs are supplied with matter. But pass beyond them, and where are we? In a world where it would be as easy to calculate men's actions by laws like those of positive philosophy, as to measure the orbit of Neptune with a foot-rule, or weigh Sirius in a grocer's scale.

And it is not difficult to see why this should be. The first principle on which the theory of a science of history can be plausibly argued, is that all actions whatsoever arise from self-interest. It may be enlightened self-interest, it may be unenlightened; but it is assumed as an axiom, that every man, in whatever he does, is aiming at something which he considers will promote his happiness. His conduct is not determined by his will; it is determined by the object of his desires. Adam Smith, in laying the foundations of political economy, expressly eliminates every other motive. He does not say that men never act on other motives. He asserts merely that, as far as the arts of production are concerned, and of buying and selling, the action of self-interest may be counted upon as uniform. What Adam Smith says of political economy, Mr. Buckle would extend over the whole circle of human activity.

Now, that which especially distinguishes a high order of man from a low order of man—that which constitutes human goodness, human greatness, human nobleness—is surely not the degree of enlightenment with which men pursue their own advantage; but it is self-forgetfulness; it is self-sacrifice; it is the disregard of personal indulgence, personal advantages remote or present, because some other line of conduct is more right.

We are sometimes told that this is but another way of expressing the same thing; that when a man prefers doing what is right, it is only because to do right gives him a higher satisfaction. It appears to me on the contrary to be a difference in the very heart and nature of things. The martyr goes to the stake, the patriot to the scaffold, not with a view to any future reward to themselves, but because it is a glory to fling away their lives to truth and freedom.

And so through all phases of existence, to the smallest details of common life, the beautiful character is the unselfish character. Those whom we most love and admire, are those to whom the thought of self seems never to occur; who do simply and with no ulterior aim—with no thought whether it will be pleasant to themselves or unpleasant—that which is good and right and generous.

Is this still selfishness, only more enlightened? I do not think so. The essence of true nobility is neglect of self. Let the thought of self pass in, and the beauty of a great action is gone, like the bloom from a soiled flower. Surely it is a paradox to speak of the self-interest of a martyr who dies for a cause, the triumph of which he will never enjoy; and the greatest of that great company in all ages would have done what they did, had their personal prospects closed with the grave. Nay, there have been those so zealous for some glorious principle as to wish themselves blotted out of the book of Heaven if the cause of Heaven could succeed.

And out of this mysterious quality, whatever it be, arise the higher relations of human life, the higher modes of human obligation. Kant, the philosopher, used to say that there were two things which overwhelmed him with awe as he thought of them: One was the star-sown deep of space, without limit and without end; the other was, right and wrong. Right, the sacrifice of self to good; wrong, the sacrifice of good to self—not graduated objects of desire, to which we are determined by the degrees of our knowledge, but wide asunder as pole and pole, as light and darkness; one the object of infinite love; the other, the object of infinite detestation and scorn. It is in this marvelous power in men to do wrong (it is an old story, but none the less true for that)—it is in this power to do wrong—wrong or right, as it lies somehow with ourselves to choose—that the impossibility stands of forming scientific calculations of what men will do before the fact, or scientific explanations of what they have done after the fact.

If men were consistently selfish, you might analyze their motives; if they were consistently noble they would express in their conduct the laws of the highest perfection. But so long as two natures are mixed together, and the strange creature which results from the combination is now under one influence and now under another, so long you will make nothing of him except from the old-fashioned moral—or, if you please, imaginative—point of view.

Even the laws of political economy itself cease to guide us when they touch moral government. So long as labor is a chattel to be bought and sold, so long, like other commodities, it follows the condition of supply and demand. But if, for his misfortune, an employer considers that he stands in human relations towards his workmen; if he believes, rightly or wrongly, that he is responsible for them; that in return for their labor he is bound to see that their children are decently taught, and they and their families decently fed, and clothed, and lodged; that he ought to care for them in sickness and in old age—then political economy will no longer direct him, and the relations between himself and his dependants will have to be arranged on quite other principles.

So long as he considers only his own material profit, so long supply and demand will settle every difficulty, but the introduction of a new factor spoils the equation.

And it is precisely in this debatable ground of low motives and noble emotions; in the struggle, ever-failing yet ever renewed, to carry truth and justice into the administration of human society; in the establishment of States and in the overthrow of tyrannies; in the rise and fall of creeds; in the world of ideas; in the character and deeds of the great actors in the drama of life, where good and evil fight out their everlasting battle, now ranged in opposite camps, now and more often in the heart, both of them, of each living man—that the true human interest of history resides.

The progress of industries, the growth of material and mechanical civilization, are interesting; but they are not the most interesting. * * * * * *

What then are the lessons of history? It is a voice sounding forever across the centuries, the laws of right and wrong. Opinions alter, manners change, creeds rise and fall, but the moral law is written on the tablets of eternity. For every false word or unrighteous deed, for cruelty and oppression, for lust or vanity, the price has to be paid at last; not always by the chief offender, but by some one. Justice and truth alone endure and live. Injustice and falsehood may be long-lived, but dooms-day comes at last to them, in French Revolutions and other terrible ways.—*James A. Froude.*

THE CHURCH OF THE FUTURE.

What did these true Knights of the Cross—these brave Barons of the Reformation—win back for themselves and for their descendants? God's free gift of liberty! The right of *all* men to read and judge the Scriptures for themselves. But Protestantism had no sooner won back this right of private judgment, than it proved false to the principles to which it had been indebted for its own existence. It at once proceeded to draw up creeds, and to frame articles, and to put forth its own peculiar "Scheme of Salvation," to hedge itself about with ecclesiastical and civil Law, and to erect an infallible Popedom of its own. * * *

The laws of God are stronger than the laws of men. The church that shall endure the wear and tear of Time, must not be reared on Dogmas which men out-grow; but on the laws of man's spiritual nature—which are laws of God. All Falsehood will ultimately die out. There is no moral darkness but what God's light will penetrate *some time.* It is not Truth and Right that are everywhere hedged about by the "pains and penalties" of Law. Truth and Right need no such guardians: they can guard themselves. Whatever is Right is reasonable, and whatever is Reasonable is Right. No Institution, no Church, that intends to the divine work of a church, namely, to spiritualize, and instruct, and elevate the moral and intellectual condition of all the People—must hope to stand, if its basis be not strictly Rational—for then its basis will be Right; or if its principles be not expansive—for then it can and will adapt itself to the growing wants, and to the moral and intellectual development of the nations in which it is located.

There are tens of thousands of educated, thoughtful men, who, because they cannot countenance the irrational things which are said and done everywhere around them in the name of Religion, look deridingly on; and stand aloof from all denominations. In addition to these there is that still larger class, the laboring men and their families, to whom Religion would not only carry Spiritual consolation, but would tend to raise and redeem them, as a class, from the degradation and social thraldom which it has come to be the opinion among us that they suffer agreeably to an ordinance of God. I do not believe this; I hope I never shall believe it. If Christianity has a mission on earth, it is to raise and bless the Poor. This is God-like labor, and worthy of the followers of Christ.

A Church by moral suasion, but by no other means, ought to repress that growing, ever-thriving Sensuality—the natural offspring of Selfishness, which is the basis and root of all degradation, and poverty, and squalid wretchedness, and all the wrong and moral evil which environ us on every side; and to cultivate and cherish that Love—the natural offspring of Education and Spiritual development, which would in the process of time exterminate these giant evils, and establish righteousness and the kingdom of God.

A Church true to these principles, is the true Parliament; the true Magistrate; the true Policeman; the true guide in all things; the truest friend of Humanity; the only representative on earth of God. What the Church of England *should* have been, the Church of the Future—if it prove worthy of the name of a Church—*must be!*

It is clear that such a Church must have an all-beneficent God as the object of its adoration; a belief in immortality for its hope; and for its earthly basis, that Reason which commends itself to every man's conscience, and is holy "in the sight of God." For Doctrines, such a church will take its stand on the divine principles enunciated in Christ's Sermon on the Mount. It must seek to be the "light of the world" by addressing itself to the universal feelings, and wants, and yearnings, and inner nature of all humanity. It must be a "city set on a hill that cannot be hid." It is not to "destroy the Law or the Prophets," but to "fulfil" the one, and bring about the sublime predictions of the other. It is not to preach "an eye for an eye, and a tooth for a tooth;" but must preach the work of Righteousness, and obtain all its conquests over evil and wrong, by Love. It is not to "love its *brethren* only," but to love *all* men and labor unceasingly to do them good. It must not be a pious-looking sham, but a truly pious reality.

It must eschew the sandy foundation of Fable, and Fancy, and ever-shifting Opinion, and build its Temple on the Rock of uncontradictable Truth; that when the rains of Error descend, and the floods of Imposture come, and the whirlwinds of Falsehood beat upon it, it might stand—firmly as the Rock which bears it. Its Religion must be Love to God, and Love to *all* humanity. It must be the Church of those who *have* no Church: it must be the friend of the friendless; the support of the weak;—it must aim to be the Church of the People. Justice must be its watchword; and the inscription on its banner—Love. * * * *

My dear Friends, to me it seems that the Church of the Future—spring up where it will, or however named—should collect the Pariahs of Society into its bosom as its *first* care.

I have already intimated that it should, in my opinion, proclaim a Religion which has long gone out of fashion—a Religion which has Reason for its basis; brotherly love, and equal justice in all things—on earth as in heaven—for its temporal aim; "the stone which the builders rejected" for the chief one of its Temple; a God of perfect Justice and Goodness and Truth, for its daily and hourly worship; that it must be a Church of refuge for the Infidel—a cosmopolitan communion—an Educated working Church, for an Educated working world—in which there is honor for its elders,—a rational discipline for the young—a means of Salvation (without let or hindrance) for all. I would have a Church, then, which should deserve to be National,—a Religion which none but the *utterly selfish*, and those who profess to pride themselves upon being *irrational*, could discountenance or reject—a church for *all*, but, in the first instance, more especially for the *Poor* who have no church, and thousands upon thousands of them no education, *no God!—Edward N. Dennys, London.*

God's Voice Nearer Than the Book.

It is perhaps God's will that we should be taught, in this our day, among other precious lessons, not to build up our faith upon a book, though it be the Bible itself; but to realize more fully the blessedness of knowing that He himself, the living God, our Father and Friend, is nearer and closer to us than any book can be; that his voice within the heart may be heard continually by the obedient child that listens for it; and that *that* should be our Teacher and Guide in the path of duty, which is the path of life, when all other helpers—even the words of the best of books—may fail us.—*J. W. Colenso.*

Toleration, and Study of the Bible.

At the Reformation it might have seemed at first as if the study of theology were about to return. But in reality an entirely new lesson commenced; the lesson of toleration, the very opposite of dogmatism. It implies in reality a confession that there are insoluble problems upon which even Revelation throws but little light. Its tendency is to modify the early dogmatism, by substituting the spirit for the letter, and practical religion for precise definitions of truth. This lesson is certainly not yet fully learnt. Our toleration is at present too often timid, too often rash, sometimes sacrificing valuable religious elements, sometimes fearing its own plainest conclusions. Yet there can be no question that it is gaining on the minds of all educated men, whether Protestant or Roman Catholic, and is passing from them to be the common property of educated and uneducated alike. There are occasions when the spiritual anarchy which has necessarily followed the Reformation, threatens for a moment to bring back some temporary bondage, like the Roman Catholic system. But on the whole the steady progress or toleration is unmistakable. The mature mind of our race is beginning to modify and soften the hardness and severity of the principles which its early manhood had elevated into immutable statements of truth.

Men are beginning to take a wider view than they did. Physical science, researches into history, a more thorough knowledge of the world they inhabit, have enlarged our philosophy beyond the limits which bounded that of the Church of our Fathers. And all these have an influence, whether we will or no, on our determinations of religious truth. There are found to be more things in heaven and earth than were dreamt of in the patristic theology. God's creation is a new book, to be read by the side of His revelation, and to be interpreted as coming from Him. We can acknowledge the great value of the forms in which the first ages of the Church defined the truth, and yet refuse to be bound by them; we can use them, and yet endeavor to go beyond them, just as they also went beyond the legacy which was left us by the Apostles. * * * *

The strongest argument in favor of tolerating all opinions, is that our conviction of the truth of an opinion is worthless unless it has established itself in spite of the most strenuous resistance, and is still prepared to overcome the same resistance if necessary. Toleration itself is no exception to the universal law: and those who must regret the slow progress by which it wins its way, may remember that this slowness makes the final victory the more certain and complete. Nor is that all. The toleration thus obtained is different in kind from what it otherwise would have been. It is not only stronger, it is richer and fuller. For the slowness of its progress gives time to disentangle from dogmatism the really valuable principles and sentiments which have been mixed up and contained in it, and to unite toleration, not with indifference and worldliness, but with spiritual truth and religiousness of life.

Even the perverted use of the Bible has therefore not been

without certain great advantages. And meanwhile how utterly impossible it would be in the manhood of the world to imagine any other instructor to mankind. And for that reason, every day makes it more and more evident that the thorough study of the Bible, the investigation of what it teaches and what it does not teach, the determination of the limits of what we mean by its inspiration, the determination of the degree of authority to be ascribed to the different books, if any degrees are to be admitted, must take the lead of all other studies. He is guilty of high treason against the faith who fears the result of any investigation, whether philosophical, or scientific, or historical. And therefore nothing should be more welcome than the extension of knowledge of any and every kind—for every increase in our accumulation of knowledge throws fresh light upon these, the real problems of our day. If geology proves to us that we must not interpret the first chapters of Genesis literally, if historical investigation shall show us that inspiration, however it may protect the doctrine, yet was not empowered to protect the narrative of the inspired writers from occasional inaccuracy; if careful criticism shall prove that there have been occasional interpolations and forgeries in that Book, as in many others, the results should still be welcome. Even the mistakes of careful and reverent students are more valuable now than truth held in unthinking acquiescence. The substance of the teaching which we derive from the Bible will not really be affected by anything of this sort. While its hold upon the mind of believers, and its power to stir the depths of the spirit of man, however much weakened at first, must be immeasurably strengthened in the end, by clearing away any blunders which may have been fastened on it by human interpretation.—*Frederick Temple, D. D.; Chaplain in ordinary to Queen Victoria—Head Master of Rugby School.*

CHAPTER XIII.

THE SYMPATHY OF RELIGIONS.

BY T. W. HIGGINSON.

NEWPORT, R. I.

Our true religious life begins when we discover that there is an Inner Light, not infallible but invaluable, which "lighteth every man that cometh into the world." Then we have something to steer by; and it is chiefly this, and not an anchor, that we need. The human soul, like any other noble vessel, was not built to be anchored, but to sail. An anchorage may, indeed, be at times a temporary need, in order to make some special repairs, or to take fresh cargo in; yet the natural destiny of both ship and soul is not the harbor, but the ocean; to cut with even keel the vast and beautiful expanse; to pass from island to island of more than Indian balm, or to continents fairer than Columbus won; or, best of all, steering close to the wind, to extract motive power from the greatest obstacles. Men must forget the eternity through which they have yet to sail, when they talk of anchoring here upon this bank and shoal of time. It would be a tragedy to see the shipping of the world whitening the seas no more, and idly riding at anchor in Atlantic ports; but it would be more tragic to see a world of souls fascinated into a fatal repose and renouncing their destiny of motion.

And as with individuals, so with communities. The great historic religions of the world are not so many stranded hulks left to perish. The best of them are all in motion. All over the world the divine influence moves men. There is a sympathy in religions, and this sympathy is shown alike in their origin, their records, and their progress. Men are ceasing to disbelieve, and learning to believe more. * * *

Every year brings new knowledge of the religions of the world, and every step in knowledge brings out the sympathy between them. They all show the same aim, the same symbols, the same forms, the same weaknesses, the same aspirations. Looking at these points of unity, we might say there is but one religion under many forms, whose essential creed is the Fatherhood of God, and the Brotherhood of Man,—disguised by corruptions, symbolized by mythologies, ennobled by virtues, degraded by vices, but still the same. Or if, passing to a closer analysis, we observe the shades of difference, we shall find in these varying faiths the several instruments which perform what Cudworth calls "the Symphony of Religions." And though some may stir like drums, and others soothe like flutes, and others like violins command the whole range of softness and of strength, yet they are all alike instruments, and nothing in any one of them is so wondrous as the great laws of sound which equally control them all.

"Amid so much war and contest and variety of opinion," said Maximus Tyrius, "you will find one consenting conviction in every land, that there is one God, the King and Father of all." "God being one," said Aristotle, "only receives various names from the various manifestations we perceive." "Sovereign God," said Cleanthes, in that sublime prayer which Paul quoted, "whom men invoke under many names, and who rulest alone, it is to thee that all nations should address themselves, for we all are thy children." So Origen, the Christian Father, frankly says that no man can be blamed for calling God's name in Egyptian, nor in Scythian, nor in such other language as he best knows.

To say that different races worship different Gods, is like saying that they are warmed by different suns. The names differ, but the sun is the same, and so is God. As there is but one source of light and warmth, so there is but one source of religion. To this all nations testify alike. We have yet but a part of our Holy Bible. The time will come when, as in the middle ages, all pious books will be called sacred scriptures,

Scripturæ Sacræ. From the most remote portions of the earth, from the Vedas and the Sagas, from Plato and Zoroaster, Confucius and Mohammed, from the Emperor Marcus Antoninus and the slave Epictetus, from the learned Alexandrians and the ignorant Galla negroes, there will be gathered hymns and prayers and maxims in which every religious soul may unite,—the magnificent liturgy of the human race.

The greatest of modern scholars, Von Humboldt, asserted in middle life and repeated the assertion in old age, that "all positive religions contain three distinct parts. First, a code of morals, very fine, and nearly the same in all; second, a geological dream, and third, a myth or historical novellette, which last becomes the most important of all." And though this observation may be somewhat roughly stated, its essential truth is seen when we compare the different religions of the world, side by side. With such startling points of similarity, where is the difference? The main difference lies here, that each fills some blank space in its creed with the name of a different teacher. For instance, the Oriental Parsee wears a fine white garment, bound around him with a certain knot; and whenever this knot is undone, at morning or night, he repeats the four main points of his creed, which are as follows:—

"To believe in one God, and hope for mercy from him only.

"To believe in a future state of existence.

"To do as you would be done by.

Thus far the Parsee keeps on the universal ground of religion. Then he drops into the language of his sect and adds:—

"To believe in Zoroaster as lawgiver, and to hold his writings sacred."

The creed thus furnishes a formula for all religions. It might be printed iu blank like a circular, leaving only the closing name to be filled in. For Zoroaster read Christ, and you have Christianity; read Buddha, and you have Buddhism; read Mohammed, and you have Mohammedanism. Each of these, in short, is Natural Religion *plus* an individual name. It is by insisting on that *plus* that each religion stops short of being universal.

In this religion of the human race, thus variously disguised, we find everywhere the same leading features. The same great doctrines, good or bad,—regeneration, predestination, atonement, the future life, the final judgment, the Divine Reason or Logos, and the Trinity. The same religious institutions,—monks, missionaries, priests, and pilgrims. The same ritual—prayers, liturgies, sacrifices, sermons, hymns. The same implements—frankincense, candles, holy water, relics, amulets, votive offerings. The same symbols,—the cross, the ball, the triangle, the serpent, the all-seeing eye, the halo of rays, the tree of life. The same saints, angels, and martyrs. The same holiness attached to particular cities, rivers, and mountains. The same prophecies and miracles,—the dead restored and evil spirits cast out. The self-same holy days; for Easter and Christmas were kept as spring and autumn festivals, centuries before our era, by Egyptians, Persians, Saxons, Romans. The same artistic designs, since the mother and child stand depicted, not only in the temples of Europe, but in those of Etruria and Arabia, Egypt and Thibet. In ancient Christian art, the evangelists were represented with the same heads of eagles, oxen, and lions, upon which we gaze with amazement in Egyptian tombs. Nay, the very sects and subdivisions of all historic religions have been the same, and each supplies us with mystic and rationalist, formalist and philanthropist, ascetic and epicurean. The simple fact is, that all these things are as indigenous as grass and mosses; they spring up in every soil, and only the microscope can tell them apart.

And, as all these inevitably recur, so comes back again and again the idea of incarnation,—the Divine Man. Here, too, all religions sympathize, and, with slight modifications, each is the copy of the other. As in the dim robing-rooms of foreign churches are kept rich stores of sacred vestments, ready to be thrown over every successive generation of priests, so the world has kept in memory the same stately traditions to decorate each new Messiah. He is predicted by prophecy, hailed by sages, born of a virgin, attended by miracle, borne to heaven without tasting death, and with promise of return. Zoroaster and Confucius have no human father. Osiris of Egypt is the Son of God; he is called the Revealer of Life and Light; he first teaches one chosen race; he then goes with his apostles to teach the Gentiles, conquering the world by peace; he is slain by evil powers; after death he descends into hell, then rises again, and presides at the last judgment of all mankind: those who call upon his name shall be saved. Buddha is born of a virgin; his name means the Word, the Logos, but he is known more tenderly as the Saviour of Man; he embarrasses his teachers, when a child, by his understanding and his answers; he is tempted in the wilderness, when older; he goes with his apostles to redeem the world; he abolishes caste and cruelty, and teaches forgiveness; he receives among his followers outcasts whom Pharisaic pride despises, and he only says, "My law is a law of mercy to all." Slain by enemies, he descends into hell, rising without tasting death, and still lives to make intercession for man.

These are the recognized properties of religious tradition; the beautiful garments belong not to the individual, but the race. It is the drawback on all human greatness that it makes itself deified. Even of Jesus it was said sincerely by the Platonic philosopher Porphyry; "That noble soul who has ascended into heaven, has by a certain fatality become an occasion of error." The inequality of gifts is a problem not yet solved, and there is always a craving for some miracle to explain it. Men set up their sublime representatives as so many spiritual athletes, and measure them. "See, this one is six inches taller; those six inches prove him divine." But because men surpass us, surpass everybody, shall we hold them separate from the race? Construct the race as you will, somebody must stand at the head, in virtue as in intellect. Shall we deify Shakespeare? It paralyzes my intellect if I doubt whether Shakespeare was a man; it paralyzes my whole spiritual nature if I doubt whether Jesus was.

I believe that all religion is natural, all revealed. What faith in humanity springs up, what trust in God, when one recognizes the sympathy of religions! Every race believes in a Creator and Governor of the world, in whom devout souls recognize a Father also. Every race believes in immortality. Every race recognizes in its religious precepts the brotherhood of man. The whole gigantic system of caste in Hindostan has grown up in defiance of the Vedas, which are now being invoked to abolish it. "He is my beloved of whom mankind are not afraid, and who of mankind is not afraid," says the Bhagvat Geeta. "Kesava is pleased with him who does good to others, who is always desirous of the welfare of all creatures," says the Vishnu Purana. In Confucius it is written, "My doctrine is simple and easy to understand," and his chief disciple adds, "It consists only in having the heart right and in loving one's neighbor as one's self." When he was asked, "Is there one word which may serve as a rule of practice for all one's life?" he answered, "Is not 'Reciprocity' such a word? what you wish done to yourself, do to others.' By some translators the rule is given in a negative form, in which it is also found in the Jewish Talmud (Rabbi Hillel), "Do not to another what thou wouldst not he should do to thee; this is the sum of the law." So Thales, when asked for a rule of life, taught, "That which thou blamest in another, do not thyself." "Thou shalt love thy neighbor as thyself," said the Hebrew book of Leviticus. Iamblichus tells us that Pythagoras taught "the love of all to all." "To live is not to live for one's self alone, let us help one another," said the Greek dramatist, Menander; and the Roman dramatist Terence, following him, brought down the applause of the whole theater by the saying, "I am a man; I count nothing human foreign to me." "Give bread to a stranger," said Quintilian, "in the name of the universal brotherhood which binds together all men under the common father of nature." "What good man will look on any suffering as foreign to himself?" said the Latin satirist Juvenal. "This sympathy is what distinguishes us from brutes," he adds. The poet Lucan predicted a time when warlike weapons should be laid aside, and all men love one another. "Nature has inclined us to love men," said Cicero, "and this is the foundation of the law." He also described his favorite virtue of justice as "devoting itself wholly to the good of others." Seneca said, "We are members of one great body. Nature planted in us a mutual love, and fitted us for social life. We must consider that we were born for the good of the whole." "Love mankind," wrote Marcus Antoninus, summing it all up in two words; while the loving soul of Epictetus extended the sphere of mutual affection beyond this earth, holding that "The universe is but one great city, full of beloved ones, divine and human, by nature endeared to each other.

This sympathy of religions extends even to the loftiest virtues,—the forgiveness of injuries, the love of enemies, and the overcoming of evil with good. "The wise man," said the Chinese Lao-tse, "avenges his injuries with benefits." "Hatred," says a Buddhist sacred book, the Dhammapada, "does not cease by hatred at any time; hatred ceases by love; this is the eternal rule." "To overcome evil with good is good, and to resist evil by evil is evil," says a Mohammedan manual of ethics. "Turn not away from a sinner, but look on him with compassion," says Saadi's Gulistan. "If thine enemy hunger, give him bread to eat; if he thirst, give him water to drink," said the Hebrew proverb. "He who commits injustice is ever made more wretched than he who suffers it," said Plato; and adds: "It is never right to return an injury." "No one will dare maintain," said Aristotle, "that it is better to do injustice than to bear it." "We should do good to our enemy," said Cleobulus, "and make him our friend." "Speak not evil to a friend, nor even to an enemy," said Pittacus, one of the Seven Wise Men. "It is more beautiful," said Valerius Maximus, "to overcome injury by the power of kindness, than to oppose to it the obstinacy of hatred." Maximus Tyrius has a special chapter on the treatment of injuries, and concludes: "If he who injures does wrong, he who returns the injury does equally wrong." Plutarch, in his essay, "How to profit by our enemies," bids us sympathize with them in affliction and aid their needs. "A philosopher, when smitten, must love those who smite him, as if he were the father, the brother, of all men," said Epictetus. "It is peculiar of man," said Marcus Antoninus, "to love even those who do wrong. * * Ask thyself daily to how many ill-minded persons thou hast shown a kind disposition." He compares the wise and humane soul to a spring of pure water, which blesses even him who curses it; and the Oriental story likens such a soul to the sandal-wood tree, which imparts its fragrance even to the axe which cuts it down.

How it cheers and enlarges us to hear of these great thoughts and know that the Divine has never been without a witness on earth! How it must sadden the soul to disbelieve them. Worse yet to be in a position where one has to hope that they may not be correctly reported—that one by one they may be explained away. * * For instance, as the great character of Buddha has come out from the darkness, within fifty years, how these reluctant people have struggled against it, still desiring to escape. "Save us, O God!" they have seemed to say, "from the distress of believing that so many years ago there was a sublime human life. * * Anything rather than believe that there is a light which lighteth every man that cometh into the world.

For this purpose the very facts of history must be suppressed or explained away. Sir George Mackenzie, in his "Travels in Iceland," says that the clergy prevented till 1630, with "mistaken zeal," the publication of the Scandinavian Eddas. Huc, the Roman Catholic Missionary, described in such truthful colors the religious influence of Buddhism in Thibet, that his book was put in the *index expurgatorius* at Rome. Balmes, a learned Roman Catholic writer, declares that "Christianity is stripped of a portion of its honors" if we trace back any high standard of female purity to the ancient Germans; and so he coolly sets aside as "poetical" the plain statements of the accurate Tacitus. If we are to believe the accounts given of the Jewish Essenes by Josephus, De Quincey thinks, the claims made by Christianity are annihilated. "If Essenism could make good its pretensions, there, at one blow, would be an end of Christianity, which, in that case, is not only superseded as an idle repetition of a religious system already published, but a criminal plagiarism. Nor can the wit of man evade the conclusion."

And what makes this conclusiveness more repulsive is its modernness. Paul himself quoted from the sublime hymn of Cleanthes to prove to the Greeks that they too recognized the Fatherhood of God. The early Christian apologists, living face to face with the elder religions, made no exclusive claims. Tertullian declared the soul to be an older authority than prophecy, and its voice the gift of God from the beginning. Justin Martyr said: "Those who live according to Reason are Christians, though you may call them atheists." "The same God," said Clement, "to whom we owe the Old and New Testament, gave also to the Greeks their philosophy, by which He is glorified among them."

How few modern sects reach even this point of impartiality? "There never was a time," says a distinguished European preacher, "when there did not exist an infinite gulf between the ideas of the ancients and the ideas of Christianity. There is an end of Christianity if men agree in thinking the contrary." And an eminent Unitarian preacher in America, Rev. A. P. Peabody, says: "If the truths of Christianity are intuitive and self-evident, how is it that they formed no part of any man's consciousness till the advent of Christ?" How can any one look history in the face, how can any man open even the dictionary of any ancient language, and yet say this? What word sums up the highest Christian virtue, if not *philanthropy?* And yet the word is a Greek word, and was used in the same sense before Christendom existed.

Fortunately there have always been men whose larger minds could adapt themselves to the truth, instead of narrowing the truth to them. In William Penn's "No Cross No Crown," one-half the pages are devoted to the religious testimony of Christians, and one-half to the non-Christian world. * * *

And, if it is thus hard to do historical justice, it is far harder to look with candor upon contemporary religions. Thus the Jesuit Father Ripa thought that Satan had created the Buddhist religion on purpose to bewilder the Christian church. There we see a creed possessing more votaries than any in the world, numbering nearly one-third of the human race. Its traditions go back to a founder whose record is stainless and sublime. It has the doctrine of the Real Presence, the Madonna and Child, the invocation of the dead, monasteries and pilgrimages, celibacy and tonsure, relics, rosaries, and holy water. Wherever it has spread, it has broken down the barrier of caste. It teaches that all men are brethren, and makes them prove it by their acts; it diffuses gentleness and self-sacrificing benevolence. "It has become," as Neander admits, "to many tribes of people a means of transition from the wildest barbarism to semi-civilization." Tennent, living amid the lowest form of it in Ceylon, says that its code of morals is "second only to that of Christianity itself," and enjoins every conceivable virtue and excellence. It is coming among us, represented by many of the Chinese, and a San Francisco merchant, a Christian of the Episcopal Church, told me that, on conversing with their educated men, he found in them a religious faith quite as enlightened as their own. Shall we not rejoice in this consoling discovery? "Yes," said the simple-hearted Abbe Huc: so he published his account of Buddhism, and saw it excommunicated. "No!" said Father Ripa, "it is the invention of the devil!"

With a steady wave of progress Mohammedanism is sweeping through Africa, where Christianity scarcely advances a step. Wherever Mohammedanism reaches, schools and libraries are established, gambling and drunkenness cease, theft and falsehood diminish, polygamy is limited, woman begins to be elevated and has property rights guaranteed; and, instead of witnessing human sacrifices, you see the cottager reading the Koran at her door, like the Christian cottager in Cowper's description. "Its gradual extension," says an eye-witness, "is gradually but surely modifying the negro. Within the last half century the humanizing influence of the Koran is acknowledged by all who are acquainted with the interior tribes." So in India, Mohammedanism makes converts by thousands (according to Col. Sleeman, than whom there can be no more intelligent authority) where Christianity makes but a handful; and this he testifies, because in Mohammedanisn there is no spirit of caste, while Christians have a caste of their own, and will not put converts on an equality. Do we rejoice in this great work of progress? No! One would think we were still in the time of the crusades by the way we ignore the providential value of Mohammedanism.

The one unpardonable sin is exclusiveness. Any form of religion is endangered when we bring it to the test of facts; for none on earth can bear that test. There never existed a person, nor a book, nor an institution, which did not share the merits and the drawbacks of its rivals. Granting all that can be established as to the debt of the world to the very best dispensation, the fact still remains, that there is not a single maxim, nor idea, nor application, nor triumph, that any single religion can claim as exclusively its own. Neither faith, nor love, nor truth, nor disinterestedness, nor forgiveness, nor patience, nor peace, nor equality, nor education, nor missionary effort, nor prayer, nor honesty, nor the sentiment of brotherhood, nor reverence for woman, nor the spirit of humility, nor the fact of martyrdom, nor any other good thing, is monopolized by any one or any half dozen forms of faith. All religions recognize, more or less distinctly, these principles; all do something to exemplify, something to dishonor them. Travelers find virtue in a seeming minority in all other countries, and forget that they left it in a minority at home. A Hindoo girl, astonished at the humanity of a British officer towards her father, declared her surprise that any one could display so much kindness who did not believe in the god Vishnu.

What religion stands highest in moral results if not Christianity? Yet the slave-trader belongs to Christendom as well as the saint. If we say that Christendom was not truly represented by the slaves in the hold of John Newton's slave-ship, but only by the prayers which he read every day, as he narrates, in the cabin,—then we must admit that Buddhism is not to be judged merely by the prostrations before Fo, but by the learning of its lamaseries and the beneficence of its people. The reformed Brahmos of India complain that Christian nations force alcoholic drinks on their nation, despite their efforts; and the greater humanity of Hindoos towards animals has been, according to Dr. Hedge, a serious embarrassment to our missionaries. So men interrupt the missionaries in China, according to Coffin's late book, by asking them why, if their doctrines be true, Christian nations forced opium on an unwilling emperor, who refused to the last to receive money from the traffic. What a history has been our treatment of the American Indians! The delegation from the Society of Friends reported last year that an Indian chief brought a young Indian before a white commissioner to give evidence, and the commissioner hesitated a little in receiving a part of the testimony, when the chief said with great emphasis, "O you may believe what he says: he tells the truth; he has never seen a white man before!" In Southey's Wesley, there is an account of an Indian whom Wesley met in Georgia, and who thus summed up his objections to Christianity: "Christian much drunk! Christian beat man! Christian tell lies! Devil Christian! Me no Christian!" What then? All other religions show the same disparity between belief and practice, and each is safe till it tries to exclude the rest. Test each sect by its best or its worst as you will, by its high-water mark of virtue or its low-water mark of vice. But falsehood begins when you measure the ebb of any other religion against the flood-tide of your own.

There is a noble and a base side to every history. The same religion varies in different soils. Christianity is not the same in England and in Italy; in Armenia and in Ethiopia; in the Protestant and Catholic cantons in Switzerland; in Massachusetts, in Georgia, and in Utah. Neither is Buddhism the same in China, in Thibet and in Ceylon; nor Mohammedanism in Turkey and in Persia. We have no right to pluck the best fruit from one tree, the worst from another, and then say the tree is known by its fruits. I say again, Christianity has, on the whole, produced the highest results of all, in manners, in arts, in energy. Yet when Christianity had been five centuries in the world, the world's only hope seemed to be in the superior strength and purity of pagan races. "Can we wonder," wrote Salvian (A. D. 400), "if our lands have been given over to the barbarians by God? since that which we have polluted by our profligacy the barbarians have cleansed by their chastity." At the end of its first thousand years, Christianity could only show Europe at its lowest ebb of civilization, in a state which Guizot calls "death by the extinction of every faculty." The barbarians had only deteriorated since their conversion; the great empires were falling to pieces; and the only bright spot in Europe was Mohammedan Spain, whose universities taught all Christendom science, as its knights taught chivalry. Even at the end of fifteen hundred years, the Turks, having conquered successively Jerusalem and Constantinople, seemed altogether the most powerful nation of the world; their empire was compared to the Roman empire; they were gaining all the time. * * * *

For four hundred years it has been safe for Christendom to be boastful, but, if at any time during the fifteen hundred years previous the comparison had been made, the boasting would have been the other way.

We see what Christianity has done for Europe; but we do not remember how much Europe has done for Christianity. Take away the influence of race and climate; take away Greek literature, and Mohammedan chivalry, and the art of printing;

set the decline of Christianity in Asia and Africa against its gain in Europe and America—and whatever superiority may be left is not enough on which to base exclusive claims. The recent scientific advances of the age are a brilliant theme for the rhetorician; but those who make these advances are the last men to ascribe them to the influence of any exclusive religion.

Indeed, it is only very lately that the claim of superiority in civilization and the arts of life has been made in behalf of Christianity. Down to the time of the Reformation it was usual to contrast the intellectual and practical superiority of the heathen to the purely spiritual claims of the church. "The church has always been accustomed," says the Roman Catholic Digby, "to see genius and learning in the ranks opposed to her." "From the beginning of the world," said Luther, "there have always been among the heathens higher and rarer people, of greater and more exalted understanding, more excellent diligence and skill in all arts, than among Christians, or the people of God." "Do we excel in intellect, in learning, in decency of morals?" said Melancthon. "By no means. But we excel in the true knowledge and worship and adoration of God."

Historically, of course, we are Christians, and can enjoy the advantage which that better training has given, just as the favored son of a king may enjoy his special advantages and yet admit that the less favored are equally sons. The name of Christianity only ceases to excite respect when it is used to represent any false or exclusive claims, or when it takes the place of the older and grander words, "Religion" and "Virtue." When we fully comprehend the sympathy of religions we shall deal with other faiths on equal terms. We shall cease trying to free men from one superstition by inviting them into another. The true missionaries are the men inside each religion who have outgrown its limitations. But no Christian missionary has ever yet consented to meet the men of other religions upon the common ground of Theism. In Bishop

Heber's time, the Hindoo reformer Swaamee Narain was preaching purity and peace, the unity of God, and the abolition of castes. Many thousands of men followed his teachings, and whole villages and districts were raised from the worst immorality by his labors, as the Bishop himself bears witness. But the good Bishop seems to have despaired of him as soon as Swaamee Narain refused conversion to Christianity, making the objection that God was not incarnated in one man, but in many. Then came Ram Mohun Roy, forty years ago, and argued from the Vedas against idolatry, caste, and the burning of widows. He also refused to be called a Christian, and the missionaries denounced him. Now comes Keshub Chunder Sen, with his generous utterances: "We profess the universal and absolute religion, whose cardinal doctrines are the Fatherhood of God and the Brotherhood of Man, and which accepts the truths of all scriptures, and honors the prophets of all nations." The movement reaches thousands whom no foreign influence could touch; yet the Methodist missionaries denounce it in the name of Christ, and even the little Unitarian mission opens against it a battery of a single gun. It is the same with our treatment of the Jews; and yet the reformed Jews in America have already gone in advance of the most liberal Christian sects in their width of religious sympathy. "The happiness of man," says Rabbi Wise, in speaking for them, "depends on no creed and no book; it depends on the dominion of truth, which is the Redeemer and Savior, the Messiah and the King of Glory."

It is our happiness to live in a time when all religions are at last outgrowing their mythologies, and emancipated men are stretching out their hands to share together "the luxury of a religion that does not degrade." The progressive Brahmos of India, the Jewish leaders in America, the Free Religious Association among ourselves, are teaching essentially the same principles, seeking the same ends. The Jewish congregations in Baltimore were the first to contribute for the education of the freedmen; the Buddhist Temple in San Francisco was the first edifice of that city draped in mourning after the murder of President Lincoln; the Parsees of the East sent contributions to the Sanitary Commission. The great religions of the world are but larger sects; they come together, like the lesser sects, for works of benevolence; they share the same aspirations, and every step in the progress of each brings it nearer to all the rest. The reign of heaven on earth will not be called the Kingdom of Christ nor of Buddha—it will be called the Church of God, or the Commonwealth of Man. I do not wish to belong to a religion only, but to *the* religion; it must not include less than the piety of the world.

If one insists on being exclusive, where shall he find a home? What hold has any Protestant sect among us on a thoughtful mind? They are too little, too new, too inconsistent, too feeble. What are these children of a day compared with that magnificent Church of Rome, which counts its years by centuries, and its votaries by millions, and its martyrs by myriads; with kings for confessors and nations for converts; carrying to all the earth one Lord, one faith, one baptism, and claiming for itself no less title than the Catholic, the Universal? Yet in conversing with Catholics one is again repelled by the extreme juvenility, and modernness, and scanty numbers of their church. It is the superb elder brother of our little sects, doubtless, and seems to have most of the family fortune. But the whole fortune is so small! and even the elder brother is so young! Even the Romanist ignores traditions more vast, antiquity more remote, a literature of piety more grand. His temple suffocates: give us a shrine still vaster; something than this Catholicism more catholic; not the Church of Rome, but of God and man; a Pantheon, not a Parthenon; the true *semper, ubique, et ab omnibus*, the Religion of the Ages, Natural Religion.

I was once in a foreign cathedral when, after the three days of mourning in Holy Week, came the final day of Hallelujah. The great church had looked dim and sad, with the innumerable windows closely curtained, since the moment when the symbolical bier of Jesus was borne to its symbolical tomb beneath the High Altar, while the three mystic candles blazed above it. There had been agony and beating of cheeks in the darkness, while ghostly processions moved through the aisles, and fearful transparencies were unrolled from the pulpit. The priests kneeled in gorgeous robes, chanting, with their heads resting on the altar steps; the multitude hung expectant on their words. Suddenly burst forth a new chant, "*Gloria in Excelsis!*" In that instant every curtain was rolled aside, the cathedral was bathed in glory, the organs clashed, the bells chimed, flowers were thrown from the galleries, little birds were let loose, friends embraced and greeted one another, and we looked down upon a tumultuous sea of faces, all floating in a sunlit haze. And yet, I thought, the whole of this sublime transformation consisted in letting in the light of day! These priests and attendants, each stationed at his post, had only removed the darkness they themselves had made. Unveil these darkened windows, but remove also these darkening walls; the temple itself is but a lingering shadow of that gloom. Instead of its coarse and stifling incense, give us God's pure air, and teach us that the broadest religion is the best.

CHAPTER XIV.

AMERICA.

THE UNITED STATES.

INWARD STILLNESS—THE DIVINE PRINCIPLE WITHIN.

There is a principle which is pure, placed in the human mind, which in different places and ages hath had different names; it is, however, pure, and proceeds from God. *It is deep and inward, confined to no form of religion, nor excluded from any, when the heart stands in perfect sincerity.* In whomsoever this takes root and grows, they become brethren.

The necessity of an inward stillness hath appeared clear to my mind. In true silence, strength is renewed, and the mind is weaned from all things, save as they may be enjoyed in the Divine will; and a lowliness in outward living, opposite to worldly honor, becomes truly acceptable to us. In the desire after outward gain the mind is prevented from a perfect attention to the voice of Christ; yet being weaned from all things, except as they may be enjoyed in the Divine will, the pure light shines into the soul. Where the fruits of the spirit which is of this world are brought forth by many who profess to be led by the Spirit of truth, and cloudiness is felt to be gathering over the visible church, the sincere in heart, who abide in true stillness, and are exercised therein before the Lord, for his name's sake, have knowledge of Christ in the fellowship of his sufferings; and inward thankfulness is felt at times, that through Divine love our own wisdom is cast out, and that forward, active spirit in us is subjected, which would rise and do something without the pure leadings of the spirit of Christ. * * In this silence we learn to abide in the Divine will, and there feel that we have no cause to promote except that alone in which the light of life directs us. * * *

This state, in which every motion from the selfish spirit yielded to pure love, I may acknowledge with gratitude is often opened before me, as a pearl to seek after.

At times when I have felt true love opening my heart towards my fellow creatures, and have been engaged in weighty conversation in the cause of righteousness, the instructions I have received under these exercises in regard to the true use of the outward gifts of God, have made a deep and lasting impression on my mind. I have beheld how the desire to provide wealth and to uphold a delicate life, has grievously entangled many, and has been like a snare to their offspring; and though some have been affected with a sense of their difficulties, and have appeared desirous, at times, to be helped out of them, yet for want of abiding in the humbling power of truth they have continued in these entanglements; expensive living in parents and children hath called for a large supply, and in answering this call the "faces of the poor" have been ground away, and made thin through hard dealing.—*John Woolman, "A Friend," New Jersey, 1720.*

THOMAS PAINE.

SAYINGS AND OPINIONS.

—I believe in one God, and no more, and I hope for happiness beyond this life.

I believe in the equality of man; and that religious duties consist in doing justice, loving mercy, and endeavoring to make our fellow creatures happy.

I do *not* believe in the creed professed by the Jewish

Church, the Greek or Turkish Church, by the Protestant Church, or by any church that I know of. My own mind is my own church. It is necessary to the happiness of man that he be mentally faithful to himself.

Infidelity does not consist in believing or disbelieving; it consists in professing to believe what he does not believe.

It is impossible to calculate the moral mischief that mental lying has produced in society. When a man has so far corrupted and prostituted the chastity of his mind as to subscribe his professional belief to things he does not believe, he has prepared himself for the commission of every other crime.

The belief of a God, so far from having anything of a mystery in it, is of all beliefs the most easy, because it arises to us out of necessity. And the practice of moral truth, or in other words, a practical imitation of the moral goodness of God, is no other than our acting toward each other as he acts benignedly towards all.

We cannot *serve* God in the manner we serve those who cannot do without such service; aud therefore the only idea we can have of serving God is of contributing to the happiness of the creation he has made. This cannot be done by spending a recluse life in selfish devotion.

—When men, either from policy or pious fraud, set up systems of religion incompatible with the word or works of God in the creation, and not only above, but repugnant to human comprehension, they were under the necessity of inventing or adopting a word that should serve as a bar to all questions, inquiries, or speculations.

The word *mystery* answered this purpose; and thus it has happened that religion, which in itself is without mystery, has been corrupted into a fog of mysteries. As *mystery* answered all general purposes, *miracle* followed as an occasional auxiliary. The former served to bewilder the mind, the latter to puzzle the senses.

Instead of studying theology, as is now done, out of the Bible and Testament, the meanings of which books are always controverted, and the authenticity of which is disproved, it is necessary that we refer to the Bible of the creation. The principles we discover there are eternal, and of divine origin: they are the foundation of all the science that exists in the world, and must be the foundation of theology.

We can know God only through his works. We cannot have a conception of any one attribute but by following some principle that leads to it. We have only a confused idea of his power, if we have not the means of comprehending something of its immensity. We can have no idea of his wisdom but by knowing the order and manner in which it acts. The principles of science lead to this knowledge; for the creator of man is the Creator of science, and it is through that medium that man can see God, as it were, face to face.

ELIAS HICKS.

The Light Within.

Now my whole drift is to gather the minds of the people to the light within, which is the same as the grace of God, the manifestation of the spirit that reproves for evil. It was this that Jesus recommended to his disciples, it was this light which George Fox preached; it is an emanation from God in the soul of man, by his power and spirit; and he is everywhere, for in Him we live, move, and have our being. * * *

And how wonderfully he has directed the birds to fly from one limb to another, and to effect that which will make them happy. And who is it that guides them? God Almighty, by the sense that he has given them, and his mercy is everywhere; not a blade of grass could grow, were he not the preserver of it. He fills all things, and is everywhere present. * * * "The grace of God that bringeth salvation hath appeared to all men." This must comprehend all mankind, who have a thousand different notions about outward exercises in religious matters, in which there is no religion at all. There is no religion in anything but in this divine grace; in being taught by it, and coming under its leading. * *

And what was this "Comforter," spoken of in the Scripture? It was the spirit of truth, the light and life of God in the soul. There never was any other Comforter, and there never will be; it is that principle which is the same yesterday, to-day, and forever; and he abideth in us.

Jesus told his disciples it would not be out of them, "For he dwelleth with you, and shall be in you." * * No, verily, there never was any other Saviour than God manifesting himself in man; for "no man knoweth the things of God, but the spirit of God." * * * Oh! that we might be encouraged to gather to this standard—don't mind the name: mind the nature, mind its effects; this is enough for us to do. Don't dispute about names,—for if we do, we are dark and blind.

Tradition and Popular Opinion.

But having for a considerable time past found, from full conviction, that scarcely anything is so baneful to the present and future happiness and welfare of mankind, as a submission to tradition and popular opinion, I have been led to see the necessity of investigating for myself all customs and doctrines of a moral and religious nature, either verbally or historically communicated, by the best and greatest of men or angels, and not to sit down satisfied with anything but a plain, clear testimony of the spirit and word of life and light, in my own heart and conscience. * * *

And how much more reasonable it is to suppose, that any inspired teacher of the present day should be led to speak more truly and plainly to the states of the people to whom he is led to communicate, than any doctrines delivered seventeen hundred years ago, to a people very differently circumstanced, I leave to any rational mind to judge. * * *

I well remember how oft my conscience has smote me, when I have been endeavoring to support the Society's belief of the Scriptures that they very far excelled all other writings, that the fear of men had too great a share in leading me to adopt the sentiment, and custom rendered it more easy; but I never was clear in my own mind, and had I carefully attended to my own feelings, I should have been preserved, I believe, in a line of more consistency in that respect.

Atonement.

Surely is it possible that any rational being that has any right sense of justice and mercy, would be willing to accept forgiveness of his sins on such terms? Would he not rather go forward and offer himself wholly up to suffer all the penalties due to his crimes, rather than the innocent should suffer? Nay, was he so hardy as to acknowledge a willingness to be saved through such a medium, would it not prove that he stood in direct opposition to every principle of justice and honesty, of mercy and love, and showed himself a pure selfish creature?

Essentials in Religion.

Inward sanctity, pure love, disinterested attachment to God and man, obedience of heart and life, sincere excellence of character, this is the one thing needful, this is the essential thing in religion; and all things else, ministers, churches, ordinances, places of worship, all are but means, helps, secondary influences, and utterly worthless when separated from this. To imagine that God regards anything but this, that he looks at anything but the heart, is to dishonor him, to express a mournful insensibility to his pure character. Goodness, purity, virtue, this is the only distinction in God's sight. This is intrinsically, essentially, everlastingly, and by its own nature, lovely, beautiful, glorious, divine. It owes nothing to time, to circumstance, to outward confessions. It shines by its own light. It is God himself dwelling in the human soul. Can any man think lightly of it because it has not grown up in a certain church, or exalt any church above it? My friends, one of the grandest truths of religion is, the supreme importance of character, of virtue, of that divine spirit which shone out in Christ. The grand heresy is, to substitute anything for this, whether creed, or form, or church. One of the greatest wrongs to Christ is, to despise his character, his virtue, in a disciple who happens to wear a different name from our own.

When I represent to myself true virtue or goodness—not that which is made up of outward proprieties and prudent calculations, but that which chooses duty for its own sake, and as the first concern; which respects impartially the rights of every human being; which labors and suffers with patient resolution for truth, and others' welfare; which blends energy and sweetness, deep humility and self-reverence; which places joyful faith in the perfection of God, communes with him intimately, and strives to subject to his pure will, all thought, imagination, and desire; which lays hold on the promise of everlasting life, and in the strength of this hope endures calmly and firmly the sorest evils of the present state—when I set before me this virtue, all the distinctions on which men value themselves fade away. Wealth is poor, worldly honor is mean, outward forms are beggarly elements. Condition, country, church, all sink into unimportance. Before this simple greatness I bow, I revere. The robed priest, the gorgeous altar, the great assembly, the pealing organ, all the exteriors of religion, vanish from my sight as I look at the good and great man, the holy, disinterested soul. Even I, with vision so dim, with heart so cold, can see and feel the divinity, the grandeur of true goodness. How then must God regard it? To his pure eyes how lovely must it be! And can any of us turn from it, because some water has not been dropped on its forehead, or some bread put into its lips by a minister or priest; or because it has not learned to repeat some mysterious creed, which a church or human council has ordained?

My friends, reverence virtue, holiness, the upright will, which inflexibly cleaves to duty and the pure law of God. Reverence nothing in comparison with it. Regard this as the end, and all outward services as the means. Judge of men by this. Think no man the better, no man the worse, for the church he belongs to. Try him by his fruits. Expel from your breasts the demon of sectarianism, narrowness, bigotry, intolerance. This is not, as we are apt to think, a slight sin. It is a denial of the supremacy of goodness. It sets up something, whether a form or dogma, above the virtue of the heart and the life. Sectarianism immures itself in its particular church as in a dungeon, and is there cut off from the free air, the cheerful light, the goodly prospects, the celestial beauty of the church universal. * * *

We have grown up under different influences. We bear different names. But if we purpose solemnly to do God's will, and are following the precepts and example of Christ, we are one church, and let nothing divide us. Diversities of opinion may incline us to worship under different roofs; or diversities of tastes or habit to worship with different forms. But these varieties are not schisms; they do not break the unity of Christ's church. We may still honor, and love, and rejoice in one another's spiritual life and progress, as truly as if we were cast into one and the same unyielding form. God loves variety in nature and in the human soul, nor does he reject it in Christian worship. In many great truths, in those which are most quickening, purifying and consoling, we all, I hope, agree. There is, too, a common ground of practice, aloof from all controversy, on which we may all meet. We may all unite hearts and hands in doing good, in fulfilling God's purposes of love towards our race, in toiling and suffering for the cause of humanity, in spreading intelligence, freedom and virtue, in making God known for the reverence, love, and imitation of his creatures, in resisting the abuses and corruptions of past ages, in exploring and drying up the sources of poverty, in rescuing the fallen from intemperance, in succoring the orphan and widow, in enlightening and elevating the depressed portions of the community, in breaking the yoke of the oppressed and enslaved, in exposing and withstanding the spirit and horrors of war, in sending God's word to the ends of the earth, in redeeming the world from sin and woe. The angels and pure spirits who visit our earth come not to join a sect, but to do good to all. May this universal charity descend on us, and possess our hearts; may our narrowness, exclusiveness, and bigotry melt away under this mild celestial fire. Thus we shall not only join ourselves to Christ's Universal Church on earth, but to the Invisible Church, to the innumerable company of the just made perfect, in the mansions of everlasting purity and peace.—*William E. Channing.*

Man's Demands, God's Commands.

Man's natural demands are God's only commands. This is a great and comprehensive proposition; and, in one sentence, answers all questions respecting arbitrary documentary Revelations, given to one or more chosen ones, to be communicated by them to the rest of mankind. The laws, or commands of God given to thee, or to me, or to any human being, are made known to us in the demands of our Nature. To know these demands is all we need to know, healthfully to supply them is all we need to do, in order that we may become all that we are designed to be and all that we are capable of being. He who most perfectly understands the demands of his Nature, body and soul, most perfectly understands the will of God; he who most perfectly supplies those demands, most perfectly obeys God. He walks with God, and he is the only man who is after God's own heart. * * *

Does human nature respond approvingly to the spirit and practice of self-sacrifice for the good of others? Does it ever and without fail feel a conscious sense of well-doing and self-respect in the feeling and the act? Is it a demand of our social nature? Can human beings associate in pairs, or in millions, harmoniously and happily, on any other basis? Can we live in society, and maintain order and harmony, except on the principle that we are never to injure others for our benefit? The universal human heart accords its deepest and most earnest approval to the spirit and practice of self-sacrifice; and recognizes the self-abnegationist who, in all circumstances and relations, is true to his great idea, as the true hero or heroine of the race; as Earth's true King or Queen.—*Henry C. Wright.*

Value of Self-Respect.

There is one person whose respect and reverence I seek and prize more than the respect and reverence of any or all others;—that person is Henry C. Wright.—*H. C. Wright.*

Sacredness of Parental Self-Abnegation.

That Father!—See that man, toiling without ceasing! Up early, and down late! Abroad to his daily labor, promptly and energetically! Work, work, work, and that with a will! Clouds and sunshine, calm and storm, heat and cold, light and darkness are alike to him. Plan and execute! Every power of body and mind are on the alert, regardless of his own comfort, health and life. He thinks not of self; he feels not for self; or if he does, it is as the stay of those who depend upon him. What is the secret of this daring, tireless energy? Enter his home, his nursery; there sleeps, creeps, or romps in joyous glee the inspiration and interpretation of his life. His child, his loving, gentle daughter, with arms encircling his neck, and in accents sweeter than tones of cherubs saying, "My father!" He lives for his child. Self-abnegation, a tender anxiety for the existence, the physical, intellectual, social and spiritual health and happiness of his child, controls him in all his actions and relations to her, from her conception to her present growth. In the relation in which she originated; in watching and guarding her development before and after her birth; in every effort made to guard her tender life against discordant and diseased influences, and subject it to those that are healthy and happy, self-renunciation, not mere self-gratification—his child's life and happiness, and not self-indulgence, have controlled his actions. He feels a proud consciousness of this fact, and the out-gushing affections, and confidence, and the harmonious, joyous nature of his child, are his great reward. She is the gem in his crown of paternal glory, which his life of self-abnegation, in his relations to her, has placed there. As that daughter grows up to womanhood, and becomes assured that in all his relations to her, her existence, health and happiness, and not mere self-indulgence, controlled her father—will not her heart twine its tenderest affections around him, in grateful and joyous martyrdom? Between a father and daughter thus begotten, developed, born and matured under the influence of self-abnegation, rather than self-gratification, the relation can bring naught but heaven to both.

That Mother!—Think of the forebodings of her heart, her ever-present anxiety and care, during the pre-natal life of her child! Her plans, her sympathies, her actions, all relate to its welfare. She is aware, and ever acts on the conviction, that every action of her brain, and every pulsation of her heart, is making its impress on the body and soul of the new life that is developed within her organism. The air she breathes, the food she eats, the liquid she drinks, the home she lives in, the company she keeps, the pleasures indulged in, her conditions of body and soul, and all her surroundings—in a word, all the experiences of her interior and exterior life are momentarily stamping themselves on the organic conditions of her child, and embodying themselves in its character and destiny, in the eternity that lies before it, and must receive it. This she knows and regards as the one fact that should guide her life. In all these actions of her physical, intellectual and social life, the new immortal life being developed beneath her heart is her one thought, the controlling power of her life. Whether she eats or drinks, works or rests, sleeps or wakes, whatever she does, she does to the glory of her child. Her one absorbing anxiety is, how to confer on her child a beautiful, healthy body and soul; and to organize into it a pure and noble character and destiny. She would give existence to one whose life, in all its great Future, shall shine brighter and brighter unto the perfect day; whose track across the horizon of Eternity, shall be like the course of the sun across the heavens, shedding only light, warmth and beauty over the world. What hopes, what visions of heroism and nobleness, fill that maternal heart, touching the destiny of her child! She spares no effort to make her child all her own heart would have it, a child of God. What though in giving it birth an agony that can never be told is hers? She, with dauntless resolution, with lofty bearing, and sublime resignation, sees the hour of her august martyrdom approach; and that hour past, she folds her babe to her bosom, and sings over it with a joy unspeakable and full of glory, a "*Gloria in Excelsis.*" See that mother bending over that infant son, with weary, wasting watchfulness; with a toil that knows no rest, an anxiety that knows no sleep, a courage that never falters, and a vigilance that never slumbers, and with an energy and daring that no dangers can appal. What is her heart's inspiration? What the power that sustains her? What turned that timid, shrinking woman into a fearless, patient heroine? Where is the secret of her power? It is the infant son that nestles in her bosom, and draws its life from hers. She sees, hears, sleeps, wakes, eats, drinks and lives, that she may bless her boy. Her very life is hid with her son in God. The mystery of that mother's life finds its only solution in her child. She is hungry that her son may eat, she is thirsty that he may drink; she awakes that he may sleep; she is cold, that he may be warm; she is sick, that he may be well; she suffers that he may rejoice; she dies that he may live.

Can that son forget that mother? Never! His existence is an ever-present memorial of her; and till conscious existence ceases, that mother will live in his tenderest and most ennobling recollections. With her patient renunciation of self for his good; with her sleepless vigilance, and tender nursing in sickness; with the tender watchfulness that anticipated his wants; with the sweet smile that chased away sorrow from his heart and sadness from his brow; with the sweet kiss that sealed her forgiveness of all his faults; with the self-forgetting love, and the tireless energy and all-enduring patience and fortitude that guarded his health and life, through helpless infancy, wayward childhood, and headstrong youth,—are associated all the tenderest and most potential memories of his life. Can the image of that self-denying mother ever be stricken from his heart? Never!

And when that son comes to know that his existence, his health and happiness, constitute the governing motive of her life, in his conception; and that, in all her relations to him, during his gestational life, she regulated her drink, her sleep, her labor, her enjoyment, and her every action with reference to his welfare; when he knows that her life before, as well as since his birth, was a life of utter self-abandonment to his life and happiness—will he not fold her to his heart and give her a place there, from which no other love can ever drive her? Can coldness, distrust, concealment, or indifference ever enter into such a relation? Can discord and conflict ever come between such a mother and a son thus conceived, born and reared? Never. And when the eyes of that mother are dim, when the beauty and vigor of her youth are gone, and the serene and noble aspects of age are settled on her brow, and her steps are feeble, the holy love and powerful arm of that grateful son, in whose eyes that mother's beauty and glory never shone so bright before, will encircle her and bear her onward to her home *within the veil*, there to watch and rejoice over him, and to await with maternal pride his coming. Such a son is of royal blood, and has a queenly mother. In her hand she holds a sceptre over an empire of greater power, and wider extent, than is that which rules an empire on which the sun never sets.—*Henry C. Wright.*

Creeds.

We believe and insist, that each and every rational and moral being, male and female, is under the highest obligation to form his or her own opinions about religion. Every one, we hold, is bound, and therefore should be left perfectly free to seek after, if happily he may find, the truth of God for himself; form his own creed, his own body of divinity; be fully persuaded in his own mind as to what is true on every question that may arise respecting the character of God, the principles of the divine government, man's accountability, the design of his life in this world, and his destiny in the world to come.

I am utterly unable to discover the benefit which ever has been or can be derived from a creed prescribed by human authority; a formula of faith; a system of doctrines devised and concocted by any man or any set of men, to be enforced upon the assent of other men, each of whom has an inalienable right to think for himself. Many and very grave evils, gross hypocricies, and atrocious cruelties, have everywhere, and in all ages, been the legitimate offspring of this assumption of authority to dictate to fellow men what they must believe.—*Samuel J. May.*

Free Thought and Free Speech.

Talk not of this or that subject being too sacred for investigation! Is it too much to assert, that there is but one object beneath the skies that is sacred—and that is, Man? Surely, there is no government, no institution, no order, no rite, no day, no place, no building, no creed, no book, so sacred as he who was before every government, institution, order, rite, day, place, building, creed and book, and by whom all these things are to be regarded as nothing higher or better than means to an end, and that end his own elevation and happiness; and he is to discard each and all of them, when they fail to do him service, or minister unto his necessities.

They are not of heaven, but of men, and may not, therefore, receive the homage of any human being. Be assured that whatever cannot bear the test of the closest scrutiny, has no claim to human respect or confidence, even though it assume to be sacred in its origin, or given by inspiration of God, but must be treated as spurious, profane, dangerous.

Let, then, the mind, and tongue, and press, be free. Let free discussion not only be tolerated, but encouraged and asserted, as indispensable to the freedom and welfare of mankind. A forcible suppression of error is no aid to the cause of truth; and to allow only just such views and sentiments to be spoken and circulated as we think are correct, is to combine bigotry and cowardice in equal proportions. If I give my children no other precept—if I leave them no other example—it shall be, a fearless, impartial, thorough investigation of every subject to which their attention may be called, and a hearty adoption of the principles which to them may seem true, whether those principles may agree or conflict with my own, or with those of any other person. The best protection which I can give them is to secure the unrestricted exercise of their reason, and to inspire them with true self-reliance. I will not arbitrarily determine for them what are orthodox, or what are heretical sentiments, on any subject. I have no wish, no authority, no right to do so. I desire them to see, hear, and weigh both sides of every question. For example:—I wish them to examine whatever may be advanced in opposition to the doctrine of the divine inspiration of the bible, as freely as they do whatever they find in support of it; to hear what may be urged against the doctrines, precepts, miracles, or life of Jesus, as readily as they do anything in their defence; to see what arguments are adduced for a belief in the non-existence of God, as unreservedly as they do the evidence in favor of his existence. I shall teach them to regard no subject as too holy for examination; to make their own convictions paramount to all human authority; to reject whatever conflicts with their reason, no matter by whomsoever enforced; and to prefer that which is clearly demonstrative to mere theory. And why do I intend to pursue such a course? Because I am not infallible, and therefore dare not put on the robes of infallibility. Because I think free inquiry is essential to the life of truth among mankind. * * * *

"Whoever is afraid," says Bishop Watson, "of submitting any question, civil or religious, to the test of free discussion, seems to me to be more in love with his own opinion than with the truth!" A noble sentiment for a man—much more for a prelate.

No sentiment has been more greatly admired, or more frequently quoted since it was uttered, than that of Jefferson: "Error of opinion may be safely tolerated, where Reason is left free to combat it."

"Philosophy, wisdom and liberty," says Sir W. Drummond, "support each other. He who will not reason is a bigot, he who cannot is a fool, and he who dares not is a slave." * *

Coleridge tersely says: "He who begins with loving Christianity better than truth, will end by loving himself better than either."

Among all the noble sayings that fell from the lips of the great champion of English freedom, John Milton, not one deserves to be eternalized more than this: "Let Truth and Falsehood grapple: who ever knew Truth put to the worse in a free and open encounter?"

"The spirit of Jesus," says the amiable and courageous Abbe de la Mennais, "is a spirit of peace, of compassion and of love. They who persecute in his name, and who search men's consciences with the sword; who torture the body to convert the soul; who cause tears to flow, instead of drying them up; these men have not the spirit of Christ, and are none of His." * * * * *

True, it does not follow that a man is in the right because he is ready to engage in controversy; for he may be devoid of sense, or disgustingly presumptuous, or extremely vain, or annoyingly combative, or incurably perverse. But this is certain:—he who is for forcibly stopping the mouth of his opponent, or for burning any man at the stake, or thrusting him into prison, or exacting a pecuniary fine from him, or impairing his means of procuring an honest livelihood, or treating him scornfully, on account of his peculiar views on any subject, whether relating to God or man, to time or eternity, is either under the dominion of a spirit of ruffianism or cowardice, or animated by that fierce intolerance which characterized Saul of Tarsus, in his zeal to exterminate the heresy of Christianity. On the other hand, he who forms his opinions from the dictates of enlightened reason, and sincerely desires to be led into all truth, dreads nothing so much as the suppression of free inquiry—is at all times ready to give a reason for the hope that is in him—calmly listens to the objections of others—and feels nothing of anger or alarm lest his foundation shall be swept away by the waves of opposition. It is impossible, therefore, for him to be a persecutor, or to call upon the strong arm of violence to put a gag into the mouth of any one, however heretical in his sentiments. In proportion as we perceive and embrace the truth, do we become meek, heroic, magnanimous, divine. * * * *

Let us speak plain: there is more force in names
Than most men dream of; and a lie may keep
Its throne a whole age longer, if it skulk
Behind the shield of some fair-seeming name.
Let us call tyrants TYRANTS, and maintain
That only freedom comes by grace of God.
And all that comes not by His grace must fall;
For men in earnest have no time to waste
In patching fig-leaves for the naked truth.

Let us call tyrants, TYRANTS. Not to do so is to misuse language, to deal treacherously with freedom, to consent to the enslavement of mankind. It is neither an amiable nor a virtuous, but a foolish and pernicious thing, not to call things by their right names. John Knox, when he was reprimanded for his severity of speech, with much significance and great good sense declared that he would call a fig a fig, and a spade a spade. "Woe unto them" says one of the world's great prophets, "that call evil good, and good evil; that put darkness for light, and light for darkness; that put bitter for sweet, and sweet for bitter."

Popular sins are never regarded by the people as sins; they are never called sins. Terms are invented to describe them which fall upon the ear without harshness, and which, whenever uttered, give no alarm to the moral sense. This is what is called in Scripture the transformation of Satan into an angel of light. Thus, they who are engaged in upbuilding the horrid slave-system in this country,—a system which presents no single feature of decency or utility, and which John Wesley comprehensively and justly called "the sum of all villainies"—the Southern slaveholders and their abettors, designate it as "the peculiar institution," as "the corner-stone of our Republican edifice." This description of it conveys no idea to the mind that is revolting or disagreeable, but quite the contrary—and yet it means theft and robbery; it means assault and battery; it means nakedness and penury; it means yokes, fetters, branding-irons, drivers and bloodhounds; it means cruelty and murder, concubinage and adultery; it means the denial of all chances of intellectual and moral culture, gross mental darkness, and utter moral depravation; it means the transformation of those who, in the scale of creation, are but a little lower than the angels, to the condition of brutes and the fate of perishable property; in one sentence, it means the denial of God as the common Father of us all, and of Christ as our common Saviour and Redeemer. Still, we wrap it up in the fine linen of a deceitful phraseology—we call it the "peculiar institution"—outwardly, we garnish this sepulchre, and make it pleasant to the eye, but carefully hide the bones, the uncleanness, and the pollution, which are festering beneath. * * *

Of all the reformers who have appeared in the world—whether they were prophets, the Son of God, apostles, martyrs or confessors; whether assailing one form of popular iniquity or another; whether impeaching the rulers in the State, or the teachers in the Church; not one of them has been exempt from the charge of dealing in abusive language, of indulging in coarse personalities, of libelling the characters of great and good men, of aiming to subvert time-honored and glorious institutions, of striking at the foundation of the social fabric, of being actuated by an irreligious spirit. The charge has ever been false, malicious, the very reverse of the truth; and it is only the reformer himself who has been the victim of calumny, hatred and persecution. His accusations are denied, his impeachments are pronounced libellous, simply because the giant iniquity which he assails has subdued to its own evil purposes all the religious and political elements of the land, and everywhere passes current as both necessary and reputable. Of Jesus it was said, "This man is not of God! he keepeth not the Sabbath day; he is a blasphemer; he hath a devil." Of the Apostles it was said, "They are pestilent and seditious fellows, who go about seeking to turn the world upside down." And Paul declares that they were treated as the offscouring of all things. Luther and his coadjutors were represented as the monsters of their times. Those excellent and wonderful men, Penn, Fox, Barclay, with the early Friends, suffered every kind of reproach, and experienced great tribulation, as infidel emissaries and fanatical disorganizers. Before the abolition of the African slave trade, Wilberforce and Clarkson were vehemently denounced as interfering with vested rights, and seeking to cripple the prosperity of England; and a murderous attempt was made to drown the latter in the river Mersey at Liverpool. It is needless to ask how those heroic and unfaltering pioneers of our race are now regarded. The mid-day sun shining in the fullness of its strength is not brighter, the firm set earth is not more solid than their fame; and down through all coming time shall they be hailed by countless processions of new-born generations as among the saviors of their race. There will be none to distrust their disinterestedness, none to question their sanity, none to scoff at their testimony. * * * In taking a retrospect of the past, the present stands ostensibly amazed and shocked at the treatment of those glorious old reformers. It sees nothing in the sternest language of the prophets to condemn; it hails Jesus as the true Messiah, and weeps over his crucifixion; it venerates the memories of the apostles and martyrs; it places Luther, Calvin, Penn, in the calendar of saints. It mourns that all these were beyond its countenance and succor, and takes infinite credit to itself, that it is animated by a far higher and nobler spirit.

All this is spurious virtue and mock piety; it is a cheap mode of being heroic and good, for it costs nothing. * * *

But let it not be so with us. Let us prove ourselves worthy of the great and good who have gone before us. Truth needs our help; let her have it. Right is cloven down in the land; let us come to the rescue. Liberty is hunted with blood-hounds, and lynch law is threatened to her advocates; let us form a body-guard around her, and bare our bosom to the shafts that are aimed at her. Christianity, as exemplified in the life of its great Founder, is tarnished, modified, perverted to the sanctioning of enormous crimes, to the justification of sinners of the first rank; let us endeavor to remove its stain, to hold it up in its pristine purity, as against all wrong, all injustice, all tyranny, and embracing all mankind in one common brotherhood.

Millions of our countrymen are in chains, crying to us for deliverance; on the side of their oppressors there is power; let us rally for their emancipation, and never retire from the conflict until victory or death be ours. The demon spirit of war is driving his chariot wheels over the bodies of prostrate thousands, and kindling the flames of hell throughout our borders; let us be volunteers in the cause of peace; and give no countenance whatever to the spirit of violence. To do all this, it will cost us something; we must think no more of the bubble reputation of the hour than did Jesus; we must have entire faith in God, and be baptized into the divine spirit of love; we must see of the travail of our souls, and be satisfied; we must be strengthened and consoled by the thought that, in addition to the sweet approval of our own consciences, we shall secure the gratitude of a redeemed posterity, and the smiles of God. * * * *

Generally speaking, I care not how highly any one praises the dead, or how great may be his professed veneration for Luther or Calvin, for Whitefield or Wesley, for David or Moses, for Jesus or Paul. As at this day all this is popular, and is everywhere well received, it gives me no evidence of any vital appreciation of the character of those intrepid reformers, on the part of the encomiast. The cowardly and time-serving, the hypocritical and pharisaical are always prompt to appear as the special champions of all departed canonized worth. * * *

To every great reform the same objections, substantially, are urged until it triumphs. First—That it is against the Scriptures. Second—That it disturbs the peace, and endangers the safety of the Church. Third—That it is generally discarded by the priesthood, who being divinely appointed, must know all about it. Fourth—That it is contrary to long-established precedent and venerated authority. Fifth—That it lacks respectability and character; those who espouse it are generally obscure, uninfluential, and none of the rulers believe in it. Sixth—It is sheer fanaticism, and its triumph would be the overthrow of all order in society, and chaos would come again. Lastly—Its advocates are vulgar in speech, irreverent in spirit, personal in attack, seeking their own base ends by bad means, and presumptuously attempting to dictate to the wise, the learned and the powerful.

Be not intimidated by any of these outcries. They are "full of sound and fury, signifying nothing." Or rather they indicate the standard around which it is your duty and my duty to rally; and that is the standard of right, whether storm or sunshine be our portion, or whatever may be the consequences.

First of all, let us maintain freedom of speech; let us encourage honest and fearless inquiry in all things. Let us recognize no higher standard than that of Reason, and dare to summon to its bar all books, customs, governments, institutions and laws, that we may prove them, and render our verdict accordingly. Whatever in this great universe is above our reason, with that we need have no controversy, nor should it give us any anxiety; whatever is contrary to our reason, that let us promptly reject, though a thousand books deemed sacred should declare it to be true—though ten thousand councils should affirm it to be right—though all nations should pronounce us to be guilty of a terrible heresy in rejecting it. If God does not address us as reasonable beings, he cannot address us as accountable beings, and hence we are absolved from every moral obligation to him; we take our place with the beasts of the field, with the fowls of the air, with stocks and stones. But he has created us in his great and glorious image; and

> "In our spirit doth His Spirit shine,
> As shines the sunbeam in a drop of dew."

Thank God, the Past is not the Present. For its opportunities and deeds, we are not responsible. It is for us to discharge the high duties that devolve on us, and carry our race onward. To be no better, no wiser, no greater than the Past, is to be little, and foolish and bad; it is to misapply noble means, to sacrifice glorious opportunities for the performance of sublime deeds, to become cumberers of the ground. We can and must transcend our predecessors in their efforts to give peace, joy, liberty to the world.—*William Lloyd Garrison.*

THE REFORMER.

We may regret that in this stage of the spirit's life, the sincere and self-denying worker is not always permitted to partake of the fruits of his toil, or receive the honors of a benefactor. We hear his good evil-spoken of, and his noblest sacrifices counted as naught,—we see him not only assailed by the wicked, but discountenanced and shunned by the timidly good, followed on his hot and dusty pathway by the execrations of the hounding mob, and the contemptuous pity of the worldly-wise and prudent; and, when at last the horizon of Time shuts down between him and ourselves, and the places which have known him know him no more forever, we are almost ready to say with the regal voluptuary of old: "This also is vanity and a great evil; for what hath a man of all his labor and of the vexation of his heart, wherein he hath labored under the sun?" But is this the end? Has God's universe no wider limits than the circle of the blue wall which shuts in our nestling-place? Has life's infancy only been provided for; and beyond this poor nursery-chamber of Time is there no playground for the soul's youth, no broad fields for its manhood? Perchance, could we but lift the curtains of the narrow pin-fold wherein we dwell, we might see that our poor friend and brother whose fate we have thus deplored has by no means lost the reward of his labors, but that in new fields of duty he is cheered even by the tardy recognition of the value of his services in the old. The continuity of life is never broken; the river flows onward and is lost to our sight, but under its new horizon it carries the same waters which it gathered under ours; and its unseen valleys are made glad by the offerings which are borne down to them from the Past, flowers, perchance, the germs of which its own waves planted on the banks of Time. Who shall say that the mournful and repentant love with which the benefactors of our race are at length regarded, may not be to them in their new condition of being sweet and grateful as the perfume of long-forgotten flowers; or that our harvest-hymns of rejoicing may not reach the ears of those who in weakness and suffering scattered the seeds of blessing?

Great truths when first told are not always believed, and for that very reason are the more needed, for it is evermore the case that the right word, when first uttered, is an unpopular and denied one. Hence he who undertakes to tread the thorny pathway of Reform—who, smitten with the love of truth and justice, or indignant in view of wrong, and insolent oppression, is rashly inclined to throw himself at once into that great conflict, which the Persian seer not untruly represented as a war between light and darkness—would do well to count the cost. To the reformer, in an especial manner, comes home the truth that whoso ruleth his own spirit is greater than him who taketh a city. Patience, hope, charity, watchfulness unto prayer, how needful are all these to success! Without them he is in danger of ingloriously giving up his contest with error and prejudice at the first repulse; or, with that spiteful philanthropy which we sometimes witness, taking a sick world by the nose, like a spoiled child, and endeavoring to force down its throat the long rejected nostrums prepared for its relief.

What then! Shall we, in view of these things call back young and generous spirits, just entering upon the perilous pathway? God forbid! Welcome, thrice welcome, rather. Let them go forward, not unwarned of the danger, nor unreminded of the pleasures which belong to the service of humanity. Great is the consciousness of right. Sweet is the answer of a good conscience. He who pays his whole-hearted homage to Truth and Duty—who swears his life-long fealty on their altars, and rises up a Nazarite consecrated to their holy service—is not without his solace and enjoyment, when, to the eyes of others, he seems the most lonely and miserable. He breathes an atmosphere which the multitude know not of—"a serene heaven which they cannot discern rests over him, glorious in its purity and stillness." Nor is he altogether without kindly human sympathies. All generous and earnest hearts which are brought in contact with his own beat evenly with it. All that is good and truthful and lovely in man, whenever and wherever it truly recognizes him, must sooner or later acknowledge his claim to love and reverence. His faith overcomes all things. The future unrolls itself before him, with its waving harvest-fields springing up from the seed he is scattering; and he looks forward to the close of life with the calm confidence of one who feels that he has not lived idle and useless; but with hopeful heart and strong arm has labored with God and nature for the Best.

And not in vain. In the economy of God, no effort, however small, put forth for the right cause, fails of its effect. No voice, however feeble, lifted up for Truth, ever dies amidst the confused noises of Time. Through discords of Sin and Sorrow, Pain, and Wrong, it rises in deathless melody, whose notes of wailing are hereafter to be changed to those of triumph, as they blend with the Great Harmony of a reconciled universe. —*J. G. Whittier.*

Forgiveness and Love.

The doctrines of forgiveness and love, taught by Jesus, are not, as men seem to suppose, mere beautiful sentimental theories, fit only for heaven: they are rational principles, which may, not only safely, but profitably, be reduced to practice on earth. All divine principles, if suffered to flow out into the ultimates of life, would prove the wisest political economy.

The assertion that society makes its own criminals, interferes with the theological opinions of some. They argue that God leaves the will of man free, und therefore every individual is responsible for his own sin. Whether the same action is equally a sin in the sight of God, when committed by individuals in totally different circumstances, I will not attempt to discuss. Such questions should reverently be left to Him who made the heart, and who alone can judge it. But I feel that if I were to commit a crime, with my education, and the social influences that prop my weakness in every direction, I should be a much worse sinner than a person guilty of the same deed whose childhood had been passed among the lowest haunts of vice, and whose after years had been unvisited by outward influences to purify and refine. The degree of conviction resisted would be the measure of my sin.

The simple fact is, human beings stand between two kinds of influences, the inward and the outward. The inward is the spirit of God, which strives with us always. The outward is the influence of Education, Society, Government, etc. In a right state of things, these two would be in perfect harmony;

but it is painfully obvious that they are now discordant. Society should stand to her poor in the relation of a parent, not of a master.

People that are most unwilling to admit that external circumstances have an important agency in producing crime, are nevertheless extremely careful to place *their* children under safe outward influences. So little do they trust their free will to the guidance of Providence, they often fear to have them attend schools taught by persons whose creeds they believe to be untrue. If governments took equal paternal care, if they would spend more money to prevent crime, they need spend far less to punish it.—*Lydia Maria Child.*

Spiritual Christianity.

In its *first* movement in Christian history that Spirit was unfettered by creeds, in the modern sense. St. Paul had no theology, according to our use of that term, and no literature to impose as law for the Church, and as the channel of grace *in the future* of Christendom.

He struggled with all his fervor to get the idea of a free and common communication of the Divine Spirit to all races, through a risen head of our humanity, enthroned over the whole Christian mind as its only mental creed and bond. What we call his theology was mostly his interpretation of the religious records and movements of *the past*—and that for an immediate, a temporary and pressing issue. He strove to convince the Jewish part of the Church that, out of their own documents, they were condemned for exclusiveness in denying the equal in all nations by the plan of Divine Providence.

* * * * * *

And the New Testament documents taken together do not present any shapen, interlocked, systematical system of Christianity to the understanding. They were never intended to fix the form, and to enfigure infinite truth for the *intellect* of a church that was to last thousands of years in an advancing civilization. It is very difficult for any scholar, studying the facts without prejudice, to make the philosophy of religion by St. James coincide with that of St. Paul; or the conceptions of the church in the Apocalypse and in Galatians identical. We do not get the light of *theological science* in equal clearness, or in harmonious hues, from these fragments of the primitive thought of the church. But we do get the spirit through them all in uniform intensity. They give us truth of the eternal order; heat, and electric currents, and charges from the invisible world in equal measures. Of what consequence is it how adequately or accordantly they convey the perceptions of the infinite reason in the mysteries of theology, if they flood us with the deeper truth of the infinite essence; if they are batteries for shedding the "*powers* of the world to come" on the torpid conscience, the disloyal or flaccid will, the corrupt imagination, the withering heart; if they make us feel the holiness, the justice, the unsounded charity of God; if they restore the proportions of things to our *moral* vision, reducing this world to a speck within the soul's world, and curtained from it by a film that may break for us to-morrow?

Ah, how brutally these marvelous records have been treated under our theories of a minute and infallible intellectual inspiration! How men have crushed and cut them to make poetry, and precept, and vision, and mystic vagueness of utterance, and Oriental hyperbole, and hot rhetoric for an emergency, and well-weighed judgments, and lyric raptures, fit together like the puzzle-maps of wood with which children play, into an outlined map of eternal wisdom, consistent and complete!

It is not more reverent and wise to look at those chapters of fragmentary scrolls of an inspiration that breathed the *forces*, and not the *science* of the Infinite into the first generations of Christendom? Shall we not thus see them set around with the pure splendor of the Spirit, deeply tinged with different human temperaments, as types of the diverse genius which the gospel has sanctified in history? * * *

And we have a right to say now, in the interest of vital

Christianity, that all theories of Christ rank and office, and all catechisms and creeds, are *indifferent* to the Spirit, so far as they belong to the speculative science of the Infinite, or to the philosophical interpretation of the Scripture. This is the great question: how near is the man to the Spirit of God? how closely does the Christ he believes in bring him to the Infinite? how richly does he interpret to him the character of the Almighty—his equity, his providence, his love? It is *working* truth, truth for redemption, truth that cleanses the passions, burns the clouded conscience, wrenches the cowardly will, and knocks at the heart with a sweet and serious pleading, in which the Spirit hides. A notional Trinity or a notional Unity it cares not for any more than it cares for your conception of how many strata are in the surface of the globe, or how the sun's light is connected with its substance. * *

Is it the spiritual truth which looks through the creed that is the all-important element so far as the person is concerned. St. Paul determined to know no other formula than the Cross of Christ. But what did it mean to him? We have seen that it meant the breaking out of divine love toward all mankind; it meant the equal spiritual rights of all races; it meant a perfect moral providence, it meant the condemnation of Pharisaism as high treason to humanity; it meant the abolition of all covenant-grace; it meant that humility, charity, self-sacrifice is the law of the moral universe; it meant that men need no more pine here as prisoners, but could burst through faith "into the air of that supernatural life which God lives eternally." In a word, it meant just the opposite of the system into which the old school Calvanism has petrified the book of Romans.

The Cross of Christ is thus preached now, in the Trinitarian Church, by men like Bushnell, and Kingsley, and Maurice, and Robertson, and Stanley, and is interpreted thus by theologians like Jowett, and scholars like Bunsen; and it is the sign of the purest faith and most adequate conception of Christianity in our time. * * *

It is the amount of quickening truth which our creed is

translucent that keeps us—just as it is the sweetness and depth of saintly beauty, and not the literal, historic or positive verity of the person or the scene that moves us in one of Raphael's groups. * * *

I do not argue that truth of creed is unimportant. I do not say that a systematical and pure theology, an adequate intellectual interpretation of the office of Christ and the meaning of Christianity, is not a most desirable thing. But I say that unless a man values and uses his Christ or his creed as a medium of the Spirit, as a lense to condense the radiance of the everlasting world upon his soul, a perfect surface-belief is of no account. * * *

Let us pray that we may yield our mind and will to the Spirit; that by its light we may see through our creeds into the all-important verities of the substantial world; that we may be instruments of Christian music, more than soldiers of Calvanistic or Unitarian camps; and that we may be lifted at last, by that Spirit, to that world where we shall experience the truth, that "whether there be prophecies they shall fail; whether there be tongues they shall cease; whether there be knowledge it shall vanish away" before the charity that "never faileth," which gives the "unity of the Spirit," and is "the fulfilling of the law."—*T. Starr King.*

A Lesson From Nature.

Now I have one tree just by my study window, with which I have managed to become very intimate. We nod to each other every morning. In the long black days (just before spring), I could see my friend was looking disheartened enough.

It had great treasures of buds; but it seemed to fold them as a child folds a treasure in its clasped fingers, and all the while to be saying, "Well, I do think this spring will never come." But, I said, "Hold on, good tree, spring is surely coming. I saw her down on the Alabama line. Here is the winter—fierce, persistent and determined to stay. Yonder, where I have been, is the spring—soft, sunny, filling the woods with her white splendor; and I can see the blossoms pouring up this way, faster than I can run on my feet to tell you." And it was so. The warm days came at last; summer was victor; and my tree stood, tremulous in her beautiful green leaves, like a bride adorned for her wedding.

Why will not men take these things into their hearts, and be as full of faith in the meaning and purpose of their lives as of their flowers? Is man alone the neglected step-child? Are his fortunes alone misfortunes? Are we much worse than the lilies? Or is it not of all things true, that as man rises nearest of all on this earth to the image of the Infinite, so he is nearest of all on earth to the Providence that enfolds and blesses all? —*Robert Collyer.*

Inspiration Present and Universal.

The Old dies that the New may sing of birth, maturity and victory. The Past, with its lengthened shadows, its defeats and triumphs, was well; so were frightful explosions in the old Plutonian period. Fossils in Silurian rocks are significant, as treasured histories of primeval life bespeaking higher organized existence. * * *

Parchments are fixtures. While neither constitutions nor creeds grow, *souls do.* As well strive to fill our arteries with the blood of Jewish patriarchs and priests, as to appropriate their thoughts, commandments or religious experiences, forgetful of the living present, hoping thereby to have our spiritual life vitalized. The yesterdays are gone, let them go! The good of the Past preserved and reconstructed, Americans have to do with the to-days, and with a brightening Future whose crowning glories should be harmonial men and women, being laws unto themselves. * * *

All those brave souls of the Past were helps, not masters or infallible guides. Wisdom did not die with them, and they must not talk to us authoritatively. Each should be his own authority. God speaks to us as frequently and as fatherly as he did to Jewish seers. Seeing in every valley a Jordan, in every sectarian church a Dead Sea, in every aspirational heart a temple of worship, in every woodland eminence a mount of ascension, and in every child an embryo angel, what *special* need of Hebrew bounty styled "*Revelation?*" Inspiration is everywhere an in-breathing from the Infinite.—*J. M. Peebles.*

GODLINESS OF LABOR.

Why is it such a fatal thing when a country has men who throw discredit on labor? Wherever a theory prevails that work is degrading, great mischief ensues; not because a false ambition withdraws needful hands from employment, for there are many kinds of work that demand diversities of gifts. If a man lay down one tool to take up another, he may still be faithful to the commonwealth. And it is not because men work badly who work under the contempt of their fellows—although there is no labor so ill done as that which is meanly requited—but some kind of necessity, hunger, the climate, or the whip, will compel men to work in spite of human scorn; and the work will correspond with the necessity. In degrading labor, the mischief is done to mankind by degrading Providence—it is a practical infidelity to the great idea that God is a Creator. See how it operates. Work runs through the universe; it is the condition of permanence and growth. Mankind is not retarded so much by inefficiency as by the arrogance that will not imitate God, for a certain per cent. of inefficiency must always accompany so many births, being only another accident of malformation. But God, in prosecuting his divine schemes, allows for inefficiency, but not for infidelity; not for the arrogance that calls it an honor to do nothing. When one variety of work is thought degrading, all work becomes impaired.

It is a revolt of the whole working organization against the order of the world. Intellect itself is betrayed when it is anxious to make it appear that no vulgar labors occupy it. It is trying to separate itself from the natural religion of mankind, and to pass off for something better than a laborer.

What intellect God puts into the strokes of every day, as he thinks it not degrading to have his petroleum ready for the tap, his veins of coal and granite ready for the blaster's drill, his oak rimmed for keelsons with the hardness of a thousand years! He puts slag into his iron, quartz into his gold, wildness and peril into his whales, and rejoices to provoke our honest labor. There is not a stroke made by pen or pickaxe, that is not in answer to the mind of God. He holds the most precious things beyond our arm's length—gems, gold, beauty; he worketh hitherto to make them, and we must work to win them—diamonds in the river channels, pearls in dusky Indian seas, liberty in every acre of the soil. How long His mind must brood before he can bring forests to lignite, and lignite to coal; before carbon will bleach and whiten into the Koh-i-nor, before the soil of a republic can be transmuted into the rights of man!

This is all the industry of God, who knows that idleness is chaos, and an idle man the soul's disorganizer. * * * *

No privilege is high enough to look down on God's imagination; for having once conceived his own right mind, he devotes eternity to Virtue and the Rights of Man.—*John Weiss.*

Free Religion and the Free State.

What are the safeguards of a Free State? Intelligence surely is one. But as that advances, it gives the individual mind the consciousness of its own dignity, its command of natural law, its freedom, its direct access to truth, its right to apply the same universal principles to all persons, races, religions. But intelligent mind alone cannot save a State; or Greece had not fallen. There is a little European State which has passed through the intestine strifes of petty cantons in which Greece perished, and come out united and free. Switzerland has large practical intelligence: her schools are the models of this century; her education of the masses leaves England and France a hundred years in the background. She has another element of stability, behind intelligence,—namely, strength of moral conviction. Now Switzerland is intensely religious. These cantonal wars have not been like the Greek, political, so much as religious; very often pure wars of sect. There is no country where the hostilities of creeds have been so inveterate. The Jew was, until very recently, under heavier disabilities in some parts of Switzerland than in any other enlightened country. Yet such is the moral energy of that people, their sense of justice, their devotion to liberty, that they have put the intensest religious antagonisms underfoot, and are most united by disparagement of mere dogma in the interest of practical duty. The little mountain fastness has been the refuge of free thought for all Europe. It has had to yield now and then a little, as recently in complying so far with the demands of a powerful neighbor as to withdraw Mazzini, the religious and political radical, from its Italian borders; but it is only to hold him closer to its own bosom. Switzerland is saved only by reverence for liberty. Her mountains are at once symbol and guardian of a Free Religious Faith.

America is trying a more radical and a broader experiment than Switzerland. We are blending the antagonisms of all races and the diversities of all faiths. We are giving equal powers to the best and the worst, to the wisest and the most ignorant, among the tribes of men. The busy, peaceful hordes of Asia re-enforce us from the West; the scum of Europe floats over to us from the East; the barbarous poor white, and his perhaps more barbarous social master, are more than half our South; the very Esquimaux peep in upon our North. And, to meet these multifold demands, we have summoned the free thought and faith, the latest science of the world. We have a new continent, new liberties, new inspirations. Do we imagine that out of these combinations there shall not come creative experience such as never came before since the world was made, not even in that analogous grand concourse of races and beliefs in the Roman Empire, out of which Christianity first emerged? Our national experiment, covering the race, demands the universal religion that shall spring from the fusion of all experiences and all gifts. Not the blood of all races only is now to be mixed: but the very day is new; the day of mind, of heart, of sun and soil. The free self-governing tribes, face to face with nature, alive with scientific ardor, conscious of unparalleled opportunity, of a spiritual vision peculiar to the hour, are no subjects for the old-world faith in a prescribed historical centre.

Let the free State make free religion; the nation of nations stand open to the coming God, whom the exclusive revelations could not reveal. Stand, each in the spiritual freedom that is open eye and ear, for the practical and intellectual service that shall further others, and soul and State alike are saved.

It is not possible to make citizenship a dependency on the Messiah. The Constitution wants no name to swear by, concedes to no one religion the sole right to guarantee the Infinite Care. And the whole stress of the time is towards the liberty thus outwardly conditioned. There is something in the very air that assures us. The common sense and practical intelligence of men and women responds to every hint that the old ecclesiastical bondage is but varnish and veneer. The track of American destiny may yet be stormy and perilous; but the Idea that makes our social and political civilization is making our religious faith. Human nature, not exceptional persons; principles before precedents; direct access of each to the light, not approach through title or grace of another; common duties, not exclusive rights; no hierarchies nor lordships, but natural citizenship the highest dignity, to which all exaltation returns,—it is one and the same key that unlocks the great questions, both in law and in faith. The same instinct that lifts the negro to political manhood, and makes democracy a success, refers Jesus to his own spiritual manhood, and vindicates religious freedom.—*Samuel Johnson.*

CULTURE DEMANDED BY MODERN LIFE.

The mind of our age is confronted with a host of urgent questions, such as the Perils of Misgovernment, the Limits of Legislation, the Management of Criminals, of the Insane, the Congenitally Defective, and the Pauper Class; the operation of Charities, the Philosophy of Philanthropy, the Relations of Sex and Race, International Ethics, the Freedom of Trade, the Rights of Industry, Property in Ideas, Public Hygiene, Primary Education, Religious Liberty, the Rights of Invention, Political Representation, and many others, which inosculate and interfuse into the great total of practical inquiry which challenges the intellect of our times; and it is this which the classical scholar evades, when he shrinks from the present and retires into the past. And well he may; for the mastery of the languages and literatures of Greece and Rome, and culture in unprogressive studies, furnish neither suitable ideas nor mental habits for this kind of work.

Science, grounding itself in the order and truth of nature, armed with the appropriate knowledge, and inspired with the hope of a better future, to which it sees all things tending, enters the great field, as properly its own, and will train its votaries to that breadth of view, that robust boldness of treatment, and that patient and dispassionate temper which imminent questions of the times so decisively demand.

In his late instructive lecture on the "Development of Ideas in Physical Science," Professor Leibig shows that it has been a slow organic growth, depending upon deeper conditions than the mere favor or opposition of Church or State. He shows that in Greece the progress of science was arrested by its slave-system, points out the necessity of abounding wealth to give leisure for thought and culture, and the importance of these social conditions which bring into intimate intercourse all classes of thinkers and workers, upon the mutual co-operation of which the advance of science and of society depends. He says: "*Freedom*, that is the absence of all restrictions which can prevent men from using to their advantage the powers which God has given them, is the mightiest of all the conditions of progress in civilization and culture;" and adds that "it can hardly be doubted that among the peoples of the North American Free States all the conditions exist for their development to the highest point of culture and civilization attainable by man."

These are weighty considerations for the educators of this country. Institutions are but expressions of ideas and habits; and the European policy, governmental and ecclesiastical, is grounded upon a culture suited to its necessities, and which has grown up with it in the course of ages. Both idolize the past; both worship precedent, and authority, and both dread independent inquiry into first principles; one recoils from Freedom as the other from Science. Freedom and Science, on the other hand, have had a coeval destiny; have suffered together and grown together. Both break from proscription and throw themselves upon Nature, and the watchword of both is Progress, which consists not in rejecting the past, but in subordinating and outgrowing it, in assimilating and reorganizing its truth, and leaving behind its obsolete forms. In the last century we threw off the trammels of the repressive system, and entered upon the experiment of Free Institutions; but it avails little to shift the external forms, if the old ideas are not replaced by new growths of thought and feeling.—*E. L. Youmans.*

THE THINKING MACHINE.

Men admire the steam engine of Watt, and the calculating engine of Babbage; but how little do they care for the thinking engine of the Infinite Artificer! They venerate days and dogmas, and ceremonials; but where is the reverence that is due to the most sacred of the things of time, the organism of the soul? We speak of the glories of the stellar universe; but is not the miniature duplicate of that universe in the living brain a more transcendent marvel? We admire the vast fabric of society and government, and that complicated scheme of duties, responsibilities, usages and laws which constitute order; but how few remember that all this has its deep foundation in the measured march of cerebral transformations. We point to the inventions, arts, sciences and literatures which form the swelling tide of civilization; but were they not all originated in that laboratory of wonders, the human brain? Geological revelations carry us back through durations so boundless that imagination is bewildered, and reason reels under the grandeur of the demonstration; but through the measureless series of advancing periods, we discover a stupendous plan. Infinite Power, working through infinite time, converges the mighty lines of causality to the fulfillment of an eternal design,—the birth of an intellectual and moral era through the development of the brain of man, which thus appears as the final term of an unfolding world. * *

The scientific method of studying human nature, important as may be its relation to the management of the insane and feeble-minded, and valuable as is its service in establishing the limits of mental effort, must find its fullest application to the broad subject of education. * * A knowledge of the being to be trained, as it is the basis of all intelligent culture, must be the first necessity of the teacher.—*E. L. Youmans.*

Growth and Self-Sacrifice.

There is a perpetual circle of beneficent change—of dissolution and reproduction. Such is the work of the year from summer to winter, from seed-time to harvest. Such is the revolution of ages and cyles of being. Descend into the recesses of the earth, into those immense catacombs where huge monsters lie packed away, each in its strong sarcophagus, like dead barbaric kings, with the wrecks of their dynasties around them.

There, in original fossil forms, behold the seeds of human civilization, and admire the process through which these things enriched the great economy by their death more than by their life. And thus it is everywhere. Loss, defeat, sacrifice, are the terms of reward and obedience, of growth and advancement

But the law of the natural (or material) is in this respect the law of the moral world. Let me then ask you to consider especially this process of growth and adornment as it appears in *human* affairs; in history and individual experience. "Except a corn of wheat fall into the ground and die, it abideth alone; but if it die it bringeth forth much fruit." See how the inmost principle of this fact appears in human action and the *discipline of character*.

Is it not true that increase of good, not only for others, but for ourselves, comes exactly in proportion as we extirpate *selfishness?* In this element, which, of course, I refer to in its mean and bad sense, all sin has its own roots; while on the other hand all virtue, all religious life, springs up in the denial of it, and the victory over it. Except man loves something, and lives for something besides himself, he does indeed "abide alone;" and his life is barren. He has wealth of blessedness and imparts none to others.

To be alone one need not go into a desert or a solitary chamber. The most gloomy, impenetrable loneliness is isolation of soul, is to live in a crowd without one pulse of sympathy or one reciprocal nerve. How lonely is a great city to such a man. Sometimes men are in such a position through no fault, but often through some inherent and haunting vice. And in this miserable sense the selfish man is alone. * * *

On the other hand, as we let narrow self-regard fall into the ground and die, as starting from the basis of lawful self-appreciation we go forward to help and bless others, and become part of the living world around us, not only does there spring up additional fruitage of good for humanity at large, but we, too, are made richer. A man feels that not only has he helped others, but that into himself has passed a joy and a power that abide forever.

Thus, in proportion as our action is broad and human, we

never die. We become identified with mankind at large, and are incorporated with all past efforts of nobleness and beneficence. Thus we go forth in the boundless light and free air of coming ages.

See how good and true men have lived in all ages and lands. Whose names are repeated from heart to heart and from lip to lip? Whose names stir the fresh blood of Liberty and the pulses of Virtue? Men in whom the contracted kernel of self has died! Others who have won a selfish glory, and cut a sword-path to fame, may linger for a time to blaze and astonish.

But these alone stand serene and beautiful, like stars, to attract the world's admiration and sway its best influences forever. It has well been said by another, "No great benefit, no extensive emancipation, whether from mental slavery, from political bondage, or from social evil, is ever wrought by humanity, unless the benevolent heart that undertakes the task has the strength of self-sacrifice and is content to lay its account with long-continued endurance and bitter agony. It is to such that the thoughts turn. When politicians express their allegiance to the cause of freedom, they pledge the memories of those who died on the field or on the scaffold. When the energies of nations awake, their minds first turn, not to those who have conquered, but to those who have fallen."

But the more closely the cause is connected with the spiritual, which is the permanent welfare of men, the more noble is the sacrifice made in its behalf, even to the wondrous death on the Cross. * * *

It is only to an limited and faithless eyesight that any righteous cause falling into the ground seems to perish. Scaffolds, despotisms, ruinous battle-fields—these are all conditions of the harvest. Truth, or justice, or liberty, swathe it with parchment cerements; dig its grave with bayonets; press it down with thorns, bastiles or slave-blocks; sprinkle it all over with the venerable dust of despotism, and in that dust trace the lines of its epitaph. It may be buried, but has it perished?

Can you bury the spirit of Christ? The earth rolls, the sun shines, the spring-winds blow, God's truth flows into the soul of men, and not a kernel of the righteous seed will fail to ripen at the last.

"God is patient for He is eternal." Let us not be dismayed in any private or public trial of this life, because our short reeds of measurement cannot mark out His great plan.

"Verily I say unto you, except a corn of wheat fall into the ground and die, it abideth alone; but if it die, it bringeth forth much fruit." What a sublime law and process does this proclaim! What vast consolation does it unfold! How pregnant with the inspiration of hope for ourselves and for the world! How calmly may we take up this truth and cling to it! Take it up and cling to it—in our trial for trust; in our action for effort; and in our survey of the general movement of things, for the indication of our faith in a just and beneficent, and advancing scheme of Providence.—*E. H. Chapin.*

Spiritual Views.

Spiritualists do not allege, or believe, that any of the phenomena in which they find proofs of immortality are miraculous. They believe in the universality of Law. They do not regard the signs and wonders that came to light in Jesus' day, as exceptions to natural law, but as phenomena which occurred under laws ever in force, but with which we are imperfectly acquainted. They see reproduced under their eyes modern types of most of these signs and wonders, and they find in such reproduction one of the strongest arguments to sustain the truth of the New Testament narative.

The *general* truth which is, after all, the essential; not each separate detail. Intelligent Spiritualists reject the doctrine of infallibility. They have no belief in *plenary* inspiration. They accept the advice of one of the Oxford Essayists, Dr. Temple, Chaplain in Ordinary to the Queen of Great Britain, when, speaking of two great volumes which he ascribed to the same author—the book of Nature and the book of Revelation—he said that if discrepancy appear between them it behooved us to consider, in the first place, whether we had not incorrectly interpreted the phenomena, and, in the second, whether the message might not have come to us perverted through the messenger. This is what orthodoxy must have to come to, if she would save the essentials of her creed.

But Spiritualists go a step further. They hold that a spiritual message itself may be an error, and that of this we must judge, reverently yet freely, as by our reason we test any earthly allegation, let it come from a source however accredited. This conviction is derived from another item in the Spiritual creed.

We believe that there are the same varieties of character in the next world as in this. We believe that when we cast off the natural body there is, indeed, a potent change from the lower to the higher, yet no instantaneous transformation of the soul; no apotheosis of some, and degradation to demon-life of others. When death calls, he neither deprives us of the virtues, nor suddenly relieves us of the vices, of which he finds us possessed. Both go with us. The moral, social and intellectual qualities which may have distinguished us in this world, will be ours in another, there constituting our identity and deciding our position. So also of the evil. That dark vestment of sin with which, in a man's journey through life, he may have become endued, clings to him through the death-change, close as the tunic of Nessus. He too retains his identity; his earthly short-comings determine his spiritual state.

We believe, then, that the spirit of man passes the ordeal without other metamorphosis than that which its release from the fleshy envelope and its acquisition of clearer perceptions effect: a great gainer, too, by this, that through the agency of the spiritual senses there is opened up a wider and more luminous horoscope; and thus drawn closer to the great Source of Wisdom; yet essentially the same spirit still. It changes, even as now it does, by the intervention of motive presented, by the agency of will, by the influence of surroundings better and nobler than those of earth. It changes, as it changed here, by its own aspirations. It inhabits a world of progress still; a world of active effort, not of passive beatitudes, nor yet of irrevocable doom.

We believe that the Christian world has been, and still is, blighted with false conceptions of Death. Men robe themselves in black when he appears; mourners go about the streets. The great punishment, the evil of evils, the primeval curse, declared to have been entailed on man by Adam's fall, is held to be that summons which calls him hence. Yet, under Omniscient Goodness, nothing so universal, so inevitable as death, ever was, or ever can be, essentially evil.—*Robert Dale Owen.*

Ministration of Departed Spirits.

While every year is taking one and another from the ranks of life and usefulness, or the charmed circle of friendship and love, it is soothing to remember that the spiritual world is gaining in riches through the poverty of this.

In early life, with our friends all around us—hearing their voices, cheered by their smiles,—death and the spiritual world are to us remote, misty, and half fabulous; but as we advance in our journey, and voice after voice is hushed, and form after form vanishes from our side, and our shadow falls almost solitary on the hillside of life, the soul, by a necessity of its being, tends to the unseen and spiritual, and pursues in another life those it seeks in vain in this. For with every friend that dies, dies also some peculiar form of social enjoyment, whose being depended on the peculiar character of that friend; till, late in the afternoon of life, the pilgrim seems to himself to have passed over to the unseen world, in successive portions, half his own spirit: and poor indeed is he who has not familiarized himself with that *unknown*, whither, despite himself, his soul is earnestly tending. One of the deepest and most imperative cravings of the human heart, as it follows its beloved ones beyond the veil, is for some assurance that they still love and care for us. Could we firmly believe this, bereavement would lose half its bitterness. As a German writer beautifully expresses it, "Our friend is not wholly gone from us: we see across the river of death, in the blue distance, the smoke of his cottage:" hence the heart, always creating what it desires, has ever made the guardianship and ministration of departed spirits a favorite theme of poetic fiction.

But is it, then, fiction? Does revelation, which gives so many hopes which nature had not, give none here? Is there no sober certainty to correspond to the inborn and passionate cravings of the soul? Do departed spirits in verity retain any knowledge of what transpires in this world, and take any part in its scenes?

All that revelation says of a spiritual state is more intimation than assertion; it has no distinct treatise, and teaches nothing, apparently, of set purpose, but gives vague glorious images, while now and then some accidental ray of intelligence looks out,

"Like eyes of cherubs shining
From out the veil that hid the ark."

But ou tof all the different hints and assertions of the Bible, we think a better inferential argument might be constructed to prove the ministrations of departed spirits, than for many a doctrine which has passed in its day for the height of orthodoxy.

First, then, the Bible distinctly says that there is a class of invisible spirits who minister to the children of men. "Are they not all ministering spirits sent forth to minister to those who shall be heirs of salvation?" It is said of little children, that "their angels do always behold the face of the Father which is in heaven." This last passage, from the words of our Saviour, taken in connection with the well-known tradition of his time, fully recognizes the idea of individual guardian spirits.

For God's government over minds is, it seems, throughout,

one of intermediate agencies; and these not chosen at random, but with the nicest reference to their adaptation to the purpose intended. * * * * * *

Is it likely, then, that, in selecting subordinate agencies, this, so necessary a requisite of a human life and experience, is overlooked? While around the throne of God stand spirits, now sainted and glorified, yet thrillingly conscious of a past experience of sin and sorrow, and trembling to the soul in sympathy with temptations and struggles like their own, is it likely that he would pass by these souls, thus burning for the work, and commit it to those bright abstract spirits whose knowledge and experience are comparatively so distant and so cold?

It is strongly in confirmation of this idea, that in the transfiguration scene, which seems to have been intended purposely to give the disciples a glimpse of the glorified state of their Master, we find Him attended by two spirits of earth, Moses and Elias, "which appeared to Him in glory, and spake of His death which He should accomplish at Jerusalem."

It appears that these so long departed ones were still mingling in deep sympathy with the tide of human affairs, not only aware of the present, but also informed of the future.

What then? May we look among the band of ministering spirits for our own departed ones? Whom would God be more likely to send us? Have we in heaven a friend who knew us to the heart's core,—a friend to whom we have unfolded our soul in its most secret recesses; to whom we have confessed our weaknesses, and deplored our griefs? If we are to have a ministering spirit, who better adapted?

Have we not memories which correspond to such a belief? When our soul has been cast down, has never an invisible voice whispered, "There is lifting up?" Have not gales and breezes of sweet and healing thought been wafted over us, as if an angel had shaken from his wings the odors of paradise? Many a one, we are confident, can remember such things; and whence come they?

Why do the children of a pious mother, whose grave has grown green and smooth with years, seem often to walk through perils and dangers fearful and imminent as the crossing Mohammed's fiery gulf on the edge of a drawn sword, yet walk unhurt? Ah! could we see that glorious form, that face where the angel conceals not the mother, our question would be answered.

It may be possible that a friend is sometimes taken because the divine One sees that his ministry can act upon us more powerfully from the unseen world than amid the infirmities of mortal intercourse.

Here the soul, distracted and hemmed in by human events and by bodily infirmities, often scarce knows itself, and makes no impression on others correspondent to its desires. The mother would fain electrify the heart of her child. She yearns and burns in vain to make her soul effective on its soul, and to inspire it with a spiritual and holy life; but all her own weakness, faults, and mortal cares, cramp and confine her, till death breaks all fetters: and then, first truly alive, risen, purified, and at rest, she may do calmly, sweetly, and certainly, what, amid the tempest and tossings of life, she labored for painfully and fitfully.

So, also, to generous souls who burn for the good of man, who deplore the shortness of life, and the little that is permitted to any individual agency in this life, does this belief open a heavenly field. Think not, father or brother long laboring for man, till thy sun stands on the western mountains,—think not that thy day in this world is over. Perhaps, like Jesus, thou hast lived a human life, and gained a human experience, to become, under and like him, a saviour of thousands. Thou hast been through the preparation; but thy real work of good, thy full power of doing, is yet to begin.

There are some spirits (and those of earth's choicest) to whom, so far as enjoyment to themselves or others is concerned, this life seems to have been a total failure. A hard hand from the first, and all the way through life, seems to have been laid upon them: they seem to live only to be chastened and crushed; and we lay them in the grave at last in solemn silence. To such, what a vision is opened by this belief! This hard discipline has been the school and task-work by which their soul has been fitted for their invisible labors in a future life; and when they pass the gates of the grave, their course of benevolent acting first begins, and they find themselves delighted possessors of what through many years they have sighed for,—the power of doing good.

The year just passed, like all other years, has taken from a thousand circles the sainted, the just, and the beloved; there are spots in a thousand graveyards, which have become this year dearer than all the living world: but in the loneliness of sorrow, how cheering to think that our lost ones are not wholly gone from us! They still may move about in our homes, shedding around them an atmosphere of purity and peace, promptings of good, and reproofs of evil: we are compassed about with a cloud of witnesses, whose hearts throb in sympathy with every effort and struggle, and who thrill with joy at every success. How should this thought check and rebuke every worldly feeling and unworthy purpose, and enshrine us, in the midst of a forgetful and unspiritual world, with an atmosphere of heavenly peace! They have overcome, have risen, are crowned, glorified; but still they remain to us, our assistants, our comforters; and in every hour of darkness their voice speaks to us: "So we grieved, so we struggled, so we fainted, so we doubted; but we have overcome, we have obtained, we have seen and found all true; and in our heaven behold the certainty of thy own."—*Harriett Beecher Stowe.*

Future Life Near and Real.

I confess to you there is something in my mind of sublimity in the idea that the world is full of spirits, good and evil, and the little we can see with these bat's eyes of ours, the little we can decipher with these imperfect senses, is not the whole of the reading of those vast pages of that great volume which God has written. * * * Doubtless there are vulgar spirits. * * On the other hand, I believe there are angels of light, spirits of the blessed, ministers of God. I believe not only that they are our natural guardians and friends, and teachers, and influencers, but that they are the natural antagonists of evil spirits. In other words, I believe that the great realm of life goes on without the body, very much as it does with the body. And as here the mother not only is the guardian of her children whom she loves, but foresees that bad associates and evil influences threaten them, and draws them back and shields them from impending danger; so ministering spirits not only minister to us the divinest tendencies, the purest tastes, the noblest thoughts and feelings, but, perceiving our adversaries, caution us against them, assail them, and drive them from us. * * * *

Out of the dust and the dim, and mists and observations of life, there come moments when God permits us to see, in a second, farther, wider, and easier, than by ordinary methods of logic we can see in a whole life. Do I undervalue logic when I say it is inferior to intuition? Intuition at a white heat teaches a man in a single moment more than logic ever teaches him. Logic constructs the walls of thought, throws up ramparts, and lays out highways; but it never *discovers*. The discovering power is intuition. There are certain times when parts of the mind lift themselves up with a kind of celestial preparation, and we see and think and feel more in a single hour than ordinarily in a year. However useful and needful reasoning may be as compared with these sudden insights, it is scarcely to be mentioned with respect.

Ordinarily we are under the influence of things which are seen, and of the senses; but now and then, we know not how, we rise into an atmosphere in which Spirit-life, God, Christ, the ransomed throng in heaven, virtue, truth, faith and love, become more significant to us, and seem to rest down upon us with more force than the very things which our physcal senses recognize. There have been times in which, I declare to you, heaven was more real than earth; in which my children that were gone spoke more plainly to me than my children that were with me; in which the blessed estate of the just man in heaven seemed more real and near to me than the estate of any just man upon earth.

There are experiences that link one with another and higher life.—*Henry Ward Beecher.*

How Ideas get Spoken—Reformers.

There is this singular peculiarity about the men who first receive ideas,—they cannot keep them. When the rising sun gilded the face of the Egyptian Memnon he answered the light with songs; so, when the light of truth gilds our mental horizon, we cry out at the beautiful vision. No sooner does the man perceive that he has a new idea, than he becomes impressed that he has a mission. It is not egotism; it is not a desire for notoriety. The same power which gave him the idea filled him with an irresistible impulse to reveal it. He cannot conceal it; he rushes forth to light the lamp of his neighbors. He cannot be diverted. Wealth, ease, comfort, home, wife, children, friends, the gentle amenities of life, may plead; and poverty, disgrace, ruin, and martyrdom with rod, fire, and dungeon may menace,—he rushes on to promulgate the idea. He has gained an insight into the everlasting, the inscrutable; and his lips glow with the words with which he sets it forth. He controlled by the soft pleasures of this life? They are ephemeral. He proselyted? Never. In him an idea, for the first time since creation, has found a tongue of flame. It is no fault of his that he becomes fanatical, and overestimates the importance of his treasure. The world gains by the equilibrium resulting from a thousand such. Stand aloof, men of the world, who cannot understand anything unless it is set down in dollars and cents, quarts and bushels. Stand aside! you are the dead freight which such fanatics are to carry through; and the only possible use you serve is a retarding influence which, out of kindness, we call conservatism, by which you keep them in sight. * * * *

The world to-day has outgrown its yesterday's thoughts. Each year adds growth to the moral and intellectual world, as the circling sun adds a new layer to the tree. Each year's growth encircles all others; or in other words, the ideas of the race are higher, its attainments more noble, and it basks in a brighter light. Each year adds to the moral and intellectual temperature of mind; makes it glow with superior truth and wisdom. This growth, slow but visible, is a progress as uncontrollable as the movement of the heavenly bodies around their central suns.

Grown toward manhood, and the infant garments cannot be strained on. * * Creeds and dogmas are such garments to the spirit. When the expanding mind is forced to take up its abode in the habiliments of the past, its best motives are crushed; its feelings are stifled; its holiest emotions dried up; and it becomes barren as the desert sands of Sahara, cold and frigid as the icebergs around the frozen poles. * *

It matters little whether born on a throne or in a manger; when reformers arise in their manhood all conventionalities crumble away, and king and peasant stand in the same light. When sublime intuitions fill their overflowing souls and they reveal man's relations to the universe and to his fellow man, distinctions vanish in the rapturous glow of eloquence, as the frost-work of night vanishes in the rays of the rising sun. Confucius was nobly born; Zoroaster stated his ideas from a throne; Mohammed was a noble; their converts count by the hundred million. Eighteen centuries ago a poor carpenter's son was cradled in a manger, and arose and with a breath overturned all the cherished idols of his time, and founded a system of transcendental purity, which is the ideal, even now, of the civilized world.—*Hudson Tuttle.*

Treatment of Criminals.

We believe that in the treatment of criminals, the first and paramount object, should be to reform them, and that the best interests of society would be promoted by the means best adapted to secure this end. It is necessary to restrain offenders against the laws of morality, but care should be taken to bring them under such moral influences as will tend to develop in them the power of self-government. The prisoner should be made to feel that the discipline to which he is subjected is dictated by love to him no less than by a regard for the welfare of the community; and he should be encouraged by the assurance that the government will gladly restore him to liberty just as soon as it can do so with safety to himself and to society. Prisons should be under the control of persons of the highest moral qualifications, and their inmates should be visited by those who feel a tender concern for their welfare.—*Pennsylvania Yearly Meeting of Progressive Friends, Longwood, Pa., 1860.*

Friends of Human Progress.

Yearly meetings at Collins, Erie County, at Waterloo, Seneca County, New York, and at Sturgis, Michigan; for free and orderly discussion.

Resolved, That while we renew and emphasize our testimony, and keep up our efforts in behalf of the practical Reforms of the day, we deem it of high importance as foundation work for character, and attainment of true manhood and womanhood, that freedom of the soul be asserted and maintained inviolate; such freedom as is loyal to the truths of the spirit within us, truths which shall grow in power and beauty, as superstitions decay, as creeds are put aside, and as books are used as helpers, and not accepted as masters.

Resolved, That we urge as an important part of true religion, what may be termed the religion of the body; that reverence for its delicate offices and sacred functions which shall lead to purity of thought and of personal habits, to control over appetite and passion, to abstinence from all that is injurious, and temperance in all that is healthful, and shall put aside all filthy and degrading practices and defilements, and make our common food and drink a daily sacrament of health and purity, fitting the body for the uses of life, and making it a consecrated temple for the immortal spirit.

Resolved, That over every Judge's bench and over the doors of every prison should be written, "Justice, Safety, Reform, uplifting of the weak and the depraved, but no vengeance." And that we would aid every change in prison discipline, and every step in the treatment of criminals that reaches above vengeance, and has in view that more perfect safety that comes with the reform of the erring.

Resolved, That we favor equal suffrage and equality of rights for woman, *because it is just and therefore full of benefit.*—

These resolutions were passed at all the meetings.

Dogma vs. Truth.

If we deny that God had revealed himself to all mankind, *our creed is little better than open atheism*, for we deny the original gift of his free grace to the human soul.

But the reverent and enlightened mind, who receives Him in the way of his coming, can read the ancient conceptions of mankind, whether in the Scriptures of the Jews, the Christians, the Vedas, the Avestas, the writings of Seneca or Plato, or the monuments of Egypt or Babylon, with a grateful interest that they have been preserved from the tooth of time. He will not, however, build his faith upon these: *for then his faith becomes a superstition, which in the end will but blind his spiritual vision and blunt the perceptions of his soul.*

In a recent address a Hindoo convert said: "I go to India to preach a universal faith; I shall not tell the people our Scriptures are all right, and yours all a delusion and folly, but I shall appeal to the beautiful and true in both to demonstrate the universality of God's love."

This is the frame of mind in which man should approach his brother. * * * And we will be willing to apply the same rule of common sense and just criticism to the Writings we have received from our Fathers, that we apply to the Scriptures of the Hindoos, or the Wisdom of Confucius. The golden rule will be ours—we will mete out unto others that which we would have them measure to us. * * * *

As Dr. Arnold says, " Faith without reason is not properly faith, but mere power-worship; and power-worship may be devil-worship, for it is reason which entertains the idea of God, an idea essentially made up of truth and goodness no less than power."

This was the great thought of Jesus; and yet to-day how much of that which is taught in his name is but mere power-worship! The truthful mind, therefore, has no other alternative but to accept the language of Dr. Arnold, and "to pronounce it not to be God's voice; for no sign of power, in confirmation of it, can alone prove it to be of God."

Dogma cannot establish the immortality of our nature to the satisfaction of a single mind. It is the soul that speaks, and the reason which listens to the knowledge which God himself conveys. *Providence has granted to all men this voice.* The avenues or channels through which divine information flows to the soul can be closed or obstructed by sin or superstition; and spiritual darkness thus intervenes. The only means by which the obstruction can be removed is *by removing the cause.*

Popular Christianity holds up the idea of belief or dogma as the constituent or first principle in religion; hence the degraded condition of the Christian world, and hence the assertion that all communication from God is confined to a book written many hundreds of years ago. * *

Evangelical Christianity is to-day seeking to engraft upon the Constitution of Washington, Jefferson, and Madison, its narrow, unphilosophical, untenable, and uncharitable creed. To correct this tendency of the Church let enlightened views be disseminated in men's minds; and the time may come, in the Providence of God, when we can adopt the language of the poet-laureate of England,—

"Ring out the old, ring in the new,
Ring out the false, ring in the true."

Will this lead us to undervalue the books of the olden time? Not so! The conceptions that ancient people have formed will become more valuable and dearer to us, because we appreciate them in the light of reason and truth.—*David Newport, Pa.* (*Member of Society of Friends—"Hicksite."*)

THE GOD-GIVEN POWER TO SEE OR RECEIVE A TRUTH, IS GOD'S COMMAND TO IMPART IT.

I regard all *truth* as coming from God, and hence eternal, universal, always good, and from its nature incapable, when rightly used, of being *anything but good*, to any person, at any time or place. There is, and can be, no new truth. Every truth, however recently discovered, has existed through all time; every philosophical or mathematical principle, every property of material bodies, is eternal. No matter when or by whom it was discovered, *it pre-existed* in the Divine Mind, and is the embodiment of a Divine thought.

When Dr. Herschel and Leverier discovered a "new planet," they were but favored to see what had always existed; the *discovery* was new, not the object discovered; and so of each principle or property in physical science. The same holds of spiritual truths, which are as much realities as physical truths. They are from the same eternal source, and communicated in like manner whenever a mind or soul is *prepared*—that is, sufficiently enlightened, expanded or purified—to receive them. Every such revelation, spiritual or physical, *is for good to mankind;* as witness the happy influences of the many physical discoveries and devices within the past century upon the comfort, convenience and interests of humanity.

"Every good and perfect gift is *from above*, from the Father of Light, with whom is no variableness nor shadow of turning;"

but these "good gifts" existing from creation have not been imparted to man, many of them, until the past half century. There must be a cause for this, something has changed, I think it is man. So far from man being a fallen being, and his *highest condition past,* the human family has advanced so that man occupies a higher plane than was before. He has come nearer to God, and been enabled to partake more of His image, both in the creative faculty, so to call it, and in the diffusion of blessings to his fellow-creatures. * * * But this *preparation* must be by man; he must put inquiries to nature; and attentively and patiently await her answers. * * *

Not that the highest degree is yet attained; great blessings, no doubt, are still in the Divine Treasury, waiting until some one is sufficiently advanced or elevated to receive them, and add them to the long list of "good gifts." * * *

Now let it be observed emphatically, that these revelations, as I term them, or the knowledge of these truths and laws that have proved of such incalculable benefit to man, have not been made to or obtained by the idle and thoughtless, but they are the reward of the industrious, patient, devoted *worker*, the close *observer*, the man who questions nature with an unshaken confidence in the uniformity of her laws, which are the laws of God, and partake of His unchangeable wisdom and goodness.

All this, in my confident belief, is equally true of spiritual realities and the revelations of spiritual truths, which make up the heart or condition of humanity. Every added one expands the mind or soul, and increases its enlightenment. Their being successively imparted is interesting evidence of the progress of humanity. They are not revealed to the idle and thoughtless, but to the industrious and devoted seeker into the depths of his spiritual nature, watchfully observing the changes in his own moral consciousness, inquiring into the causes by which these changes are produced, and by the aid of that Light which is freely furnished, discovering spiritual truths never before revealed. By this means he becomes deeply instructed in spiritual things, learns the nature and power of spiritual influences and forces, and that they are as real and invariable as those that govern material bodies. When not restrained by considerations of policy arising from Society organizations, there is the same noble impulse to impart what has been discovered, to share with others the treasure found, and place it in the stock of common knowledge.

In every department of science, whose votaries make known every discovery, or what was believed to be such, as soon as it was made, there has been a great and steady advance. One discovery prepared the way for another.

In the *spiritual* department, if so it may be termed, the case has been very different. The field has been largely occupied, but the advance, if whatever change has been produced can be called an advance, has been comparatively very slow. For this there must be some cause, and this must be with *man*, not *God*. He would surely reveal truths connected with man's higher life and eternal interests as freely and fully as He has revealed those in other departments.

The hindering cause or causes are principally two. A conviction has obtained that all revelation has ceased, that the whole mind and will of God respecting man is contained in the Bible; that every spiritual discovery or illumination must conform to what is therein recorded, thus regarding any advance as unhoped for and impossible, and that the *only* means of progress in a knowledge of spiritual truths is to study this Book.

The second impediment is a prevailing belief that a knowledge of spiritual truths is not obtained through devotedness, inquiry and observation directed to the influences of our consciousness, but that God reveals these truths, not naturally, but supernaturally, to a favored few, and also that there must be a great discrimination when and to whom these truths are imparted; so that those who have been enabled to see more advanced and elevated truths, are restrained from disseminating them lest they should thereby disturb the harmony of the religious organization of which they are members. In this respect, Society organization, though possessed of so many advantages, has been a bond and restraint, preventing its development and growth.

With these views, which I honestly entertain, it will be seen why I regard the God-given power to receive a Truth, to be God's command to communicate it; believing it to be for the benefit of the race and not of the individual alone. Doubts have a right place in the mental and spiritual economy. They lead to a deeper and more careful examination of the subject in search of evidence to establish the Truth. Plant Truth, propagate and cultivate Truth, and then in accordance with the theory of "natural selection" that the strongest will prevail, Truth being stronger than all opposing principles, and possessed of greater vitality and power, will flourish and spread. —*Benjamin Hallowell, Maryland* (*Member of Society of Friends—"Hicksite."*)

The Lesson of Quakerism—The Inward Light.

The distinctive doctrine of Quakerism is the affirmation of "the immediate teaching and influence of the Holy Spirit" in the human soul. It has no elaborately wrought creed, or articles of faith. Among Friends there is a general unity of belief concerning the immediate teaching of the spirit; but a diversity of opinion in relation to other points of doctrine. It is not my aim to plead for sect, either Orthodox or Hicksite. The estimate of human nature which the doctrine of the "Inner Light" necessitates is an exalted one. Logically it subordinates everything else. "The witness within" sits in judgment upon every message, verbal or written, upon every action as well. There is no room left for a Bible of absolute authority, none for the functions of an exclusive Mediator and Saviour. *All* are children of the Father, and joint heirs in his divinely-human household. We do not need to seek to drag Jesus down, or to lessen his legitimate scope of influence. It should be our business, as it was his, to lift all humanity up to the same level of immediate, conscious communication and fellowship with God. This has been pre-eminently the mission of Quakerism.

The Rights of Women.

George Fox was an early defender of the right of women to speak in churches. Hearing of a great union meeting to be held at Leicester, wherein Presbyterians, Independents, Baptists, and Episcopalians were to unite in the discussion of religious topics, George Fox attended it. During the progress of the meeting, a woman started a question about some saying by the Apostle Peter. The presiding priest, instead of entertaining or answering her question, said to her, "I permit not a woman to speak in the church;" though he had before given liberty for any one to speak. This so outraged Fox's sense of justice and propriety, and so kindled his zeal, that he stepped up and asked the priest, "Dost thou call this place (the Steeple House) a church? Or dost thou call this mixed multitude a church?" But the priest, Yankee like, answered, by asking him what a church was; when Fox replied that "The church was the pillar and ground of truth, made up of living stones, living members, a spiritual household, which Christ was the head of; but he was not the head of a mixed multitude, or of an old house made of lime, stones and wood." This caused such a stir that the priest came down out of his pulpit, others came out of their pews, and the meeting broke up in confusion. Many followed Fox to an inn, where the discussion was continued, and several were converted by him to Quakerism, among them the woman who asked the question and who was forbidden to speak in the church.

Other women were convinced by his teaching, and shared with men, with quiet courage and rare moral heroism, the fearful persecution and untold sufferings in which all were involved by devotion to the truth as it became known to them.

PEACE.

From the beginning, Friends have been advocates of Peace. A Quaker civilization would abolish armies and navies; do away with all war and preparations for war. It would eliminate altogether the principle of destructive force from governmental organizations. Carried out to its ultimate, it would abolish sheriffs, magistrates and lawyers, and obliterate the lines of distinction between Church and State. Politics would become religious in the best sense, and religion would have to do mainly with human needs in this phase of life. There would be due self-respect, and therefore respect on the part of each for the rights of all. The bare mention of such a state of society, contrasted with the present, only serves to show the broad margin of difference between the doctrines of most other sects and those of Quakerism, and between the so-called Christian civilization of to-day, and what is contemplated in the teachings of Jesus, as attainable by men and women. However distant in the future may be the full realization of this beneficent, peaceful dispensation, all who have faith in the capacity of human progress, and in an advancing civilization, must needs keep it steadily in view.—*A. M. Powell, N. Y.*

QUIETISM AND WORK.

Generally the trials and sins of men come of magnifying the present incident, putting too much emphasis upon what they would gain, making undue account of the besetments and annoyances of the hour. They fail to endure as seeing the invisible. * * * Shall we never overcome these intoxications and exaggerations, and see and dwell in the real and unchanging? We need to transfuse the transient with the perennial, and behold each day overarched with the forever.

The royal souls, remarkable for their possession and strength, mounting superior to all and living above sin, seem to have been those who were penetrated wtth this element, able to keep constantly in eye the great considerations. They never drank intoxication, maintained a perfect sobriety and sanity throughout. * * In presence of the grave, of onflowing time, silence of the everlasting, the passions of men are hushed : the resentments cease to follow there. With perfect consideration ever, we should be in perfect poise, never a ruffle upon the bosom of the deep sea of our peace.

It is plain, however, that there are qualifications for all this thing, counter-truths that must not be overlooked. If there were no want, no incitement, there would be no movement, no action or life. The supreme world speaks to us as law. Existence is not quiescence : the virtues are not passive solely. There are stakes to be contended for, heights to be won, victories to be earned. We are in time, and our present possession is not infinite. It would seem the very solution itself of the contradiction is a contradiction. The repose is in action : the rest is by motion. The eternal is to be sought by successive advances in time : we are to grasp the transcendant, the ideal, in the actual; substance, in the forms. We are to renounce, to realize; and to pursue, to realize; to seek, to cling to, to fasten upon, to reach the intangible and everlasting.

All the great deeds of history have been done under an intensity of impression, a power of conviction, a sense of *must*, that burned and melted all before it. It seems to be essential to any performance that the mind should be charged, we might say overcharged, with the imperative weight of the work. Eternity is to be so realized in time, and the god takes our eyes with illusion. Life is a conflict, and ever a kind of contradiction : two opposing elements are converged and blended in each single instant. To fulfill well our mission we must see time also, and read the imperative command of the moment and the hour. The high wisdom is to read aright, and to marry and blend action in repose, perfect doing with perfect peace.

It is an old feud that has divided the quietists from the workers : it has always been hard to reconcile the antagonisms, and there has been some lack of appreciation and fairness on both sides. These two sects have always, that is, among the earnest people, divided the world. On the one side is meditation, on the other exertion; on one, satisfaction, at least calm, on the other thirst, solicitude, the ambitions of doing. They charge haste, and impatience of accomplishment, and a certain intolerance, upon the doers: these charge indisposition to work, a lazy optimism, and criminal indifference, upon those. One is the saintship of zeal, and frequently of heat and impoise: the other is the saintship of inner containing, and not seldom of unlawful renunciation. The full union and reconciliation of the two traits we do not yet find in society or individuals. It is a very nice medium to hit. The optimism must be conquest, the faith that is intense love and serene victory, the zeal of devotion, the recognized claim of the everlasting, and resting in the everlasting, the two virtues blent indissolubly into one as in the godhead in the heavens. Perhaps it will need more age and ripeness to the race, finer births, to make approximation to the true ideal to any large extent possible. * * We need to be reminded constantly of the unshifting, the eternal element. There is so much of stir, pressure, and heat, so little of poise in the world. But this is not all: we need action, a true recognition, and royal fealty. There is great lack of this, a criminal optimism, a disposition to excuse ourselves, and dwell in trust and quiescence, inertia, rather than in wrestling, prevailing prayer. So the world, much as it needs teachers of the former, still needs prophets and evangelists of the latter.—*C. D. B. Mills, Syracuse, N. Y.*

Christ's Character—The Real Gospel.

The world itself is changed, and is no more the same that it was; it has never been the same since Jesus left it. The air is charged with heavenly odors, and a kind of celestial consciousness, a sense of other worlds is wafted on us in its breath. Let the dark ages come, let society roll backward, and churches perish in whole regions of the earth, let infidelity deny, and what is worse, let spurious piety dishonor the truth; still there is a something here that was not, and a something that has immortality in it. Still our confidence remains unshaken, that Christ and his all-quickening life are in the world, as fixed elements, and will be to the end of time. For Christianity is not so much the advent of a better doctrine, as of a perfect character; and how can a perfect character, once entered into life and history, be separated and finally expelled? It were easier to untwist all the beams of light in the sky, separating and expunging one of the colors, than to get the character of Jesus, which is the real gospel, out of the world.—*Horace Bushnell.*

Natural Religion.

But some may say there are no motives in Natural Religion, no commands of God to be obeyed with gain, or disobeyed with loss.

No man has talked with God, God has talked with no man. But the commands are there, written in the constitution and relation of things; written on the body, and the soul, and the earth, and the heavens. Is there no motive to abstain from drunkenness but the command of God in the Bible? Drunkenness will bring sickness, poverty, disgrace, sorrow to friends, *delirium tremens*, premature death, debasement of soul. Are not these sufficient motives? This which is true of drunkenness, is true of everything in the world.

Why should we keep the Sabbath? Because God commanded it? The Mohammedans keep Friday; the Jews, Saturday; the Christians, Sunday. There is not a word in the Bible to indicate that we are to rest on the first day of the week! There is a positive command to keep the seventh; yet we refuse to keep the seventh, and do keep the first. All days are alike holy. The motive to keep Sunday is not in the command of God, there exists no such command; the motive is in the welfare of society.

A great many people fear that if we break away from the supernatural, we break away from religion. No: we only break away from superstition.

Among the believers of all revealed religions there are some base, some noble, some irreligious. As an eminent author has justly remarked, the shortness of time has furnished as many arguments to the debauchee as to the devotee. That scheme which says a man must repent in order to be saved, says also that one may repent at any time—on a sick bed and in old age; and that in repentance all sins will be washed away. On this theory, therefore, many people conclude to take their fill of sin in their healthy years, hoping to find time to repent in their old age or on the bed of death. A belief in Natural Religion will do more to prevent iniquity than any other, because nature cannot be improved. Her penalties are sure: they are sufficient and only sufficient. Exact justice, which cannot be escaped, nature metes to all. When people believe this, they will be careful not to violate nature's laws.

Watts says, and he utters the spirit of Christendom, "Blind unbelief is sure to err." All that is true, but more, also is true. "Blind belief is sure to err." Hundreds of people, through a lingering superstition of the power of faith, cling to old notions and doctrines as though there were merit in believing, and they will therefore believe to the last moment. There is no merit in belief. We ought to believe just so far as there is reason, and no farther. An honest doubter is as acceptable to God as an honest believer; the merit is in the honesty, not in the doubt nor belief. In Natural Religion, faith without evidence is sin. We believe in faith; we cherish it; but no farther than we find a rock foundation on which it may rest.

The great obstacle which stands in the way of Protestants is the prejudice that there can be no imperfection in the Bible. They refuse to hear anything except what is taught from its pages or said in its defense. The great requirement of the present, is to get our hearts open, and our ears open, so as to learn all there is to learn in the world. All that helps truth helps religion. Natural religion accepts a cheerful face and believes in a cheerful heart. Sorrow is inevitable with imperfection, but in order to be religious, it is not necessary to artificially increase it. Man is the only laughing animal, and a good laugh is as acceptable to God as a good cry. Both have their uses. The long-faced, austere, ascetic Christianity is not natural. The pain that comes is to be bravely borne, but we are not to seek it. Seek the sunshine—make life as pleasant and joyous as it can be made.

Take good care of human nature, and you take good care of religion. Out of the best human hearts grows the best religion, as largest crops grow from the finest soil. Cultivate, make rich, make broad, make sympathetic, make true and noble the souls of men, and you are sure to grow the noblest religion. Human nature in its healthy development bring forth good.—*Herman Bisbee, Wisconsin.*

Immortality in the Light of Science.

The earliest and most durable records of humanity are records of spiritual impulses, hopes, faiths,—gropings of the human mind to adjust its relations, speculatively and practically, with some mysterious Power believed to rule the universe,—reachings out and up of the finite into the infinite. But all the facts on this side of human experience these scientists ignore. They confine their attention to physical phenomena, and do not consider the phenomena of faith, reverence, worship. And yet these latter phenomena, whatever their origin, make up half of the recorded history of mankind, and present the facts that bear most intimately on this question of immortality. That surely can be no complete science which ignores them. And there is another class of phenomena, which, however much scientific men may now deride them, and however much of fraud and charlatanism may be mixed up with them, will persist, I believe, in forcing themselves upon human attention until science shall give them a just investigation and recognition. I refer to the phenomena of mesmerism, clairvoyance, animal magnetism, along with which whatever is well authenticated in "Spiritualism" is to be placed. What shall we say of that bond between two lives, hundreds of miles apart in space, which, like an electric wire, gives instantaneous intelligence of the experience of the one to the other? Of this we have well-authenticated instances, and among persons not easily deluded and not addicted to implicit acceptance of every new thing that appears. Science may treat these reports all alike with incredulity and contempt (as many of them deserve to be treated); but then life, as science confesses, is riddle upon riddle, and its secrets are not yet all guessed. And I believe it will be found in the end that this class of phenomena to which I now refer, and which are so closely related to the mysterious connection that exists between mind and body, will, when investigated and classified, have an important bearing on the revelation of things pertaining to the future that are now inscrutable to reason.

One other defect I have to note in the argument of those men of science who undertake positively to deny immortality. They frequently leave the calm, judicial tone of pure science, which simply reports facts and lets them fall, as it were, of their own gravity into system, and write like interested advocates of their hypothesis. They become partizan and dogmatic. Some of them are guilty of as pure dogmatism as are the theologians and ecclesiastics whom they treat with such disdain. When Büchner, for instance, warms into indignant eloquence over the tediousness and horror of the very conception of eternal existence, which he contrasts with the welcome repose of annihilation, we see that he has left the character of the student of science and put on the robes of the priest. The passage betrays that he is not writing from facts, but from a prepossessed opinion. So when, in opposition to the theory that the soul may have in its future life a body similar to its present, but more refined and ethereal, he declares that "the human body is composed of the most delicate and most perfect organs and cannot be conceived to become still finer and more perfect," we are reminded of that theological dogmatism which undertakes to assert that this or that doctrine must answer the needs of men for all time, that a certain religious system is completely rounded and contains all possible truth, or that some historical character has given an example ultimate and absolute for all human attainment and can never in all the eternities be surpassed.

The primordial substance, force, power, whatever it is in essence, from which all things have been evolved, must have been, as we have already seen, germinal with intelligence as well as with material energy and form. This fact in some shape is admitted by these scientists. Buchner allows a "formative principle in the organic and inorganic world." Dr. Carpenter, writing on the subject of *vital force*, discussing the question whether it is something apart from matter itself, says: "What the germ really supplies is not the force, but the directive agency." Something of this kind has to be admitted in order to account for the fact that things are produced not by hap-hazard, but according to certain types; that one germ-cell for instance, develops into a bird, and another, not distinguishable from it, into a man. Even though the types have all come by the gradual action of "natural selection" from one type, that does not avoid the necessity of admitting a "formative principle" somewhere. This "formative principle," or "directive agency," may not be a separate entity from the matter in which it works. We need not necessarily conceive of it as a creative spirit or force apart from matter and acting upon it from the outside. Let it be inherently involved in the very existence of matter,—something inseparable from its original substance: still, it implies intelligence, purpose, volition. Matter and spirit may be one and indivisible, but both must be represented in the primary essence of the universe, since both have appeared in the phenomena of the universe. The scientific conception of them must be that they are equally eternal in essence. And the whole history of the universe, its varied evolutions, developments, manifestations of force, productions of organism, types of being, systems and creatures, may be scientifically represented as the result of the mutual action of these two elements. The directive agency is working its way out of chaos into and through material forms, and rising constantly to higher manifestation of itself therein. In man it comes to self-conscious ness. Doubtless by the principle of correlation we may trace a thread of identity between the inanimate law of the inorganic world, the instinct of the vegetable and animal kingdoms, the semi-reason and volition of the higher species of the brute creation, and the self-conscious intelligence and free moral choice that belong to civilized man. These may all be regarded as phases and stages in the progress of the same formative principle. It may even be admitted that there are some glimmerings of self-conscious intelligence, and even perhaps of a moral sense, in animal races that are below man, and that were antecedent to him in the process of evolution. Still when the organism of man is reached after this long process of development, the elements of this primary formative principle expand and flower into vastly more wonderful phenomena,—into conscious reflection, moral perception and purpose, will and foresight; into self-sacrificing beneficence and love; into not merely *perceptions* of existing order and beauty and goodness, but abstract *conceptions* of an ideal Excellence beyond anything that sense or experience reveals; and, more than all, into a creative, intelligent energy, which is capable of taking up nature's thought and processes, and voluntarily carrying them forward, in a sense, to still higher completion. All these powers did not, it is true, suddenly appear in full fruition with the appearance of human beings on the planet. They, too have come by the slow gradation of development. But they have appeared in man as they have appeared in no race below or anterior to him. And they make man what no other order of beings on earth is, a rational observer and student of nature, and an intelligent, free co-worker with her forces. We may say, indeed, that with the human race a new form of force, a new development of vital energy, comes into the universe. It is the force of personality. Man has the ability to convert by rational choice the resources and powers of nature to the service of his purposes. He is free to make all forms of force and life that were before him tributary to his being. Thus he has the power voluntarily and consciously to progress upon his own nature. That capacity of progress (through the law of "natural selection," or by any other method) which, in the development of organic life anterior to him, has been shown in the advance from type to type, reappears in him transmuted into intelligent and moral volition. Henceforward progress is secured, not by the production of one type from another, but by conscious development within the human type. The productive directing agency having become consciously creative in man, his nature is germinal with all future types, and he is able himself to realize them without any break in his conscious identity. An ideal is ever before him, and ever he advances to its attainment, ideal upon ideal continually leading him on. And this is true of the individual and of the race.

Even if we keep, then, on the ground of these scientific materialists, remaining faithful to the doctrine of the correlation and conservation of forces and allowing it to be applied to mental phenomena, we may still say that in the intellectual, moral, and spiritual contents of consciousness, man carries elements of being that are indestructible. Let them be phenomena: they are phenomena that presuppose a substance that has existed from eternity and that cannot be conceived as passing out of existence. Admit that they would not have come, save through the physical organism with which they are connected; still, the germ of them is not the organism, but existed anterior to it, and helped in its production. That is, the directive energy, the formative principle, from which side of the primitive substance of things mind must be said to have come, has been as necessary in the production of the physical organism as the physical organism has been necessary to the phenomena of human consciousness. We can say, indeed, nothing better, nothing more correct metaphysically and scientifically, of the phenomena of consciousness, of these perceptions of truth, virtue, beauty, which the human mind possesses, than that they are the inherent qualities of the eternal substance of all intelligence, brought to manifestation, through the human organism, in finite personality. This gives to man a base of everlastingness in the universe. And in that capacity of progress of which I have spoken, and to which we are able to assign no limit,—that progress of the human type, through creative intelligence and choice, which corresponds to the anterior progress from type to type,—man carries the elements also not merely of everlastingness, but of personal continuance. As mechanical force rises into chemical force, and chemical force into what must still be called "vital force" (though what the term signifies may be in dispute), and vital force rises and expands in various forms of manifestation till it comes to its highest form in the personal consciousness of man, so, without any break in the law, may this new force of human personality open into some other form of life, and still preserve individual identity. The mighty energy that is enwrapped in the human will, the indomitable sense of duty that tramples down tempting pleasures and impels man to conflict and self-sacrifice for the right, the wealth of love that he lavishes and that no limit of years exhausts, the unsatisfied spirit within him forever peering over the walls of knowledge in search of new realms of truth,—as these testify to a past eternity which has been used in producing them, so do they point forward to a future eternity which they are to use as conscious creative forces in the universe.—*William J. Potter.*

Future of Earth and Man.

The earth's foundations were laid deep and enduring in the eternity of the past; and after unceasing preparations for untold ages, the grand factory for making men out of granite commences to produce tolerable specimens of the race, with the promise of vastly better in the future: but just as it does so, these people believe it will be burnt up, swept with universal destruction, that it may be refitted for a handful of "saints," certainly no better than the average of their neighbors, who are to occupy it forever. No danger! That the earth will cease to exist as it began to be, there is no doubt; but its end lies far away in the ages to come, when its fruit is ripe and its work is done.

A tree that takes twenty years to arrive at maturity will last for a hundred years at least; and since the earth has grown during many millions of years, as we now know, we may safely calculate on its continuance for millions of years to come. Our eyes have not yet beheld the whole of its surface. Shall our inheritance be taken from us before we have seen it? We have not used the stores laid up for us in this world's cellar; nay, we are finding new ones almost every day, and therefore have good reason to believe that we have not yet discovered all the treasures prepared for us. Shall the earth be destroyed before we have received its gifts or appropriated its blessings?

The world is a noble vessel, freighted with a thousand million souls, furnished with boundless stores in her deep hold, fairly started for a distant port, every sail at last set, having the best of captains, who will hardly run her upon a rock for the sake of making a raft out of the wreck for a handful of noisy passengers, leaving the rest to perish.

After we have decided that the world shall endure for ages, the question next arises, What will be its future condition? Is it the forest monarch, its trunk rounded to its full capacity, its branches matured, its fruit perfect, the years of the future adding nothing to its glory? or is it a tree with its heart unknit, its best branches undeveloped, its beauty unmatured, its fruit imperfect, waiting for that which time alone can bring?

Old as geology represents the world to be, it still more clearly shows its youth; and the philosopher calmly waits for its improvement, as an intelligent parent does for that of his child.

No man ever saw the earth in a better condition for man's occupancy than it is to-day.

"Abraham saw no fairer stars
Than those that burn for thee and me."

Amid countless mutations, it will still march on to its great and glorious destiny. Behind the eastern hills lie brighter days than have yet dawned, and the earth shall rejoice in their glory.

Progress is the law of our globe, as geology abundantly testifies. If we could but glance at its history for fifty or a hundred years, we might doubt it; but sweeping over the ages of the mighty past, and contrasting its early appearance with those widely succeeding, we can doubt no longer. We see it a puling infant in its fiery cradle, curtained with sulphurous clouds; then with the bare, flinty rock for its floor, and life as impossible as in a fiery furnace, its air more poisonous than the breath of a volcano, and its rain as corrosive as sulphuric acid. In time, rocks are ground to mud, and the simplest of plants spread their rootlets through it in search of nutriment. The air loses its sulphur and its carbon, which are stored away for distant uses. The water becomes purer, and all elements better fitted for the development and sustentation of life, which advances from the seaweed to the cedar, the wheat, and the rose-bush; from the unsensitive radiate, through mollusk, fish, reptile, bird, and mammal, to intelligent man. If the world has thus improved in the past, what more reasonable than that it shall continue to improve in the future? If it has marched with such an unfaltering step in the pathway of progress for such an immense period, who can doubt that it will continue so to do? Why should progress cease at this period in the world's history? If there was any reason for improvement when there was nothing to behold it but the leaden eye of the fish, or to care for it but the dull reptile, how much more reason now that man is here, eagerly watching every advance, his happiness increasing at every step of its progress!

Not only does the knowledge of the past that geology gives enable us to predict the general improvement of the earth as man's abode, but by it we can indicate more particularly the direction that this improvement will take. First, volcanoes will die, and earthquakes cease. * * *

I regard man as the fruit of the tree of life; and, if he is, beyond the fruit the tree cannot go. A tree advances from root to stem, from stem to branch, from branch to leaf, and from leaf to blossom and fruit, each rising in importance above the other; but when the fruit is attained, all that can be done is to perfect it. The root of the great tree of life is the radiata, their raying, ramifying arms and fingers forming its spreading radicles; the trunk of this tree, the mollusca; their shelly covering, its bark. The jointed bodies of the articulates form its branches: the vertebrates are the leaves. Every leaf has a mid-rib passing through its center, from which ribs go to each side of the leaf to strengthen it, as in vertebrates the back-bone passes through the center of the animal, and ribs proceed from it on both sides. The blossoms are the mammalia or milk-producing animals; and its fruit, humanity, waiting for the ages to ripen it. This grand old tree has been advancing for ages, renewing its rootlets, shedding its old bark, losing unnumbered branches in the storms of the past, and dropping myriads of leaves and blossoms, but, with a sound heart, reproducing better than it lost, and fruiting in good time, with the promise of the best when that fruit is fully ripe. But what evidence is there that man is the fruit of this wonderful tree? What peculiarity is there in the fruit of a tree that distinguishes it from every other part? It contains a living principle which possesses unlimited duration, and, under favorable circumstances, may unfold into a tree equal or superior to that from which it sprang. Let a piece of the root be separated from the tree, and it speedily dies, and is resolved to dust: in like manner, bark, branches, blossoms, leaves, perish when their connection with the parent plant is dissevered. The fruit alone contains the power of continuous existence within itself. Drop it on the ground or bury it, and it lives and grows, and sends its type down the ages: so man. The polyp, the snail, the worm, the fish, reptile, bird and beast may die when death comes, and return to the undistinguised dust from which they sprang; but man possesses that over which death has no power, and the extinction of one life is but the dawn of another of greater power and beauty. Some there are who doubt this: to such this argument will have no weight; but to those who believe in the soul's future, and to others who, like myself, know that we continue to live hereafter, the reasonableness of this will be apparent.—*William Denton.*

TRUE PRAYER.

In its essence, prayer is something deeper than words. Words are but one of many forms in which true prayer may find expression; nor has everything that passes for prayer a right to bear the name. Volubility of tongue is commonly in the inverse ratio to prayerfulness of spirit. When the soul prays best, the lips are sealed. A torrent of words poured forth with pious whine, shouted or screamed, perhaps, at the top of the voice, is too often the soul's ostentatious proclamation of its own prayerlessness. Deep feeling is no master of rhetoric. I would rather listen to the rumbling of cartwheels over stone pavements than to a rhetorical prayer. The one is honest, the other is dishonest, noise.

True prayer is the soul's deep homage to goodness and beauty and truth,—the profound thirst for divine life, its thrill of reverential worship before infinite and eternal Being, its deep self-identification with the One and All. It is the unutterable repose of the tired spirit in the boundless and living Whole,—the ending of ignorant struggle against the omnipresent Power that fills infinitude with itself and holds us all in the bosom of changeless law. It is not extinction of the private will, in hopeless submission to a Fate whose right is its might, but rather the glad identification of the private will with the deepest currents of the universe, its conscious and active trust in the "higher thoughts and higher ways" of the universal Mind. It is the mighty gravitation of the soul to its Source, the strong attraction of its love for the Supreme Loveliness, its joyous flight above the clouds into the serenest radiance of the empyrean. What is it *not*, that is deep, real, vital, in man's experience? It is earnestness, it is courage, it is truthfulness, it is purity, it is principle, it is love, it is the uplifting of the heart to God and self-dedication to all that is God-like. It is the outflashing of the inner light into the outward life. It is the supreme experience that makes an oasis in the desert of desolate years.

The spirit of prayer is thus the Soul of Nature breathing through the soul of man. Wherever it lives and moves, it as inevitably creates some form of self-expression as a gushing spring creates for itself a channel. But its forms of expression are as diverse as the faces and the characters of men. It would be as idle as presumptuous to prescribe one and the same form for all. Let each heart utter its own life in its own way. Everything is a prayer, a true and genuine prayer, that *expresses* an inward endeavor and longing for diviner character. It may utter itself without words in the heightened color of the cheek, the quick suffusing of the eye, in the unconscious bowing of the head, in the swifter throbbing of the heart, in the escape of a contrite sigh, in the electric thrill of the nerves at the sight of beauty or goodness; all these, and countless others, may be prayers more full, more complete, than the blended supplications of a mighty multitude.

However it may utter itself, whether with or without voice, this uplifting of the heart to the Absolute Best is the fountain of noble living and high character; and prayer, truly conceived, means each and every expression of this inward self-consecration. Truly to pray is to be conscious of a deep devotion to the ideal and perfect Good, and to put this inward devotion into some sincere expression. The one prayer incumbent upon all is to live nobly; beyond this, there is no obligation. Yet I count it a mark of spiritual misdevelopment, or at least undevelopment, when no outgush of heart-worship ever clothes itself in words,—when no inward jubilee or profound yearning ever seeks relief in direct speech to the omnipresent and indwelling One. Whether I were commanded or forbidden to pray in words, the two grievances would be equal; the vocal prayer is mockery if it be not spontaneous and free, and if it be spontaneous and free, it will not be repressed.

True prayer, therefore, is neither an attempt to enlist Omnipotence in the service of our little private jobs, nor an attempt to undermine the foundations of the universe by overthrowing the changelessness of its laws. Were it either of these, it would be infinitely childish and ridiculous, as pulpit prayers too often are. But true prayer, gushing spontaneously from a full heart, is the simple outbreathing of a peaceful and reverential spirit. Even the joy of Nature is a prayer. The sea prays in the splendid sparkle and everlasting dash of its waters. The earth prays in the uplifting of its mountain peaks like worshipping hands. The stars of night pray with radiant eyelids forever trembling as if to repress tears of adoring joy. The universe is everywhere at prayer, laying on the altar the thank-offering of its own beauty and peace. Shall the soul of man alone be mute, and pour forth no song of thanksgiving and delight? Like the birds in spring, it must utter itself in music.—*F. E. Abbott.*

FIFTY AFFIRMATIONS.

[The following outlines are offered as a purely individual interpretation of the free religious movement, it being proper to state that few, if any, of its other friends will wholly agree with it.]

Religion.

1. Religion is the effort of man to perfect himself.

2. The root of religion is universal human nature.

3. Historical religions are all one, in virtue of this one common root.

4. Historical religions are all different, in virtue of their different historical origin and development.

5. Every historical religion has thus two distinct elements,—one universal or spiritual, and the other special or historical.

6. The universal element is the same in all historical religions; the special element is peculiar in each of them.

7. The universal and special elements are equally essential to the existence of an historical religion.

8. The unity of all religions must be sought in their universal element.

9. The peculiar character of each religion must be sought in its special element.

Relation of Judaism to Christianity.

10. The idea of a coming "kingdom of heaven" arose naturally in the Hebrew mind after the decay of the Davidic monarchy, and ripened under foreign oppression into a passionate longing and expectation.

11. The "kingdom of heaven" was to be a world-wide empire on this earth, both temporal and spiritual, to be established on the ruins of the great empires of antiquity by the miraculous intervention of Jehovah.

12. The Messiah or Christ was to reign over the "kingdom of heaven" as the visible deputy of Jehovah, who was considered the true sovereign of the Hebrew nation. He was to be Priest-King,—the supreme pontiff or high-priest of the Hebrew church, and absolute monarch of the Hebrew state.

13. The "apocalyptical literature" of the Jews exhibits the gradual formation and growth of the idea of the Messianic "kingdom of heaven."

14. All the leading features of the gospel doctrine concerning the "kingdom of heaven," the "end of the world," the "great day of judgment," the "coming of the Christ in the clouds of heaven," the "resurrection of the dead," the condemnation of the wicked and the exaltation of the righteous, the "passing away of the heavens and earth," and the appear-

ance of a "new heaven and a new earth," were definitely formed and fixed in the Hebrew mind, in the century before Jesus was born.

15. John the Baptist came preaching that "the kingdom of heaven is at hand." But he declared himself merely the forerunner of the Messiah.

16. Jesus also came preaching that "the kingdom of heaven is at hand," and announced himself as the Messiah or Christ.

17. Jesus emphasized the spiritual aspect of the Messianic kingdom; but, although he expected his throne to be established by the miraculous intervention of God, and therefore refused to employ human means in establishing it, he nevertheless expected to discharge the political functions of his office, as King and Judge, when the fulness of time should arrive.

18. As a preacher of purely spiritual truth, Jesus probably stands at the head of all the great religious teachers of the past.

19. As claimant of the Messianic crown, and founder of Christianity as a distinct historical religion, Jesus shared the spirit of an unenlightened age, and stands on the same level with Gautama or Mohammed.

20. In the belief of his disciples, the death, resurrection and ascension of Jesus would not prevent the establishment of the "kingdom of heaven." His throne was conceived to be already established in the heavens; and the early church impatiently awaited its establishment on earth at the "second coming of the Christ."

21. Christianity thus appears as simply the complete development of Judaism,—the highest possible fulfilment of the Messianic dreams based on the Hebrew conception of a "chosen people."

Christianity.

22. Christianity is the historical religion taught in the Christian Scriptures, and illustrated in the history of the Christian church.

23. It is a religion in virtue of its universal element; it is the Christian religion in virtue of its special element.

24. The Christian Scriptures teach from beginning to end that "Jesus of Nazareth is the Christ of God,"—that is, the Hebrew Messiah. This, the Christian Confession, was declared both by Jesus and the apostles to be necessary to salvation or admission into the "kingdom of heaven."

25. The Christian church, from its origin to the present day, has everywhere planted itself on faith in the Christian Confession, as its divinely appointed foundation,—the eternal "rock" against which the "gates of hell shall never prevail."

26. The Christian Confession gradually created on the one hand the theology, and on the other hand the hierarchy, of the Roman Catholic Church. The process was not, as is claimed, a corruption, but a natural and logical development.

27. The Church of Rome embodies Christianity in its most highly developed and perfect form, as a religion of authority based on the Christian Confession.

28. Protestantism is the gradual disintegration of Christianity, whether regarded theologically or ecclesiastically, under the influence of the free spirit of protest against authority.

29. "Liberal Christianity,"—that is, democratic autocracy in religion,—is the highest development of the free spirit of protest against authority which is possible within the Christian church. It is, at the same time, the lowest development of faith in the Christ,—a return to the Christian Confession in its crudest and least developed form.

30. Christianity is the religion of Christians, and all Christians are believers in the Christ.

31. The Christian name, whatever else it may include, necessarily includes faith in Jesus as the Christ of God. Any

other use of the name is abuse of it. Under some interpretation or other, the Christian Confession is the boundary line of Christianity.

Free Religion.

32. The Protestant Reformation was the birth of Free Religion,—the beginning of the religious protest against authority within the confines of the Christian church.

33. The history of Protestantism is the history of the growth of Free Religion at the expense of the Christian Religion. As love of freedom increases, reverence for authority decreases.

34. The completion of the religious protest against authority must be the extinction of faith in the Christian Confession.

35. Free Religion is emancipation from the outward law, and voluntary obedience to the inward law.

36. The great faith or moving power of Free Religion is faith in man as a progressive being.

37. The great ideal end of Free Religion is the perfection or complete development of man,—the race serving the individual, the individual serving the race.

38. The great practical means of Free Religion is the integral, continuous and universal education of man.

39. The great law of Free Religion is the still small voice of the private soul.

40. The great peace of Free Religion is spiritual oneness with the infinite One.

41. Free Religion is the natural outcome of every historical religion,—the final unity, therefore, towards which all historical religions slowly tend.

Relation of Christianity to Free Religion.

42. Christianity is identical with Free Religion so far as its universal element is concerned,—antagonistic to it so far as its special element is concerned.

43. The corner-stone of Christianity is faith in the Christ. The corner-stone of Free Religion is faith in Human Nature.

44. The great institution of Christianity is the Christian Church, the will of the Christ being its supreme law. The great institution of Free Religion is the coming Republic of the World, the universal conscience and reason of mankind being its supreme organic law or constitution.

45. The fellowship of Christianity is limited by the Christian Confession; its brotherhood includes all subjects of the Christ, and excludes all others. The fellowship of Free Religion is universal and free; it proclaims the great brotherhood of man, without limit or bound.

46. The practical work of Christianity is to Christianize the world,—to convert all souls to the Christ, and ensure their salvation from the wrath of God. The practical work of Free Religion is to humanize the world,—to make the individual nobler here and now, and to convert the human race into a vast Co-operative Union devoted to universal ends.

47. The spiritual ideal of Christianity is the suppression of self and perfect imitation of Jesus the Christ. The spiritual ideal of Free Religion is the development of self, and the harmonious education of all its powers to the highest possible degree.

48. The essential spirit of Christianity is that of self-humiliation at the feet of Jesus, and passionate devotion to his person. The essential spirit of Free Religion is that of self-respect and free self-devotion to great ideas. Christianity is prostrate on its face; Free Religion is erect on its feet.

49. The noblest fruit of Christianity is a self-sacrificing love of man for Jesus' sake. The noblest fruit of Free Religion is a self-sacrificing love of man for man's own sake.

50. Christianity is the faith of the soul's childhood; Free Religion is the faith of the soul's manhood. In the gradual growth of mankind out of Christianity into Free Religion, lies the only hope of the spiritual perfection of the individual and the spiritual unity of the race.—*F. E. Abbott.*

Physical Condition of Humanity.

I think there is hope when a religion is presented to the people which is not only in favor of free thought and free speech, but which endeavors also to benefit the physical condition of humanity. There never was, there never can be, such a thing as true pleasure in vice or crime; and yet the land is full of them, because, as I think, the social condition of the people is not cared for as it ought to be at the present moment. I agree with the sentiment of that great social reformer, Robert Owen, that the characters of men are formed for them, instead of by them; and, consequently, I think the influence of circumstances in this country, rather than any natural or inherent depravity in mankind, accounts for the degradation and vice and crime that prevail in every section of the country. Let us not then suppose that it is owing to any natural or inherent depravity that this state of things exists, but only in the fact that the true remedy for social evils has not yet been put into practice; but, when the remedy is applied the reform will be complete. And it is a great sign of the times, my friends, that Radicals and Liberals and free-thinking men are doing what lies in their power for the promotion of this great reform.

Let men, if they can do no better, dream of a hereafter, to which I have no kind of objection; but the hereafter must be according to the present, and, if people live well in the present, they have the best preparation for the future. But to go into the future unprepared by the present may, perhaps, for anything I know to the contrary, be the same routine over again. But be that as it may, I am getting beyond my depth: I do not know anything about these matters; I do not pretend to know. Being finite, frail, and imperfect, I do not presume to understand the infinite, and therefore I confine my thoughts here; for I think there is enough to do in this world, and more than enough, to occupy all our time in improving the condition of the people here. And those who believe in the hereafter, should not object to the doctrine, because he who is right to-day will probably be right to-morrow. That there are those in the community who entertain these aspirations, and are endeavoring, by the aid of social science, to improve society and even religion itself, is one of the hopeful signs of the times.

"Raising their voices in a chant sublime,
They sing the glory of the coming time,
When error shall decay, and truth grow strong,
And right shall reign supreme, and vanquish wrong."

Horace Seaver.

THEODORE PARKER.

Teachings.

With Protestant ministers the Bible is a Fetish; it is with Catholic priests, only to them the Roman Church is the Master Fetish, the "Big Thunder," while the Bible is but an inferior and subordinate idol. For ultimate authority the minister does not appeal to God manifesting himself in the world of matter and the world of man, but only to the Bible; to that he prostitutes mind and conscience, heart and soul. Ministers take the Bible in a lump as divine; all between its lids as the "Word of God," infallible and miraculous; he that believeth not shall be damned; and no amount of piety or morality can make up for not believing this. No doctor is ever so subordinate to his drug, no lawyer lies so prone before statute and custom, as the mass of ministers before the Bible.

—The whole universe of matter is a great mundane psalm to celebrate the reign of Power, Law and Mind. Fly through the solar system from remotest Neptune to the Sun, study each planet, it is the same. Ask every little orange leaf, ask the aphis that feeds thereon, ask the insect corpses lying by millions in the dead ashes of the farmer's peat-fire, the remains of mollusks that gave up the ghost millions of years before man trod the globe,—they all, with united voice, answer still the same,—power, law, mind. In all the space from Neptune to the sun, in all the time from silicious shell to the orange leaf of to-day, there is no failure of that power, no break of that law, no cessation in its constant mode of operation, no error of that mind, whereof all space is here, all time is now. So the world is witness continually to power, to never-failing law, to mind that is everywhere; is witness to that ever-present Power which men call God. Look up and reverence; look down and trust.

—One of the most remarkable things in this world is the abundance of beauty, feeding and comforting man's finer and nicer faculties. God, after setting before us what we turn to bread, and garments, and houses, and musical instruments, and books, gives us the benediction of beauty as an unexpected grace after meat. In all this, I see the loveliness of the Infinite Father and Infinite Mother. Not a lichen scars the rock, not a star flames in the sky, but it tells of the infinite loveliness of the infinitely loving God.

—Industry is the business of men. It is a dignity, and only idleness a disgrace, a wrong, a curse. If you earn nothing by head or hand, by heart or soul, then you are, and must be, a beggar or a thief, and neither pay for your board or lodging.

—Let amusement fill up the chinks of your existence, but not the great spaces thereof. Let your pleasures be taken as Daniel took his prayer, with his windows open—pleasures which need not cause a blush on an ingenuous cheek.

—Think of a young man growing up, conquered by his appetites—the soul veiled by the body, the smutch of shame on all the white raiment of God's youthful son, who can stoop the pride of his youth so low, and be a trifler, a drunkard, a debauchee! The mind of man despises it, and woman's holy soul casts it aside with scorn. Stern as you may think me, and as I am, I can only weep at such decay as this,—flowers trod down by swine, the rainbow broken by the storm, the soul prostrate and trodden by the body's cruel hoof.

—The whole sum and substance of human history may be

reduced to this maxim—that when man departs from the divine means of reaching the divine end, he suffers loss and harm.

Every vice meets its own terrific punishment. What if the Honorable Mr. Devil does keep his coach and six? It is Mr. Devil who rides in it, and no six horses will ever carry him away from himself. What if the young men invite him to sit on their platforms, and so do him honor? It only exhibits his devilship before the people in that high seat. He had better have shrunk into the lowest corner.

—We are all connected with the World of Matter; with the World of Man; and with the World of God In each of these spheres we have duties to do, and rights to enjoy, which are consequent on the duties done. We may derive our habitual delight from any one of these three sources—the material, the human, and the Divine; or we may draw from all these. We may content ourselves with the lowest quality of human delights, or we may reach up and get the highest and dearest quality thereof. Complete and perfect piety unites all three—the great Thought of the Infinity of God; the great Feeling of absolute love for Him; and the great Will, the resolution to serve Him. The superstitious man thinks that God must be feared first of all; and the internal worship of God is accordingly, with that man, fear, and nothing but fear. Fanaticism is Hate before God; as superstition is Fear before him. Fanaticism is a far greater evil than Superstition; but in our day it is far less common. Mysticism is sloth before God, as Superstition is Fear, and Fanaticism is Hate. It exists still in some of the churches, which cultivate only emotions of reverence, of trust, of love, and the like, but never let the love of God come out of the heart in the shape of the love of man.

But the true idea of God, and the Religion which is to come of it—which is love of that God and keeping all his commandments—will work such a revolution in man's affairs as Luther, nor Moses, nor yet mightier Jesus ever wrought. God in Genesis represents the conception of the babyhood of humanity. But manhood demands a different conception. All round us lies the World of Matter, this vast world above us and about us and beneath; it proclaims the God of Nature; flower speaking unto flower, star quiring unto star; a God who is resident therein, his law never broke. In us is a World of *Consciousness*, and as that mirror is made clearer by civilization, I look down and behold the Natural Idea of God, Infinite Cause and Providence, Father and Mother to all that are. Into our reverent souls God will come as the morning light into the bosom of the opening rose.

—This party (Spiritualism) has an idea wider and deeper than that of the Catholic or Protestant, namely : that God still inspires men as much as ever; that He is as immanent in Spirit as in space.

For the present purpose the doctrine may be called Spiritualism. That relies on no church tradition or Scripture, as the last ground and infallible rule. It counts these things *teachers*, if they teach,—not masters; *helps*, if they help us,—*not authorities*. It relies on the divine presence in the soul of man, the eternal word of God, which is Truth as it speaks through the faculties he has given. It believes God is as near to the soul as matter is to the senses, thinks the canon of revelation not yet closed, nor God exhausted. It sees him in Nature's perfect work; hears him in all true Scriptures, Jewish or Phœnician; feels Him in the inspiration of the heart; stoops at the same fountain with Moses and Jesus, and is filled with living water. It calls God Father, not King; Christ brother, not redeemer; Heaven home, and Religion Nature. It loves and trusts, but does not fear. It sees in Jesus A MAN, living manlike, highly gifted, and with beautiful and blameless fidelity to God. * * But he lived for himself, died for himself, worked out his own salvation, and we must do the same; for one man cannot live for another, any more than he can eat and sleep for another. It lays down no creed, asks no symbol, reverences exclusively no time nor place, and therefore can use all time and every place. It reckons forms useful to such as they help. Its temple is all space, its shrine the good heart, its creed all truth, its ritual works of love and utility, its profession of faith, a divine life. It takes all the helps it can get; counts no good word profane, though a heathen spoke it,—no lie sacred, though the greatest prophet said the word. *Its redeemer is within, its salvation within,* its heaven and its oracles of God. It falls back on perfect religion,—asks no more, is satisfied with no less.

A PRAYER.*

Our Father, we thank thee for this world thou hast placed us in. We bless thee for the heavens over our heads, burning all night with such varied fire, and all day pouring down their glad effulgence on the ground. We thank thee for the scarf of green beauty with which thou mantlest the shoulders of the temperate world, and for all the hopes that are in this foodful earth, and for the rich promise of the season on every side of us.

We thank thee still more for the nature which thou hast given us, for these earthen houses of the flesh wherein we dwell, and for this atom of spirit, a particle from thine own flame of eternity, which thou hast lodged in the clay.

We thank thee for the large inheritance which has come down to us from other times. We bless thee that other men labored, and whilst thou hast rewarded them for their toil, we also have entered into the fruit of their labors, and gather where we have not strewed, and eat where we toiled not.

We thank thee for the noble institutions which other days have bequeathed to us. We thank thee for those great and godly men, speaking in every tongue, inspired by thy spirit, whom thou hast raised up from age to age, bearing witness of the nobleness of man's nature, and the nearness of thy love towards all the sons and daughters of men,—their lives a con-

*Music Hall, Boston, June, 1857 This prayer, with others, was reported by a friend, without Mr Parker's knowledge.

tinual flower of piety on earth, drawing men's eyes by its beauty, and stirring men's souls by the sweet fragrance of its heavenly flame. Most do we thank thee for him who, in an age of darkness, came and brought such marvelous light to the eyes of men; for the truths he taught and the glorious humanity he lived, blessing thee that he was the truth from thee, that he showed us the life that is in thee, and himself travelled before us the way which leads to the loftiest achievements.

We thank thee for those whose great courage in times past broke the oppressor's rod and let the oppressed go free. And we bless thee for the millions of common men, following the guidance of their leaders, faithful to their spirit, and so to thee, who went onward in this great human march, in whose bloody footsteps we gather the white flowers of peace, and lift up our thankful hearts to thee.

Not the less we thank thee for the men and women of great steadfastness of soul in our time, who have been faithful witnesses against iniquity, who light the torch of truth, and pass it from hand to hand, and sow the world with seeds whence in due time the white flowers of peace shall also spring. We are glad that thou pourest out liberally to all who lift up earnest hearts unto thee. We thank thee for the great truths which are old, and for the new truths also which are great, and for the light of justice, and the new glories of philanthropy which human eyes have beheld in this age for the first time.

O Lord, we thank thee that the glories which kings and prophets waited for have come down to us, and that thou hast revealed to babes and sucklings those truths which other ages yearned for and found not.

O, Thou who art Father and Mother to the civilized man and the savage, who seest with equal tenderness the sinner and the saint, having no child of perdition in thy great hnman family, we remember before thee our several lives, thanking thee for the joys which gladden us, the work which our hands find to do, the joy of its conclusion, and the education of its process.

We are conscious of our follies, our transgressions, our stumblings by the wayside, and wanderings from the paths of pleasantness and peace. We know how often our hands have wrought iniquity, and we have been mean and cowardly at heart, not daring to do the right which our own souls told us of; and we pray thee that we may suffer from these things, until, greatly ashamed thereof, we turn from them and lead glorious and noble lives.

We thank thee, O Father, for those who make music about our fireside, whose countenance is a benediction on our daily bread, fairer to us than the flowers of earth, or the stars of heaven. We thank thee for those newly born into this world, bringing the fragrance of heaven in the infant's breath; and if we dare not thank thee when our dear ones are born out of this world, and clothed in immortality, yet we thank thee that the eye of our faith can follow them still to the land where tears are wiped away, and the change is from glory to glory.

O Thou who art infinite in thy power, thy wisdom, and thy love,—who art the God of the Christian, the Heathen, and the Jew, blessing all mankind which thou hast made to inhabit the whole earth,—we thank thee for all thy blessings, and pray that mindful of our nature, and of thy nearness to us, we may learn to live to the full height of the faculties which thou hast given us, cultivating them with such large and generous education that we shall know the truth and it shall make us free, that we may distinguish between those ever living commandments of thine and the teachings of men, that we may enlarge still more the affections that are in us, and that there may be in us such religious trust that all our daily work shall be one great act of service, and sacramental as our prayer.

Thus may we be strengthened, able at all times to run and not be weary, to walk and never faint. Then, when our work on earth is finished, and the clods of the valley are sweet to our weary frames, may we spend eternity in the progressive welfare of thy children. And here on earth may the gleams of that future glory come upon us in our mortal life, clearing up the difficult paths, and strengthening our hearts. So may thy will be done, on earth and in heaven.

A. B. ALCOTT.

Sayings.

—If one's life is not worshipful, no one cares for his professions. Piety is a sentiment: the more natural it is, the wholesomer. Nor is there piety where charity is wanting. "If one love not his brother whom he hath seen, how can he love God whom he hath not seen." None are deceived as to the spirit of their acquaintances: the instinct of every village, every home, intimates true character. We recognize goodness wherever we find it. 'Tis the same helpful influence, beautifying the meanest as the greatest service by its manners, doing most when least conscious, as if he did it not. Let us have unspoken creeds and these quick and operative.

—Persist in being yourself, and against fate and yourself. Faith and persistency are life's architects, while doubt and despair bury all under the ruins of any endeavor. You may pull all your paradises about your ears save your earliest; that is to be yours sometime. Strive and have; still striving till striving is having. We mount to heaven mostly on the ruins of our cherished schemes, finding our failures were successes. Nor need we turn sour if we fail to draw the prizes in life's lottery. It were the speck in the fruit, the falling of our manliness into decay. These blanks were all prizes had we the equanimity to take them without whimpering or discontent.

—There is no appeal from the decisions of this High Court of Duty in the breast. The Ought is the Must and the Inevitable. One may misinterpret the voice, may deliberate, disobey the commandment, but cannot escape the consequences of his election. The deed decides.

—Nor is any man greatest standing apart in his individualism; his strength and dignity come by sympathy with the aims of the best men of the community of which he is a member. Yet whoever seeks the crowd, craving popularity for propping repute, forfeits his claim to reverence and expires in the incense he inhales. Stand fast by your convictions and there maintain yourself against every odds. One with yourself, you are one with Almighty God, and a majority against all the world.

—Love you none? Then are you lost. Love is the key to felicity; nor is there a heaven to him who has it not.

—There is nothing like comparative divinity for emancipating the mind from traditional teachings. Like travel it opens out new and distant regions of the globe of knowledge, and shows the real relations of things to one another.

—What becomes of an age whose youth knows too much? Like the old princes eager to pluck the forbidden pleasures from the stem; the brazen, following fast childhood's golden period, and leaping wildly into the iron, the five points of license; the beautiful bashfulness, nature's ornament and foil, the preserver of chastity, torn, trodden, and lost!

—A period of the world like ours, when thought is so actively engaged in all subjects affecting human welfare, must be deficient in the spiritual element if it have not a solvent for fusing the current creeds, and recombining these in a fresher faith, sufficient for the present, if not for some future generations. In the general diffusion of light, no one can hold the community of minds under the shadow of his special thought, since the revelations made to all races in times past are culminating in a purer dispensation, suited to the new needs of the centuries.

Religion and Science.

Fear and wonder are the chief elements of superstition. These are supplied by ignorance. Courage and composure come of knowledge, and grow with it.

The study of the natural sciences—including as it does, the habit of requiring strict proof—constantly diminishes that credulity through which superstition enters, and on which it feeds. Reason and knowledge are conscious of their fallible workings; and therefore do they tolerate differences of opinion. They inspire diffidence as much as ignorance does positiveness. Natural science has already done much to weaken and dispel superstition. It has put astronomy in the place of astrology, and made alchemy and the hunt for the "Philosopher's Stone," and for the "Universal Solvent," give place to Chemistry. It has liberated millions from their degrading bondage to the authority of sacred books, and left their reason as free to play upon the pages of the Bible as us upon the pages of any other book. While the mass of men construct their God out of their dreams and delusions, they who study the natural sciences are carried up through certainties to the certain God. The one imagine, and the other prove the existence and character of God.

The religion of human nature is harmony, not only with human nature, but with all Nature and with God. For every part of Nature is harmonious with every other part of it, and all Nature is in harmony with the Author of all Nature.

And what will become of the Bible when men shall cease to take it as an authority, and to worship it as a fetish, and to possess and prize it as a charm or an amulet? Rather ask, what will become of it in the *mean time*, and during the superstitious regard for it. For there is no little danger that an age of growing intelligence, disgusted with the exaggerated claims for the Bible, will reject it. But when this book shall, like any other book, be submitted to human judgment, and men feel at liberty to discriminate between the merits of its different parts—as, for instance, the incredible story of Jonah and the whale, and the felt truth of the sermon on the Mount—then will it be a new and inestimable blessing.

Will there, when the priests are gone, be still a demand for preachers? Yes, greater than ever! What will they preach?

Will they, like the priests, spend the time in telling their hearers what religion is? Oh, no; a minute a month will suffice for that! In a dozen words they can say that loving God supremely and the neighbor as ourself, or more briefly, that being true to ourself, is religion; or still more briefly, that being ourself is religion. But the question remains, What will they preach? They will preach duties, they will tell their hearers what religion calls for in the heart and life. And what shall we do for churches when the present ones shall have died out with the priests? We shall have infinitely better; for we shall then have temples in which reason will do as much to enlighten and elevate, as superstition does in the present churches to darken and degrade.

I affirm the supreme importance of religion. The next life is but the continuation of this; and we begin there just where we leave off here. If we are upon low planes here, we shall enter upon low planes there. If here we sustain high relations to wisdom and goodness, we shall there also.—*Gerritt Smith.*

Disappointment—A Teacher in God's School.

God keeps a school for his children on earth; and one of his best teachers is named *Disappointment.* He is a rough teacher; severe in tone and harsh in handling, sometimes, but his tuition is worth all it costs us. We do not pretend to be a very apt learner, but many of our best lessons through life have been taught us by that same stern old schoolmaster, Disappointment.

One lesson we learned was not to be selfish, or imagine that this world was all made for us. If it had been, the sun would have shone just when *our* hay needed curing, and the rains would have fallen only when *our* garden thirsted for water. But we found that God ordered things to please himself, and not us. And when our schemes were broken up, and our journey spoiled by the storm, the stern schoolmaster said: "The world was not made for you alone. Do not be selfish. Your loss is another's gain. The rain that spoils your hay makes your neighbor's corn grow the faster. The fall in wheat that cuts down your profits will help the poor widow in yonder cottage to buy bread for her hungry little mouths next winter. Your loss is another man's gain. Don't be selfish."

On a grand scale, sometimes, this lesson is taught. When a certain ambitious self-seeker once clutched at the dominion of all Europe, stern Disappointment met him in his path of invasion, flung a Russian snow-storm in his face, and out of the tiny snow-flakes wove a white shroud to wrap the flower of French chivalry. The lesson that the proud usurper would not learn at Aspern and Eylau was taught him in the agonies of Borodino, and in ghastly blood-prints on the frozen banks of the Beresina. His successor, the third Napoleon, has been taught, lately, the same lesson: "All Europe does not belong to you." So, too, have we, in the defeat of our humbler plans of self-seeking, been made to hear the sharp teacher say: "Do not be selfish. God did not make this world just for you. Other people have rights as well as yourself." This lesson was worth all it cost us.

A *second* lesson which Disappointment has taught us is, that our losses are not only gains, sometimes, to others, but very often the richest gains to ourselves. In our short-sighted ignorance, we had "devised a way," and set our hearts upon it. Had we been allowed to pursue it, we must have been led by it to ruin.

The record-book of every Christian's life has some pages in it which were written at the bidding of that severe teacher, Disappointment. Tears may have blotted and blurred the page at the time. But as we turn over that page now, and read it in the light of experience, we can write beneath it: "Thank God for those losses! they were my everlasting gain. Thank God for those bereavements! they have saved my soul from being bereaved of heaven. All things work together for good to them that love God; to them who are the called according to his purpose."

My friend, if you and I ever reach our Father's house, we shall look back and see that the sharp-voiced, rough-visaged teacher, Disappointment, was one of the best guides to train us for it. He gave us hard lessons. He often used the rod. He often led us into thorny paths. He sometimes stripped off a load of luxuries; but that only made us travel the freer and the faster on our heavenward way. He sometimes led us down into the valley of the death-shadow; but never did the promises read so sweetly as when spelled out by the eye of faith in that very valley. Nowhere did he lead us so often, or teach us such sacred lessons, as at the cross of Christ. Dear, old, rough-handed teacher! We will build a monument to thee yet, and crown it with garlands, and inscribe on it: *Blessed be the memory of* DISAPPOINTMENT.—*Rev. Theodore L. Cuyler, N. Y.*

SPIRITUAL DYSPEPTICS.

There is a class of weak-handed and feeble-kneed professors in Christ's church who are self-made invalids. Their spiritual debility is the direct result of their own sins and short-comings. In their case, as in the physical hygiene, disease is the inevitable punishment of transgression against the laws of health.

Is not the inebriate's bloated and poisoned frame the immediate legacy of his bottle? Is not a shattered nervous system the tormenting bequest which a high-pressure career of sensuality leaves to the transgressor? The indolence which never earns its daily bread cannot earn the appetite to enjoy it; the gluttony which gorges the stomach is but fattening an early banquet for the worms. Dyspepsia is only God's appointed health-officer, stationed at the gateway of excess, to warn off all who approach it, and to punish those who will persist in entering the forbidden ground. In like manner spiritual disease is the inevitable result of committed sin, or neglect of religious duty. It requires no profound skill to detect the cause of Mr. A.'s dyspepsia, or Deacon B.'s spiritual palsy, or poor Mr. C.'s leprosy. How can a Christian be healthy who never works? How can a man's faith be strong who never enters his closet? How can a man's benevolence be warm who never gives? A want of appetite for giving always brings on a lean visage in the church; but I do like to hear my neighbor M. pray at the monthly concert, for the fluency of devotion is quickened by his fluency of purse. He *dares* to ask God's help in the salvation of sinners, for he is doing his own utmost too. And I have known one resolute, sagacious, Christ-loving woman to do in a mission-school what Florence Nightingale did in the hospitals of Scutari; that is, teach the nurses how to cure, as well as the sick how to recover.

If this brief paragraph falls under the eye of any spiritual dyspeptic, let us offer him two or three familiar counsels. My friend, your disease and debility are your own fault, not your misfortune. It is not a "visitation of God," but a visitation of the devil, that has laid you on your back, and made you well-nigh useless in the church, in the Sabbath-school, and in every enterprise of Christian charity. Having brought on your own malady, you must be your own restorer, by the help of the divine physician.—*T. L. Cuyler.*

THE FULLNESS OF GOD.

What a transcendent idea that is in Paul's prayer for his brethren: "That ye might be *filled with all the fullness of God!*" When, therefore, we meet with a man or woman who almost never disappoints us; who is always "abounding" in the work of the Lord; who serves God on every day as well as the Sunday; who is more anxious to be right than to be rich; and who can ask God's blessing on the bitterest cup;—when we meet such a one, we know that down in the clefts of the soul is Christ, the well-spring!

In a thousand ways will the inward fountain of Christian principle make itself visible. We see it in the merchant who gives Christ the key of his safe, and never soils it with a single dirty shilling. We see it in the statesman who cares more to win God's smile on his conscience than a re-election to office. We recognize it in the minister who is more greedy for souls than for salary. We see it in the young man who would rather endure a comrade's laugh than a Saviour's frown; in the maiden who obeys Christ sooner than fashion. I sometimes detect this well spring of cheerful piety in the patient mother, whose daily walk with God is a fount of holy influence amid her household. I know of poor men's dwellings in which grows a plant of contentment that is an exotic rarely found in marble mansions. Its leaves are green and glossy; it is *fed from the Well.*

In dying chambers we have often heard this spiritual fountain playing, and its murmur was as musical as the tinkle of a brook

"In the leafy month of June."

Perfect love had cast out fear. Peace reigned. Joys sparkled in the sunlight of God's countenance. There was a well there which death could not dry—the "well of water springing up into everlasting life."—*T. L. Cuyler.*

The New Religion.

The great word of religion has always been piety. To feel right towards God, and to worship Him in the acceptable way, have always been considered the chief if not the sole duties of man. Docrines have been set forth and emphasized as the quickener and support of sentiment. Rituals have been elaborated as the most fitting language and gymnastics of devotion. Fast and penance, gorgeous rites and pomps and paraphernalia have been invoked to deepen and give emphasis, volume and articulation to the soul's worship of Deity.

It has been almost universally held that God was infinitely better pleased with prayers addressed to Him than with silent discharge of duty, sweet resignation to the inevitable ordinations of nature, or the tender and helpful service of men. Grace at meals, an exhortation in the conference-room, an hour in church, a subscription to some mission or pious enterprise, have always been held and thought more acceptable in the sight of heaven than honesty in business, fidelity to private and public trusts, personal culture, and consecration to the noblest human interests and aims. Consequently Christian ethics and exhortations have chiefly run in pietistic grooves. The face has been turned skyward. The world has been looked upon as merely a point of departure, and the duties of man to man, and the sweet and holy charities of life, have been ignored or forgotten. This is the old religion, of which not a little still remains.

Those who study carefully the significance of Christ's teachings and example, reading between the lines of the gospels and feeling the spirit that still animates the words that were written in sympathetic ink, will find that with him religion was chiefly if not entirely philanthropy. He did not ignore Deity, he identified the Father with the child, and made loving service of the child the truest and most acceptable worship of the Father. Justice, mercy, kindness, charity, forgiveness, self-sacrifice—these are the supreme Christian virtues. He did not ignore piety, but made the motive and soul of philanthropy. He does not forbid worship, but gives it a new and sublimer form in human helpfulness and uplifting. And whatever is done to alleviate the distress, ameliorate the condition, improve the morals, educate and elevate any and every class of men everywhere on earth, is in accordance with the principles and spirit of true Christianity, and part of the new religion whose essence is philanthropy, and whose love for God is the inspiration and result of helpful service of men.

The old religion has kept the ground and had things pretty much its own way hitherto. But within fifty years what is truest and most central in Christianity has got expression, and now utters itself with new clearness and force every day. The community has breathed in the new spirit, and its lungs dilate and its heart expands with the quickening influence. The age is beginning to glow with an enthusiasm for humanity. Never before was there so strong an interest in, and so deep a sympathy for, the poor suffering and the wronged. Never before was the work of humanity so highly prized, so honored by the world. No characters are so revered and loved, and have so strong a hold upon the hearts of the people everywhere, as those who have toiled and sacrificed for the good of their fellow-beings. The world is fast opening its eyes to the fact that philanthropy is the other and larger half of piety, the visible human side of religion, and that without it there can be no healthy spirituality, no saving faith, no communion with him who spent his life in doing good and died for his fellow men, nor with Him who gives Himself to his children in the bounty of the world and in their every breath. The faith that does not blossom into love of man does not spring from the Christian vine; the form that does not kindle a flame of pure sympathy for mankind is a worse than encumbrance to true worship; the sect or church that does not forget itself in sheltering the homeless, befriending the outcast, saving the lost, and inciting and inspiring its members to noblest efforts in behalf of their fellows and for human good, has yet to prove its right to the Christian name.

And evermore this new religion must increase in power and influence. Already it has invaded the sects, crept into the churches, put a new face upon the old beliefs and liturgies, and extemporized methods of activity that grate upon the old sanctities as secular and strange. It is this new religion—which works outside of churches, which makes churches of its own, calling them reforms, charities, hospitals, asylums, societies, com missions and clubs—which is undermining the old faster than any of our modern infidelities, and supplanting it with a shorter, happier, holier, and more helpful faith. The church of the future will be the church of the Good Samaritan. The saints our children will canonize and enshrine in blessed memories, will be the helpers and healers of humanity. And whosoever giveth a cup of cold water to one athirst in the spirit of love, shall be counted a follower of the Son of Man. This religion, which is piety and philanthropy both in one, is the only religion that has inherent vitality enough to live, or is of any use in the world, or can give strength and inspiration.—*Theodore Tilton.*

The Sanctity of Marriage.

In the Buddhist "Path of Virtue," it is written: "If one man conquer in battle a thousand times a thousand men, and if another conquer himself, he is the greatest of conquerors." This noble form of conquest is not taught by the sophistries of those who would bring "instantly the millennium" by removing all outward restraint, not only from "the higher love of the spirit," but from the free impulses of passion. Vain effort! Freedom would at once degenerate from license and order, which is "Heaven's first law," into anarchy and chaos. Psyche must free herself from the dominion of Venus, before she can arise to the abode of celestial love. Let the soul gain a strong and steadfast mastery over sense, and the dwelling of the gods is reached, albeit hedged about by the sanctions of morality and law.

I grant that legislation on this subject is imperfect. The law-makers of the world have in some dim sense divined the "heart's ideal of monogamic marriage," and have endeavored to make their enactments tally with this "higher law." But they have blundered: first, by creating a legal inequality between man and woman in marriage; and second, by affording too limited means of release from it to those unendurably oppressed by this inequality, or who find by bitter experience that they have wilfully or ignorantly made the fatal mistake of not conforming to the conditions of so intimate and sacred a relation. There should be a door of legal escape, and a city of refuge in public opinion, for the wrongly mated whose loveless lives are daily embittered by a refinement of slow torture that leaves no outward scar, but wrings the heart with unspeakable anguish; for women who find themselves and their children subject to insult and injury from passionate and ferocious companions, and for women with husbands made savages and fiends by strong drink, who see their homes desolated and desecrated, their children cruelly assaulted, and are themselves exposed to brutal abuse, and the horrible fear of adding other helpless victims to the domestic holocaust. The political economist, and the patron of social science, should hold it an imperative duty to see tha' women have the means of escape from subjection to such besotted monsters, in order that society may be saved from the imbecile, discordant, vicious, and murderous product. For all the victims of false marriages, the hand of law should be stretched out in merciful deliverance. In view of their misery, how narrow and heartless is the effort on the part of respectable moralists to create a public sentiment against their lawful and honorable release—to emphasize the doctrine that "when once a marriage is made and consummated, it should be as fixed a fact as the laws of nature."

This sweeping assertion can be made only of conjugal unions based on and fostered by affection, and then we may say, not that they "should be," but that they are by nature permanent. The trouble is, there is too little love in the world. In all the relations—between brothers and sisters, parents and children, friends and neighbors, husbands and wives—there is a dearth of pure affection. People do not even love themselves as they ought; if they did, they would not debase the temple of the spirit by sensual indulgence, but strive, "whether they eat or drink, or whatsoever they do," to have "the body sit lightly on the soul." Pythagoras controlled the instinct for physical gratification, aud rejected the temptation to personal aggrandizement, so as to live for the sake of wisdom, and his ear caught the music of the spheres. But too often self-love degenerates into selfishness, and the higher faculties are submerged. When this demon presides over the conjugal relation, the angel of love is banished from the hearthstone. Love is unselfish; it seeks the good and happiness of the beloved object. When this divine principle reigns in the hearts of the wedded, the supreme condition of a lasting union is attained. For love is not a fleeting sentiment that comes and passes with the hour, buı an abiding presence that glorifies the ·object of affection, purifies, enlarges, and ennobles the heart in which it dwells, and gives its own evidence of constancy. Passion is variable, but love is steadfast. "Every heart prays and pines for that holy and protecting love which will not change." The spirit seeks the permanent, it lays hold on the eternal, the principles which are garnered in its essence are indestructible, and among them is holy love. When this is awakened the heart is at rest,

> "Knowing that what is excellent,
> As God lives, is permanent."

On this changeless affection is based the true marriage. When the wedded are discordant and wretched, it is not because love is inconstant, but because they do not mutually possess this precious treasure. Let them put away selfishness, and invite and cheris the divine guest. People fancy that they love. Do they seek the happiness of the adored object, or their own gratification? Do they treat with tender consideration the bodies and souls of their chosen, or neglect the courtesies and amenities, and self-denying services, and cordial expressions of sympathy that link friends together outside of marriage, and ensure lasting fraternity? Let love reign, and discord and desire for change will cease. Le love reign, and marriage will be a holy and deathless bond between answering souls, like that of the dual force within the mighty undulations of matter, named by true religion "Our Father and Mother God."

For the man and woman who purely and truly love each other and are guided by the law of justice, marriage is not a state of bondage. Indeed, it is only when they become by this outward acknowledgment publicly avowed lovers, that freedom is realized by them in its full significance. Thereafter they can be openly devoted to each other's interests, and avowedly chosen and intimate friends. Together they can plan life's battle, and enter upon the path of progress that ends not with life's eventide. Together they can seek the charmed avenues of culture, and strengthened by each other, can brave the world's frown in the rugged but heaven-lit path of reform. Home, with all that is dearest in the sacred name, is their peaceful and cherished retreat, within whose sanctuary blooms the virtues that make it a temple of beneficence.—*Mary F. Davis.*

The Heavenly Kingdom Within Us.

This kingdom is not of the external world, neither does it belong exclusively to the spiritual regions. We have had the fair fields of the Summer Land pictured to us, and the laws of that spiritual realm partially revealed; we are told of the "Debateable Land;" but these wise teachers know well that not sun or earth or stars constitute the real spiritual kingdom. Its presence is within every human soul; its certain possession is in the everlasting now. This life is only a peninsula of this kingdom; its borders and avenues lead through the faculties of the human consciousness. * * *

There is the development of the kindly spirit, the gentle amenities of life, the friendships, the charities, that give us some glimpse of this inner kingdom; there is love that reveals the inner sense, and if these fail to reveal its presence, there comes death. That is only one of the avenues that lead to it. It is much more important to know what this spiritual kingdom shall do for you now, than to know how much that is called you goes to *the* spiritual realm. It is vastly more important to know what it is doing for the world to-day, than to know if you shall wear the same lineaments and think the same thoughts there. You will surely wear your own face there and none other.

The sun that shines in the Summer Land and through the doorways of the spiritual kingdom illumines while it does not burn, lights you through the darkened ways of life, and reveals to you the immortal possessions that are yours as a spiritual being.

Spiritual manifestations are the avenues through which you are led to this inner kingdom. Be sure you do not make light of them. Make a fact essential, for it is as valuable as the stars that shine. Neither should you over-rate them. You love to be astonished, to be terrified, but most you should like to know what message your friend brings. It is more important that your soul should be awakened to a consciousness of itself than all else. Hail with gladness all that can do that. * *

The spiritual kingdom is not limited or confined to any period or epoch. You bear it with you wherever you go. It is to you at once prophecy and fulfillment. Without it the poet's song were a dream of despair; without its love the heart would grow sere; death, that mystery and fulfillment, would be the demon's mockery to humanity. This kingdom is not born of Christ, nor of any time or any religion, but of the soul's consciousness. It is not born of states or powers, but these are born of it. Man would stand a mad idiot, a wild thing, without this supernal kingdom within.

You that have heard its voice, that have watched your own inner consciousness, know that your soul is greater than time, death and all that comes to you. The soul is greater than the body, because in it every possibilty is enshrined; within it are the silent manifestations of the Deity. There are your Franklins, your Kanes, and many more that will risk everything to find out what open sea lies near the north pole. Livingston has been dead many times in Africa, and is not afraid of the many deaths, that he may know what lies in that unknown land and what people inhabit its unexplored countries. Man lives on earth to-day to conquer; to wrest from her bosom, scarred by the fierce contests of nature, the secret of life. The time shall come when every force shall be subjected to man.

Does this prove the soul's empire is only in matter? It is because the soul is supreme, the spirit greater than matter, that man is not afraid of heat or cold, of summer or winter. This soul tnat is afraid of nothing—shall it be afraid of immortality?

Nothing less than a universe will satisfy its longings. As

the poet calls not all his soul out in one song, as he that is inspired breathes not out all his life in one inspiration, but says till eternity there shall be more songs, more inspirations, so the soul can only sing the supreme song and yet know diviner ones still are to be breathed out. The song that is in you to sing, sing it, and the work that is in you to do, do it. Bind up the broken heart, and to-morrow there comes a bird fluttering at your window, and brings back your song with a diviner note. Yonder is a spirit well-nigh dead by sadness; comfort it, lift it up, strengthen it, and next year more sad souls shall come to you and you shall be glad that you were born. This is what the spiritual kingdom can do within you. In the center of your kingdom sits your soul. There will abide those sacred prayers and saintly thoughts that have come from the minds within your kingdom. There will be your fellows in love and hope, and aspiration, and all around shall be the families of your kingdom, and the bond between you shall be love, and the law shall be love, and the kingdom shall be to you greater than all the world, with its principalities and powers.—*Cora L. V. Tappan.*

Liberty.

The aim of the people is liberty. In every corner of the known earth, at this day, the cry is "liberty." Liberty for the body; liberty for the soul. The cry has gone forth. That thought stimulates every brain and every heart. Hence, from before every pulpit, around the desk of every writer, the cry comes, "Liberty for the soul."

Oh, Mystery! thou art indeed the mother of the abominations of the earth. Can there be truth and mystery together? Is it a possibility that God's works, if he be our Father, shall be a mystery to us, his children? There is no mystery save your own ignorance, and your submission or tyranny one to another. All the wonders of the Almighty's gospel have unrolled themselves in the light of knowledge, or are now becoming manifest to the investigating spirit of man.

The vail of mystery being lifted discloses the fact that the Almighty is the God of the living, not the God of the dead; that the living are his ministering spirits; that they can and do come to earth; that they are the ministers of light and knowledge, who, in all ages of the world, have gone forth to minister to the heirs of salvation.

Progress is a portion of the eternal gospel of nature, which the ages tell; which the history of all nations teaches; which the advance of every art and every science indicates; which the history of the planets, suns, and stars proclaims; which man himself spells out from the cradle to the grave, in a perpetual series of progressive experiments, each one leading to the culminating point when his spirit is set free, to put in practice the results of the follies, the trespasses, the hopes, the wishes, the aspirations which he has gained in his earthly career.—*Emma Hardinge.*

Sanctity of Maternity.

The Romish Church has acted upon a true instinct in making Mary illustrious among women. Art, a far truer system than Papacy, has done the same thing. She has been one of the grandest and most fruitful Inspirations—the typical mother and child multiplied in various forms for the eyes and souls of all women, saying to them, "Go thou and do likewise." And the universal human heart, even though blind and cold, pays a certain involuntary homage to the mothers whose children have acted the Christ-part in their generation.

Spirituality magnifies maternity, sees its real glory, and rejoices in it, as never other sovereign rejoiced in her earthly crown and scepter. It gives the mother at once pride and humility—pride, in her great office, though a manger be its cradle—humility, in herself as an instrument in the Divine hand for its accomplishment. "Behold the handmaid of the Lord;

be it unto me according to thy law. My soul doth magnify the Lord, and my spirit hath rejoiced in God, my Saviour. For he hath regarded the low estate of his handmaiden; for, behold, from henceforth all generations shall call me blessed. For he that is mighty hath done to me great things; and holy is his name." This is the language of every true spiritual mother.

We acknowledge with unstinted speech and feeling, the fullness of the Holy Spirit in the mother; and have a worshipful feeling toward her, as its pure, responsive recipient; a feeling which all mothers command in the degree that they are pure, divine, and aspiring, in maternity.—*Eliza W. Farnham.*

Wise Reverence for Motherhood.

The Christian Church, considering the birth of Jesus exceptional in all respects, has never discovered the philosophy of the fact that Joseph "knew not" Mary from the hour when the announcement of the new life was made till the birth of the child; nor has the medical profession discovered, or, if discovered, has not taught the imperative necessity of such condition to secure to motherhood that undisturbed operation of the forces within her body, and the passivity of mind which are vitally important to her own well-being and that of her offspring. When "the harp of a thousand strings" is attuned to a new key by the unfoldment of a new life within itself, every string is thrilled with exquisite vibration, either of delight or torture. Shall any soul save the owner dictate what hands shall sweep its chords? Whether they shall receive impulse from any? Or whether, like the Æolian harp, it shall, all untouched by mortal hands, vibrate only to the celestial harmonies which ever wait upon the incarnation of the soul in human form? * *

The fundamental truth of the duty of motherhood to make itself an intelligent instrument of creative power, and to provide suitable ante-natal conditions, and suitable provisions for the rearing of offspring after birth, and to subordinate every form of selfishness to its demands, is hardly thought of, still less appreciated. * * *

We cannot behold the grandeur of manhood till it is born of and through an enlightened, self-poised motherhood. I desire and shall labor to extricate woman from a deeper mire of helplessness than legal disability. From that she should also be freed, to secure freedom in all relations; but she wants, first, courage to assert the right to her own body as the instrument of reason and conscience, and the fulfilment of the function of motherhood, subject to no authority but the voice of God in her soul. * * * *

O Christian mothers! who look for the coming of that state of peace and good-will which was heralded by the earthly advent of Jesus, can you hope for its consummation so long as mother-souls stamp upon unborn offsping the impulse of murder? That undisturbed maternity which brought into fleshly existence the Prince of Peace, must obtain in human society before it can be free from the polluting tendencies, the discordant and warring elements, which deform and blight humanity. All the traditions of the past, before Jesus, enforce the same idea of the office of undisturbed maternity. The saviours of different forms of religion, preceding Christianity, were also immaculate conceptions, born of God and motherhood. This is a truth of deeper than theological import—a vital and indispensable necessity for the salvation of humanity. Motherhood should be a shrine unpolluted by one touch of selfishness and lust. O woman! this would and will be thy recompense for all the sufferings and agonies which pertain to physical womanhood and motherhood. * * *

Now, if by reason of irresistable desire, the body can be stamped ineffaceably, and the powers of mentality be developed so wonderfully, can it be a question that upon the moral nature, the more highly spiritual tablet, impressions as deeply graven and ineffaceable will be recorded? Such being the fact, what is the first duty of motherhood? Where has God written a law more clearly or imperatively than in the power of maternity over offspring? A power which cannot be hindered in its operation, either for good or ill. Where, then, does any other relation find justification for interference with its sacred function? Where does womanhood find justification for neglecting to claim for it that condition of purity which is its first necessity? Is it cause for marvel that the education which has taught that submission to the unguided passion of man is one of the most laudable wifely virtues, and the hindrance of motherhood consequent upon this outrage of the sacred office, should result in spiritual monstrosites? Till woman comprehends her duty and responsibility as the creative instrument, to secure the best conditions and work intelligently according to her highest knowledge and convictions, diseased and passion-tossed natures will continue to fester upon society; and till she educates her sons, in tender infancy and during growing boyhood, to the truth that manhood is responsible to the same moral obligations and is equally degraded by the same impurities as womanhood, and thus revolutionizes the now false standard of a sliding scale of morals for our sex, and asks as strong condemnation for the sins of one as the other, we shall continue to have occasion to blush for the debased libels upon true manliness which now disfigure society. But I pray you be not dismayed, nor resign yourself to inaction, because the disorder seems so inextricable. There is no wrong but shall be done away, unless evil instead of good is almighty. Look at the change accomplished in the degree of enlightenment, the tone of sentiment, the possibility of reaching the minds of people by instructive teaching in various forms, within a quarter of a century just past. Man has done his work in searching out and setting forth the physiological laws which bear upon the relation of marriage and parentage. His teaching, together with the deteriorating health of American women, has aroused the intellect of both sexes. The teachings of phrenology and physiology have prepared the way for higher and deeper teachings pertaining to the laws of parentage. * * *

The practice of infanticide is becoming one of the crying evils of our time, and there is but the alternative of an undesigned and undesired maternity, at which the soul of the mother not only shrinks, but stands outraged, and which has, through centuries past, entailed upon humanity the unhappiness and misery recorded—or a free, unhindered, God-inspired motherhood.

* * * The Infinite Patience has waited through the ages for the human mind to grow into an appreciation of principles, and out of the sphere and dominion of animal appetites. Let us imitate that patience and work faithfully for the truth that is revealed to us. The protest of the great army of the outraged and desecrated motherhood of the past wails adown the ages, and transforms itself into an appeal to every woman's soul to claim for posterity the rights of its office to work with God in that empire which cannot be shared, and should not be interfered with, by any relation. The creative function has a dominion all its own, spiritually as well as physically. Here God and motherhood should be the holy of holies. Selfishness has no right to lift the veil. Teach thy daughter that in this sphere she is, by every consideration of her own well-being and that of her offspring, ruler supreme. We have a literature which may aid and instruct, but there is no power which can, with the knowledge, impart an elevated tone of feeling, no method which can so effectually preserve the purity of the tablet while it receives the impress of knowledge, as familiar converse with the holy mother-heart. Be courageous then, O woman, and bequeath to the future the qualities, by transmission, and the knowledge, by instruction, which shall lift it out of the dominion of appetite and selfishness, that we may rejoice finally in the redemption of motherhood and the salvation of humanity.—*Mrs. L. B. Chandler.*

WOMAN'S TRUE POSITION.

There is nothing of greater importance to the well-being of society at large—of man as well as woman—than the true and proper position of woman.

This subject has claimed my earnest interest for many years. I have long wished to see woman occupying a more elevated position than that which custom for ages has allotted to her. The kind of homage that has been paid to woman, the flattering appeals which have too long satisfied her—appeals to her mere fancy and imagination—are giving place to a more extended recognition of her rights, her important duties and responsibilities in life. Woman is claiming for herself stronger and more profitable food. The increasing attention to female education, the improvement in the literature of the age, are among the proofs of a higher estimate of woman in society at large. Therefore we may hope that the intellectual and intelligent are being prepared for the discussion of this question, in a manner which shall tend to ennoble woman and dignify man.

Free discussion upon this, as upon all other subjects, is never to be feared; nor will it be, except by such as prefer darkness rather than light. It was sound philosophy uttered by Jesus, "He that doeth truth cometh to the light, that his deeds may be made manifest, that they are wrought in God."

This age is notable for its works of mercy and benevolence, for the efforts that are made to reform the inebriate and the degraded, to relieve the oppressed and the suffering. Women as well as men are interested in these works of justice and mercy. They are efficient co-workers, their talents are called into profitable exercise, their labors are effective in each department of reform. The blessing to the merciful, to the peacemaker, is equal to man and to woman. It is greatly to be deplored, now that she is increasingly qualified for usefulness, that any view should be presented calculated to retard her labors of love.

Why should not woman seek to be a reformer? If she is to shrink from being such an inconoclast as shall "break the image of man's lower worship," as so long held up to view; if she is to fear to exercise her reason, and her noblest powers, lest she should be thought to "attempt to act the man," and not "acknowledge his supremacy;" if she is to be satisfied with the narrow sphere assigned her by man, nor aspire to a higher, lest she should transcend the bounds of female delicacy;

truly it is a mournful prospect for woman. We would admit all the difference that our great and beneficent Creator has made in the relation of man and woman, nor would we seek to disturb that relation; but we deny that the present position of woman is her true sphere of usefulness; nor will she attain to this sphere, until the disabilities and disadvantages, religious, civil, and social, which impede her progress, are removed out of her way. These restrictions have enervated her mind and paralysed her powers.

So far from her ambition leading her to attempt to act the man, she needs all the encouragement she can receive, by the removal of obstacles from her path, in order that she may become a true woman. As it is desirable that man should act a manly and generous part, not "mannish," so let woman be urged to exercise a dignified and womanly bearing, not "womanish." Let her cultivate all the graces and proper accomplishments of her sex, but let not these degenerate into a kind of effeminacy, in which she is satisfied to be the mere plaything or toy of society, content with her outward adornings, and with the tone of flattery and fulsome adulation too often addressed to her. True, nature has made a difference in her configuration, her physical strength, her voice, &c.—and we ask no change, we are satisfied with nature. But how have neglect and mismanagement increased this difference! It is our duty to develope these natural powers by suitable exercise, so that they may be strengthened by reason of use. In the ruder state of society woman is made to bear heavy burdens while her "lord and master" walks idly by her side. In the civilization to which we have attained, if cultivated and refined woman would bring all her powers into use, she might engage in pursuits which she now shrinks from as beneath her proper vocation. The energies of men need not then be wholly devoted to the counting house and common business of life, in order that women in fashionable life may be supported in their daily promenades and nightly visits to the theater and ball-room.

Nor will woman fulfill less her domestic relations, as the faithful companion of her chosen husband and the fitting mother of her children, because she has a right estimate of her position and her responsibilities. Her self-respect will be increased; preserving the dignity of her being, she will not suffer herself to be degraded into a mere dependant. Nor will her feminine character be impaired. Instances are not few of woman throwing off the incumbrances which bind her, and going forth in a manner worthy of herself, her creation, and her dignified calling. Did Elizabeth Fry lose any of her feminine qualities by the public walk into which she was called? Having performed the duties of a mother to a large family, feeling that she owed a labor of love to the poor prisoner, she was empowered by Him who sent her forth to go to the kings and crowned heads of the earth, and ask audience of these; and it was granted her. Did she lose the delicacy of woman by her acts? No. Her retiring modesty was characteristic of her to the latest period of her life. It was my privilege to enjoy her society some years ago, and I found all that belonged to the feminine in woman—to true nobility, in a refined and purified moral nature. Is Dorothea Dix throwing off her womanly nature and appearance in the course she is pursuing? In finding duties abroad, has any "refined man felt that something of beauty has gone forth from her?" Is she compromising her womanly dignity in going forth to seek to better the condition of the insane and afflicted? Is not a beautiful mind and a retiring modesty still conspicuous in her?

Indeed, I would ask, if this modesty is not attractive also, when manifested in the other sex? The retiring modesty of William Ellery Channing was beautiful, as well as many others, who filled elevated stations in society. These virtues, differing as they may in degree in man and woman, are of the same nature, and call forth our admiration wherever manifested.

The noble courage of Grace Darling is justly honored, leading her to present herself on the coast of England, during the raging storm, in order to rescue the poor, suffering, shipwrecked mariner. Woman was not wanting in courage in the early ages. In war and bloodshed even, this trait was often displayed. The courage of Joan of Arc is made the subject of popular lectures. But more noble moral daring is marking the female character at the present time, and better worthy of imitation. As these characteristics come to be appreciated in man too, his warlike acts, with all the miseries and horrors of the battle-ground, will sink into their merited oblivion, or be remembered only to be condemned. The heroism diplayed in the tented field must yield to the moral and Christian heroism which is shadowed in the signs of our times.

Who knows but that if woman acted her part in governmental affairs, there might be an entire change in the turmoil of political life. It becomes man to speak modestly of his ability to act without her. If woman's judgment were exercised, why might she not aid in making the laws by which she is governed? Lord Brougham remarked that the works of Harriet Martineau upon Political Economy were not excelled by those of any political writer of the present time. The first few chapters of her "Society in America," her views of a Republic, and of government generally, furnish evidence of woman's capacity to embrace subjects of universal interest.

When, in the diffusion of light and intelligence, a convention shall be called to make regulations for self-government on Christian principles, I can see no good reason why women should not participate in such an assemblage, taking part equally with man.

Let woman then go on—not asking favors, but claiming as a right the removal of all hindrances to her elevation in the scale of being. Let her receive encouragement for the proper cultivation of all her powers, so that she may enter profitably into the active business of life; employing her own hands in ministering to her necessities, strengthening her physical being by proper exercise, and observance of the laws of health. Let her not be ambitious to display a fair hand, and to promenade the fashionable streets of our city, but rather coveting earnestly the best gifts, let her strive to occupy such walks in society as will befit her true dignity in all the relations of life. No fear that she will then transcend the proper limits of female delicacy. True modesty will be as fully preserved in acting out those important vocations, as in the nursery or at the fireside ministering to man's self-indulgence. Then in the marriage union the independence of the husband and wife will be equal, their dependence mutual, and their obligations reciprocal.—*Lucretia Mott.*

Spiritual Teachings.

Man is a myriad-stringed instrument, facing every point of the infinite radius, and able to receive and repeat all the harmonies of the universe. His bosom contains the germs of all conceivable grace, personal perfection, and spiritual beauty. The glory of sun and stars is eclipsed by the glory of that reason, of that soul that can weigh and measure sun and star.

The way of life is wonderful; it proceeds by abandonment to the currents of eternal power. Tendencies are streams of power setting into us from the eternal deeps of Spiritual Being, and indicate at once the duties and destinies of the times.

Man is found to be the divinest creation on the planet. The idea of man is rising. He is no longer to be controlled by institutions. They are made for him, not he for them. It is the age of spiritual and political liberty, because it is the age of spiritual inspiration.

Let us no longer distrust our spiritual powers. Let us no longer be enslaved with these external things; let us use them, and not let them use us; and remember it is only when in the higher moments of our interior life we do consciously feel the surges of the everlasting nature, that we can realize the sweet and holy significance of immortal life.

—The rays of man's selfish intellectuality fall on the soul like moonbeams reflected from an iceberg; only to freeze the germs of our spiritual affections, which yearn to be ingulfed in divine love and beauty.

—All substance and power is ONE, or no universe could arise out of them. Hence man is the autocrat of creation. He carries, sheathed within his flesh, the potent secret of all things.

Man fronts two worlds at once; with something of the animal and something of the angel in him. He belongs to substance, yet lives amid the shadows; he lives in the world of forms, while the eternal perfections of which these forms are symbols live in him; he sees the symbols with his eyes, but he feels the divine verities signified with his spirit.

—But there is no permanent element of wealth but truth, justice, love, wisdom—the eternal verities of the soul and of God. It is not what we do, it is not our history, that makes us divine—it is what we *are*, and what *we are to be forever.*

—There is no middle ground between natural religious inspiration and the great spiritual idea. The farthest star sends its beams down into our world, and celestial chemistry picks them to pieces, and ascertains thereby the constituents of distant suns. So with the light of immortal life. Its idea, an intuition in us, is the eternal recognition of the far-fallen beams of celestial being—of Spiritual life. Intuition of the spiritual and divine is the spontaneous spiritual chemistry of the soul. There are no "discrete degrees" in nature between "matter" and "spirit;" there is no qualitative chasm or vacuum over which, from either side, influences cannot pass.

The expanded earth and unfolded heavens are manifestations of an Eternal Spirit. The rocks, hills, valleys, rivers, ocean, and stars gleam with the white splendors of the Divine Reason. The Spiritual idea of substance is arising from science. All bodies are now proved to be only petrified forms of force; all forces are proved, by their mutual transformability, to be only modes of the action of some common, simple, homogeneous, invisible or spiritual Power; and all power is eternal, infinite and divine. For how could man receive life, power, substance, light, heat, gravitation, electricity, beauty, and wisdom, if he were not composed at bottom of substance, and power, and law, one and identical with these?

If the solid rocks we tread had not, by the laws of disintegration and organization, ascended into the composition of the human structure, geology would be a sealed book, an impossible study to man. If the star-beam had never been wrought up into the composition of your baby in the cradle, he would never in his manhood see these glimmers through the midnight air. If the sunlight had never kissed itself into the structural intelligence of your boy, he never would know of its existence, or feel its warmth, or recognize its beauty and power. How can that which is spirit, if it be totally different from matter, as some have supposed, be connected with matter? What law exists between two unlike and opposite substances, which, as a chain, can unite these two extremes?

Therefore I say unto you, the substance *of* the world is the intelligence *in* the world; and that intelligence is revealed primarily, not *to*, but *in* man. Wherefore, revelation is of two kinds—objective and subjective; or external and phenomenal, and interior and substantial. Now what is inspiration? Is it not the cognition by the personal soul of the existence and flow of the Eternal? It cometh from the relation of the personal to the impersonal, of the relative to the absolute, of the dependent to the independent, of the shadow to the substance.

—The aim of science should be to fathom those hidden, secret, invisible forces, of which the suns and stars are the merest precipitations and residue. If there be a God, then "matter" is but spiritual sediment; "suns" are only shadows of eternal Reason; so that the spirit *in* Nature and *in* man is the only permanent, solid and enduring substance.

—The fraternity of souls and the paternity of God rest at last on the identity of the original substance of each being. If human spirits are the children of God—if the idea of the fatherhood of God be not a delusion—then the substance of the Creator is the foundation of each soul. Yea, the identity of the primordial essence of the human and the Divine Spirit, is the only logical basis; and it is on this foundation alone that religion itself is possible.

—For if God be Spirit and Infinite there is no room for any other substance than spirit. Spirit is the primordial Power at the center, and the original substance at the foundation of the world. Personality, therefore, cannot be predicated of a Boundless Being, of the Infinite Beneficence. Individuality is, necessarily, relative and dependent, and pre-supposes the absolute and independent, which is Infinite Spirit, eternal law. But Infinite Spirit is absolute, not relative; is independent, not limited.

—The spiritual philosophy has facts by the million—facts which appeal to every possible condition of mind, from the most sensuous to the most spiritual-minded; while for the deep and intuitive thinker it has the most transcendent and spiritual ideas. The unlettered can be surprised by the movement of a table without contact of visible power; while under the inspiration of the gifted seer and poet, the great fields of eternal day break on our wrapt vision. It opens on the one hand the great question of physiological psychology, and on the other, the profound questions of transcendental theology. Hence it promises to reach all the world and every soul thereof. It is the democracy of religion and of philosophy combined. It is the Catholicism of Rationalism, with a fact, an idea, a reason, and a symbol, for every possible mood of man. In bridging over the grave, it connects the poorest barefooted, ragged child of earth—whose kindred watch him from the homes of the pure and the free, weeping when he strays, and rejoicing when he returns to the true path—with the highest archangel of the Summer Land.

—Demonstrate the naturalness of spiritual forces and laws, and the realm of the divine is brought within reach of science. Science may then push its discoveries up into the immortal world; may, must link the two worlds together in the bonds of a scientific as well as sacred fellowship, and so banish all hobgoblins, all ghosts, all superstitions, and all senseless religious fanaticism from the world.

—When we perceive the unity of nature; when we regard the mutual transformability of bodies, and of all forces; when we discover in the analyzed sunbeam and star-beam the elements which have been precipitated and hardened into rocks, and coal, and iron, and other metals; when we behold everywhere the reign of the same invisible power, ever changing in form, but ever the same in *esse*—the soul is carried on and on in the tide of inspiration, up to the same great central conception that spirit "is all, and in all."

Substance is necessarily eternal; phenomena necessarily limited in time and space. Induction deals only with shadows; deals only with form, not substance; deals only with phenom enalities. The universe swings between these two vortices: First, downward and outward, into forms of appearance; second, upward and inward, into thought, into consciousness, into eternal Light.

Does any one suppose that men first inferred that there was such a thing as love by induction? No! the human heart loves as spontaneously as the the bird sings, because it cannot help it.

—Nature is a unity—an undivided empire; and to him who affirms the God in it, there is no escape from the spiritual fraternity of all things, and of all spheres of being. Spiritual Communion is the glorious flower of all religious experience; the answer to all prayer; the ultimate of all study, the goal of all science and scholarship. Spirit is the foundation of all things; continued inspiration from God the one condition of all life, high and low, and hence communion with Nature, universal. There is no world too fine for the spirit in man; no angel too pure to work for us earthlings; and no spiritual aristocracy allowable in this God's world.

Believe me, brethren, there is a grander world than that in which these shadows dance across the sensible horizon; there is a diviner life, a serener consciousness, a more golden condition, than that of the body and its relations to the world.

—Spiritualism is the only resort of all Christian progressives, who hold on to the idea of God, and to the possibility of a natural divine life; and Atheism is the only resort of all those who cannot so hold on. Just where Spiritualism differs from Theology it agrees with the religion of Jesus. It is alive, fresh, spontaneous, progressive. But what is the genius, spirit, scope of the great Spiritual Movement? What are its ideas, methods, sources of power, and aims? Is it all confined to the fact of intercourse between the two worlds? Nay, far from it. He who accepts the fact of spiritual intercourse, must take all that goes logically with that fact as part of the truth of the whole movement.

Spiritualism shows how the career of a soul in this life affects its condition in the next. Is it not proper, then, for it to deal with the conditions of this life? We felt that the ministering angels of the spiritual world inspired and pushed us on to the work, as well as the deep voice of our inmost spiritual nature. Our aim is the attainment of that "perfection and truthfulness of mind which is the secret intention of Nature." Verily, our aim is too large to admit a creed or sect. We hold that the "chief end of man" is the highest and most harmonious development of all the powers of life to a complete and consistent whole.

—The gospel of this epoch is for progress—for the enfranchisement of woman, and her admission, on terms of equality with man, to all the rights, privileges, and immunities of life. It demands justice to all classes of citizens. It calls on government to make all equal before the law. It opens itself to science and philosophy, and all truth, from every quarter of the globe. While in religion the advent of the Spiritual Dispensation, emancipating millions in our own land as well as in Europe, the decay of the Papal hierarchy, and the revival of the spirit of Art, and its consecration to Nature, attests the immense activity and spiritual energy of this century. All these facts are the sure signs of coming benefits.

Supernaturalism is now rapidly sinking into hopeless decrepitude and remediless decay. Under the influence of liberal scholarship, free thought, fearless criticism, and the great Spiritual Movement, joined with the late discoveries in science, popular theology is being actually destroyed.

Behold, the seventh great religious revolution of the world is upon us. Brahminism, Buddhism, Judaism, Classicalism, Mohammedanism, and even modern Christianity, are, regarding their claims, only failures. All have failed to save man from ignorance, crime, war, slavery and woe. Now the race advances, either to Atheism or to a universal Spiritualism.—*Selden J. Finney.*

THE "FREE RELIGIOUS" MOVEMENT.

Let us not be misunderstood. We are not brought to affirm the indifference of religions: still less are we tempted to assert their equality in dignity or worth. That some are nobler than others is a fact too evident to be overlooked. One is leaf, another blossom, another fruit. Indeed, to compare them is less easy than to contrast them. Strung along in a line from the world's infancy to its maturity, they represent the stages of the world's growth. The sentiment of the Infinite is the creative source of them all. But that sentiment, how variably is it blended! It may be found somewhere to exist as pure sentiment, unmixed with intellect. The religions of India combine sentiment with fancy. The religions of the Semitic race are a combination of sentiment with moral sense. In China the sentiment has a large infusion of the filial, domestic, and ancestral spirit. We need not hesitate to say, that Christianity is the crowning glory of religions thus far; but we must not turn a deaf ear to eulogiums which other faiths receive from their adherents. The Christian claims that his religion is the religion of the highest races, and the most developed civilizations. He declares that it associates the religious sentiment with the greatest number of regal powers, with the most sympathy, conscience, intelligence and imagination; that its theology is the grandest piece of speculative construction yet achieved; its churches the noblest monuments of organized feeling and purpose yet erected; its cultus the most complete expression of the heart's desire, the most comprehensive ministration to its need yet devised; that its sacred books are, as a whole, so much richer than those of any other faith, that they are not altogether unworthy to be called "The Bible." In the purity of its moral standard; the sublimity of its moral ideal; the spendor of its cardinal virtues; the sweetness of its spiritual graces; the strength of its upward-soaring wing; the tenderness of its human regards; its skilful blending of judgment and grace; the awfulness of its abysses; the transcendency of its heights; the vastness of its pictorial representations; the magnificence of the frescoes with which it has covered the adamantine walls of the world; the softness of its angels; the terror of its fiends; the domestic qualities of its Godhead, Father, Mother, and Child; the stateliness of its drama of redemption, whose stage is the heaven-canopied universe, whose scenes are the epochs of history, whose *dramatis personæ* are all created beings, nay, the uncreated Being himself,—in these, and in a hundred respects besides, Christianity, in the view of its disciples, is the queen of faiths.

But the older faiths of India, Persia, China, Judea, speak of their glories and superiorities, too, as rapturously as this faith does. And if we look forward, measuring by the rule of present intelligence, we see those who regard Christianity as very imperfect.

Is Christianity the full and final faith? Does it satisfy philosophy? Does it exhaust feeling? Is it synonymous with reason? It is a gorgeous romance. Is it a complete story of the heart's life? Is it even poetry for the modern imagination? Does it satisfy the dreams of the mature world? Is it our Tennyson, or our Browning? Our George Eliot, or even our Charles Dickens? Is it open to no criticism? What statement will you make of it that commands general assent? When Mr. Abbott says Christianity culminates in Romanism, every Protestant nostril dilates with scorn. When Protestantism unfolds its scheme, the Liberals shake their heads. The Liberals produce their interpretation, and an audible smile ripples over the countenance of the by-standers. India is ready to welcome Christ, Keshub Chunder Sen declares; but it can make nothing of the system of dogmas that bears his name. Philosophy looks on Christianity, and says: "Yes, it is very impressive as a fact in history, very imposing as an institution, very beautiful as a demonstration of sentiment, very sonorous as an example of rhetoric, very superb as a piece of art, a master-work of architecture, painting, and song; but before an advanced intelligence can accept it, there must be important modifications. The dogmas must be restated, the definitions revised, the histories rewritten, the traditions recast. All its theories must be reconsidered, its views of human nature, human life, human destiny. Its Bible must be expurgated, its worship spiritualized, its cultus adapted to actual needs. Nay, its standard of virtue is open to objection. its graces do not sit altogether gracefully on modern men." In fact, this highest form of religion is less supreme in its domain than the lower forms are in theirs. It does not answer social or intellectual calls. * * * * * *

How much more natural is it to say that the soul grows its beliefs; that they answer to the stages of its development, correspond to its moods of feeling, conform to the soil and atmosphere which it supplies. The Bibles are the soul uttering its deepest convictions; the worships are the soul aspiring; the creeds are the soul believing; the churches are the soul associating its powers of sympathy; the prophets are the preaching soul; the priests are the sanctifying soul; the saints are the soul consecrated; inspiration is a deep breath of spiritual air; revelation is the uncovering of the world's meaning, the dropping of scales from the eye, the look behind the veil.

Regarded thus, religion is not an *impression* made by God on the heart of his child, but rather an *expression* of the child's heart towards God; and the religions of the world are less truly regarded as voices out of the eternal silence, than as voices sent *into* the eternal silence. * * *

The Free Religionist affirms the supremacy of the religious sentiment, and its inexhaustible vitality. The splendor of its past performances justifies the hope of other performances equally timely and noble in the times before us. He does not propose to make a muddle of religions, to reduce them to a minimum, and accept a residuum of carbonic in place of the diamond. It is not his plan to strike an average among the world's faiths. He makes the highest pledge of a higher. He does what the liberal believers in all the sects are doing; but he does it in obedience to a larger law.

Let me venture to state a few of the first principles which are suggested by our position in the general religious world.

It is the traditional view that religion, belonging to the supernatural sphere, comes down upon the human mind to control it.

It is the rational view that, the sphere of the supernatural being included in the compass of the mind, religion is one of the mind's expressions.

It is usually taught that the founders of religions were either divine beings, or human beings miraculously taught.

We teach that the founders of religions were exalted types of human nature.

The common belief is, that religion necessarily comes with miracle.

Our belief implies that religion comes by due process of spiritual preparation and unfolding.

The elders said, the Sovereign Wisdom broods over men, disclosing itself from time to time, and demanding obedience to its dictations.

We say, the Sovereign Wisdom is disclosed within men in proportion as they enlarge their intelligence.

Tradition runs, that God stands to the world as the potter to the clay.

Our faith runs, that the divine forces are manifest in and through the organic universe.

It is an old persuasion that God makes himself known in his ways, attributes, and intentions.

It is our persuasion that no knowledge of him is exact, and that all we have our faculties procure for us.

We grew up to think that Jesus exhausted the capacities of human nature.

We have come to think that Jesus expressed the sentimental side of human nature alone, leaving it philosophical side in the shadow.

It is the common faith that man is an exile seeking a home beyond the grave, to which religion introduces him.

It is our faith that man is at home here, and that religion tells him how beautiful and noble his home may become.

It is the old idea that man is in bondage to sin.

It is the new idea that sin is imperfection and may be outgrown.

The religion of the day prescribes a form of cultus.

Our religion prescribes a law of culture.

It is generally believed that the pivot of all modern history is the hour when God revealed himself.

We believe that history is a series of chapters in the autobiography of mankind, each fresh manifestation of mind being a fresh disclosure of the divine intention.

It is the popular impression that science must be held subordinate to revelation.

It is the rational impression that science is revelation.

According to the ruling notion, piety is escape from the world, and refuge in God.

According to the new notion, piety is fidelity to the aims and uses of the world.

Pious opinion declares future blessedness to be the end of the elect.

Reason declares moral uprightness, character, to be the noblest attainment.

It is a principle in what is ordinarily called religion that culture draws men away from the the spiritual life.

It is a principle in free religion that culture, in its large sense, is a means to the spiritual life.

The common prejudice is that religion must regard liberty with suspicion.

It is our judgment that the fullest liberty is essential to rational faith.

It is a vulgar axiom that the spirit of the age must submit to be dominated by religion, which is the same yesterday, to-day, and for ever.

It is with us a primary truth that religion must, in the future as in the past, accommndate its forms to the spirit of the age.

These you will observe are suggestions, not dogmas. Free religion has no creed.—*O. B. Frothingham.* (*Address at meeting of Free Religious Association, Boston,* 1870.)

Fear of the Living God.

"It is a fearful thing to fall into the hands of the living God.—*Hebrews, X,* 31.

I wonder how many people know that this text is in the Bible. I wonder how many know that it is in the New Testament. I wonder how many of those who know of its existence understand what it means, or ever tried to understand it. If it were written thus: "It is a fearful thing to fall into the hands of the living Satan," or, "it is a fearful thing to fall *out* of the hands of the living God"—that would be intelligible. But the passage as it runs is loaded, every word, with incomprehensibleness to modern Christians. I will not try to carry you back to the state of feeling about God which prevailed two thousand years ago. Two thousand years is a long time; and when everything else that people thought and did looks so very strange to us, what they thought and did about religion should not surprise us.

I might explain the sentence I have quoted by two others in the same chapter, the one immediately preceding this—"We know him who hath said, Vengeance is mine, I will repay;" the other concluding the chapter—"For our God is a consuming fire." But to explain these sentenees so that they would seem true to a modern mind would be as hard as to explain the text. Let us give up all attempt, then, to get fully into the mind of those dark ages of Faith, and see what there may be in our modes of thought that throws light on these strange words.

Is it not common now to think of God as standing for moral law, judgment, retribution? Is he not the representative of the accusing and avenging conscience? When is he instinctively thought of? In dark days, in gloomy times, in periods of fear, when calamity befals, or sorrow comes, or death approaches, or the sense of guilt oppresses the mind. How is he commonly thought of then? As the being who darkens the day, makes the time gloomy, produces the fear, sends the calamity, causes the sorrow, inflicts the death, holds over the sense of guilt the rod of penalty. He is the awful Being. At the mention of His name men droop their heads, lengthen their faces, subdue their voices, let the light out of their countenances, and recall their misdoings. The word "punishment" calls up the thought of God. The mention of hell suggest Him. His attributes are the great swelling attributes that appal. He is Omnipotent; men are pigmies before Him; they are grasshoppers; He can blow them away as dust; they are as asleep. He is Omniscient. He knows what everybody is about, knows what they are thinking of, what they are feeling; has a detective in every bosom. All over Christendom people tremble as they think of that Justice that holds every one to the letter of the Law, and makes each answerable for his deeds without regard to all those fine considerations which diminish the weight of personal responsibility. All over the world God is a terror. It is the effort of religious men to make him felt as a terror. Hear men pray to him. Read the Church litanies. Listen to the warning counsel given to wilful, vicious, and criminal people: "Be careful. You are watched. The Avenging Angel is dogging your footsteps. You are rushing to your doom." Christian men and women have not yet outgrown the feeling that the living God is an unsleeping policeman, incessantly walking his rounds. * * * * *

Multitudes have trusted themselves to the Living God, and have found it sweet to do so. Broad thinkers, cutting themselves adrift from the quiet moorings of their Faith, have launched away under the guidance of knowledge, and, instead of falling sheer into the gulf of unbelief and despair, have found themselves floating over sunny waters, beneath heavens lit with the glory of new constellations; have discovered islands and continents never heard of before; have made acquaintance with fresh territories of thought, and have learned how beautiful it was to be citizens of the world, free to come and go where they would, in full faith that the further they went the more wondering, reverential, and loving they would become, provided they went in sober earnestness and faith.

Venturing to believe in humanity, we have tried republican institutions; and in proportion to the fidelity of our experiment has been the demonstration of its success. Mr. Carlyle's frightful picture of "shooting Niagara" provokes a smile. In live humanity we find there is a live Deity; and so far from its being a "fearful thing" to fall into his hands, we are only praying that we may have grace to fall into his hands more entirely. If anything will save us from the fearfulness of the ancient systems of government, which assumed that the living God dwelt in a palace and left it only to prowl round the gardens and awe intruders, it is trust in the principle that people are best governed when they govern themselves.

It was believed in the olden time that the State must maintain religion; that if it did not, the evil one who was constantly going about seeking whom he might devour would snap up many souls, as a vulture snaps up chickens, and would bring the whole land to the barrenness of infidelity. The State *did* cease to have any concern with religion, and never was so much piety, so much personal faith or conviction, so much deep individual concern for spiritual things. The wicked one who prowled about seeking whom he might devour, proved to be the living God stirring in his children's hearts the embers of the personal religious life.

It was believed in the olden time that either the Church or the despotic State must undertake the support of the schools. It was a fearful thing to fall into the hands of the malicious demon of ignorance which infested the world. But on the voluntary system, which throws on the people the responsibility of educating themselves, the schools not only increased in numbers but improved in quality; there is better teaching, better discipline, better school architecture and regulation. And so on in other things. We have found that the whole universe is filled with the Living God; that the Living God is not living jealousy, or wrath, or cunning, but living truth and goodness and beneficence. We have learned to see Him in the elements that bring us health, comfort, prosperity, happiness. We have learned to see Him in the elements which bring discipline, experience, wisdom. We have learned to see Him in air and light, in the fine gases, in muscle, nerve, fibre and tissue, in organs and functions. We have learned to see Him in intelligence and affection, in the glow of aspiration and in the courage of a noble will. We have learned to see Him in the wise economies that administer life, in the knowledge that centuries have built up, in the principles that brace us in our difficulties and solace us in our grief. We have come to the belief that the dreadful thing is to fall *out* of the hands of the Living God, to fall out of knowledge and reason and truth and charity, to fall out of confidence and trust, to remain so shut up in our narrow houses of belief or custom that we do not know what the Living God is, and are continually fancying that he is living ogre or living devil. * * *

It is a fearful thing when one who has never questioned his belief first begins to question it, and stepping out of his old home of Faith, sees what looks like a howling wilderness about him. It is a fearful thing when one who has always dwelt on problems he could master, and has felt perfectly at home with the ordinary questions of his lot, finds himself face to face with problems he cannot master, and gropes about him in the dark for an answer to questions that baffle his intelligence. All experimenting of this kind is a fearful thing—all venture into the land of the unknown, though it has been going on for thousands of years, and has always resulted in the nobleness of mankind. Nothing is so fearful as Novelty in custom or institution. However confident their anticipation of heaven, none are ready to die. But experience teaches us that the fearfulness is for the instant. The momentary shock of the plunge over, a new set of powers comes into play; a new order of satisfactions reveals itself to view; a new and broader existence is disclosed. We come to learn that to live under law, to live justly, healthfully, obediently, trustingly, is the farthest possible from being a fearful thing. The liar, the thief, the traitor, the murderer, would all be the happier for falling into the hands of the Living God. I plead for the substitution of a spirit of quiet repose for a spirit of fear, as we think of the power that holds our destiny in its hands. I plead for a spirit of courage in meeting emergencies, facing difficulties, coming in contact with trials, encountering what seems to be evils, entering upon new and untried paths of life. Let us be sure that there is no demon but the demon of doubt, fear, ignorance, in our own timid bosoms; that out of doors all is light and power.—*O. B. Frothingham.*

Religious Liberty.

For myself, I belong to a sect (Baptist). I love it and I honor it. I believe its history to be one of transcendant glory. I believe that the brave men and women who have belonged to it in different ages and in different lands, have stood in the front rank of those who have demanded "soul liberty;" and at the stake, at the whipping-post, in the prison, everywhere by their blood they have sealed this precious testimony. But I am sometimes afraid that my sect, having passed out from under the harrow of persecution, being no longer a scorned and outcast people, having grown to magnificent proportions of strength, of culture, of education, of wealth, and of power, are beginning to forget the glorious lessons of the past, and are tempted to build up simply an ecclesiastical structure, and to put their hand of power upon those who wish only to repeat the announcements which our ancestors so gloriously and so bravely made. All church history is but a repetition of this experience, and therefore it comes to pass that in every age this battle must be fought over again. Through eighteen long centuries, now in this land and now in that, now by this people now by that people, now by a resistance to civil tyranny, now by a protest against ecclesiastical despotism, this assertion of the liberty of every man to believe for himself, answering only to God, and not to human tribunals, has been made again and again. I believe that it is made here to-day not in any spirit of wild enthusiasm or distorted fanaticism, but in a calm, earnest, studious, and honest way.

Now, in this land which we call free, in this age which we call glorious, we need not perhaps so much for our own sakes as for the sake of those who shall come after us, to assert the principle which more than two long centuries ago was the very axiom of Protestantism,—the absolute right of every human soul to interpret for itself the whole word of Scripture. No longer do the thunderbolts forged at the Vatican, and hurled by the angry hand of the Pope, excite alarm, but merriment only, on the part of those against whom they are directed. The horrid chambers of the Inquisition are deserted, the dreadful mechanism of torture lies idle and rusted, the whipping-post and the scaffold to-day claim no victims to religious bigotry; but there is a more subtle, and if possible, a more accursed persecution, which, to-day even, is employed by too many who vainly dream they are doing God service. It is the persecution which seeks to brand with odium and write "outcast" upon brave and honest souls, who simply differ from their fellows on questions of intellectual interpretation or doctrinal statement, while their behavior and lives are on the side of justice, of brotherhood, and of love. I think, therefore, that we need to take to ourselves the lessons which are so beauteously illustrated in the life and behavior of Jesus; that it is not what a man says he *believes* that makes him either to be accepted or to be rejected, but it is what a man *does*. A life of justice, a life of purity, a life of chasteness, a life of temperance, a life of benevolence, a life that puts out its hand of defence over the weak and the oppressed, a life that dares to defy wealth and power, even, if they are upon the side of wrong,—is not such a life a life of unquestioned righteousness? For myself I hold it to be a cardinal and vital dogma, that Jesus of Nazareth is the Saviour of the world. I believe him to be God incarnated, manifested in flesh. When I look upon him stretched upon the Cross of Calvary, when I behold that crown of thorns, those wounded hands and feet, that side pierced by the cruel foeman's spears, my soul sees there my vicarious atonement and sacrifice, and by the shedding of that blood I believe my sin to be pardoned. That, to my soul, is a profound, deep, earnest, and absorbing belief. But if any other man judge differently, I am not constituted an ecclesiastical tribunal to try him, or to pronounce a verdict of condemnation against him. I think of what Jesus himself said, "Who art thou that judgest another man's servant? To his own master he standeth or falleth." I recollect that the severest and bitterest rebukes which passed the lips of the gentle Nazarene were those which were hurled at the scribes and pharisees who sat at Moses' seat, who wore broad phylacteries, who loved the uppermost seats in the synagogue, who paid tithes of mint, anise, and cummin, and yet who devoured widows' houses, and forgot the wider law of justice and love. I transfer that lesson to to-day, and think that it is not the outward ecclesiastical relationships which men hold that will save them, or cause them to perish, but that vital communion between God and their own souls is the one thing necessary to salvation.

This much we need, it seems to me,—a more earnest, a more profound, a more devout and hearty work in our day and land, to save from the woes and suffering, that do encompass them about, the millions of the children of want. Let us not be so industrious for the erection of gorgeous church edifices, for the devising of elaborate ceremonials, for the defence of ordinances or of doctrines, however needful we may think them to be; but let us be very zealous and careful in our work and errand of mercy to do that which is just and true and right and good. Whether, therefore, a man belong to one sect or another, whether he belong, as St. Francis Xavier, to the old Romish communion, or, as Emanuel Swedenborg, to the Church of the New Jerusalem, or, as the glorious Channing, to a broad and Catholic faith, or whether he belong to no outward ecclesiastic organization whatever, these questions, it seems to me, fade and sink away into insignificance in comparison with this vital and absorbing question. Are we conscious of the deep responsibility that rests upon us during the brief day of our earthly life, that we perform life's errand and mission well? When I myself rest this weary head under the green sod, and some child or beloved friend shall stand there some summer day, when nature weaves a garniture of blossoms above me, and the birds in the boughs of trees overhead are making the air musical, I take God this moment to witness, I would rather have it said of me, "There lies a man who was a friend to the widow and to the orphan, who spoke a word for the slave, for the outcast, and the suffering, and who, in all the works of sweet humanity and righteousness, followed after the footsteps of Jesus," than to have it said of me, "He was mighty in the defence of his faith, and established the dogmas of his sect."

Do you recollect what Garibaldi, the apostle of Italian liberty and unity, said, just before he made his memorable attack upon Rome? He called his soldiers together, and said,

"Let those who choose hunger and wounds and death follow me." To-day I seem to hear the Captain of our salvation, calling out to us and saying, "Let those who choose self-denial, those who choose crucifixion to the world and to self-indulgence, walk after my steps!" We are not to climb some giddy height of ecclesiastical preferment; we are not to win for ourselves fortune; but we are to do justly and to do well, in God's name, and with God's help, trusting that the day may speedily come when differences in the interpretation and apprehension of truth may be changed into unity of spirit, in that better and perfect creed of our Lord, where clouds and shadows come not, and where every soul is filled with immaculate purity and love.—*Rev. C. H. Malcom, Newport, R. I.*

Being and Doing.

Doing is necessary, for what avails the spirit if it be not embodied in some outward form? It expires, it evaporates. We must actualize it in life and noble deeds. But you esteem the tree for its *fruit-bearing power*, and not alone for its present crop. It has a higher value than its immediate yield. So character is greater than conduct, for it is the source of conduct. * * * At the divine judgment the question will not be simply what have you *done*, but what are you? Perhaps in that sifting of being from doing, of character from conduct, the supposed sinner shall turn out a saint, and the reputed saint be sent to the lowest place. And herein lies much of the immorality of the popular doctrine which holds out the hope of heaven and the fear of hell as motives to lives of charity, temperance, honesty, and good-will; for deeds done thus, on speculation, as means to a selfish end, are as morally valueless as ecclesiastical penances and practices. The Protestant who salves over his conscientious scruples for sin by leaving a few dimes' worth of tracts at our front doors, is on the same level of moral life with the Catholic who measures his piety by the number of his pater nosters.

Summing up then: which is best? to make your works better than yourself, or to make yourself so good that no work can adequately represent you? For still it remains true that you can never put *the highest* into words or deeds. Speech is limited, words are insufficient to express the richest and fullest life of the soul. Speech is human, the soul is divine; finite works can never justly represent the infinite source from whence they sprang. * * *

What the age needs is this constant affirmation of the spirit against the materializing influences of our common daily life, and the present one-sided development of scientific thought. "The soul," said an old philosopher, "is the measure of all things." Spirit alone can adequately interpret to us the problems of the world of matter and the universe of man. * * The fleshly eye sees the sparrow fall to the ground, the spirit reassures itself with the thought that the Father sees it fall. Unfeeling hands press the crown of thorns upon the sensitive brow, but the spirit discerns the roses crowning the thorns, and is at peace.

It is the soul which gives birth to the distinctions, good or evil, right or wrong, for the soul is the measure of the universe. So in human life, our deeds are characterless in themselves; and merely *symptomatic* of our inner being. What you *are* lends significance to what you *do.* Strive then, first of all, for that sublime faith, that vital piety, that stability of character, which is the infallible *source* of large-hearted deeds. * * * Deeds must spring spontaneously from the divine life within the soul. In this harmonious interaction lies the only possible guarantee for a healthy normal life. But let us recognize the soul as the true center of our moral being, and be able to say, with Lavater, "May my deeds be like my words, and my words be like my heart."

Then our works will no longer be forced and unrepresentative, but genuine, spontaneous and efficient!

"Thou must be true thyself,
If thou the truth wouldst teach;
Thy soul must overflow, if thou
Another soul would reach;
It needs the overflowing heart
To give the lips full speech.
Think truly, and thy thought
Shall the world's famine feed;
Speak truly, and thy word
Shall be a fruitful seed;
Live truly, and thy life shall be
A great and noble creed."

Charles W. Wendte, Chicago, Ill.

R. W. Emerson—Teachings.

—To the poet, to the philosopher, to the saint, all things are sacred, all events profitable, all days holy, all men divine. A man should learn to detect and watch that gleam of light which flashes across his mind from within, more than the luster of the firmament of bards and sages. We lie in the lap of immense intelligence, which makes us receivers of its truth and organs of its activity. The relations of the soul to the Divine Spirit are so pure, that it is profane to seek to interpose helps.

—Whenever a mind is simple, and receives a divine wisdom, old things pass away—means, teachers, texts, temples fall; it lives now, and absorbs past and future into the present hour. All things are made sacred by relation to it. When a man lives with God, his voice shall be as sweet as the murmur of the brooks and the rustle of the corn. The soul raised over passion beholds identity and eternal causation, perceives the self-existence of Truth and Right, and calms itself with knowing that all things go well.

—Nothing can bring you peace but yourself. Nothing can bring you peace but the triumph of principles.

—Proverbs, like the sacred books of each nation, are the sanctuary of the intuitions.

—O my brothers, God exists. There is a soul at the center of Nature, and over the will of every man, so that none of us can wrong the universe.

—The way to speak and write what shall not go out of fashion is, to speak and write sincerely. A man passes for what he is worth. Very idle is all curiosity concerning other people's estimate of us, and all fear of remaining unknown is not less so. Never was a sincere word utterly lost. Never a magnanimity fell to the ground, but there is some heart to greet and accept it unexpectedly.

—This over-estimate of the possibilities of Paul and Pericles, this under-estimate of our own, comes from a neglect of the fact of an identical nature.

—The essence of friendship is entireness, a total magnanimity and trust. Every violation of truth is not only a sort of suicide in the liar, but is a stab at the health of human society. Trust men and they will be true to you; treat them greatly, and they will show themselves great, though they make an exception in your favor to all their rules of trade. I see not any road of perfect peace which a man can walk, but after the counsel of his own bosom.

—As there is no screen or ceiling between our heads and the infinite heavens, so is there no bar or wall in the soul where man, the effect, ceases, and God, the cause, begins. We lie open on one side to the deeps of spiritual nature, to the attributes of God.

—Some thoughts always find us young, and keep us so. Such a thought is the love of the universal and eternal beauty. With each divine impulse the mind rends the thin rinds of the visible and finite, and comes out into eternity, and inspires and expires its air. The heart which abandons itself to the Supreme Mind finds itself related to all its works, and will travel a royal road to particular knowledges and powers. Ineffable is the union of man and God in every act of the soul.

—All goes to show that the soul in man is not an organ, but animates and exercises all the organs; is not a function like the power of memory, of calculation, of compassion, but uses these as hands and feet; is not a faculty, but a light; is not the intellect or the will, but master of the intellect and the will; is the background of our being in which they lie—an immensity not possessed, and that cannot be expressed.

—Let man then learn the revelation of all nature and all thought to his heart; this, namely: that the Highest dwells with him; that the sources of nature are in his own mind, if the sentiment of duty is there. But if he would know what the great God speaketh, he must "go into his closet and shut the door," as Jesus said. God will not make himself manifest to cowards. He must greatly listen to himself, withdrawing himself from all the accents of other men's devotion. Even their prayers are hurtful to him, until he has made his own. Our religion vulgarly stands on numbers of believers. Whenever the appeal is made—no matter how indirectly—to numbers, proclamation is then and there made that religion is not. He that finds God a sweet enveloping thought to him never counts his company. When I sit in that presence, who shall dare to come in? When I rest in perfect humility, when I burn with pure love, what can Calvin or Swedenborg say?

—But the idea which now begins to agitate society has a wider scope than our daily employments, our households, and the institutions of property. We are to revise the whole of our social structure, the State, the school, religion, marriage, trade, science, and explore their foundation in our own nature. What is man born for but to be a Reformer, a Re-maker of what man has made; a renouncer of lies; a restorer of truth and good, imitating that great Nature which embosoms us all, and which sleeps no moment on an old past, but every hour repairs herself, yielding us every morning a new day, and with every pulsation a new life? Let him remove everything which is not true to him. * * * * *

But there will dawn erelong on our politics, on our modes of living, a nobler morning in the sentiment of love. Our age and history for these thousand years has not been the history of kindness, but of selfishness. Our distrust is very expensive. The money spent for courts and prisons is ill laid out. We make, by distrust, the thief and burglar, and incendiary, and by our court and jail we keep him so. An acceptance of the sentiment of love throughout Christendom for a season, would bring the felon and the outcast to our side in tears, with the devotion of his faculties to our service. See this wide society of laboring men and women. We allow ourselves to be served by them, we live apart from them, and meet them on the street without a salute. We do not greet their talents, nor rejoice in their good fortune, nor foster their hopes, nor in the assembly of the people vote for what is dear to them. Thus we enact the part of the selfish noble and king from the world's foundation. See, this tree always bears one fruit. In every household, the peace of a pair is poisoned by the malice, shyness, insolence, and alienation of the domestics. * * * Let our affections flow out to our fellows; it would operate in a day the greatest of all revolutions. The State must consider the poor man, and all voices must speak for him. Every child born must have a just chance (with work) for his bread. Let the amelioration in our laws of property proceed from the concession of the rich, not from the grasping of the poor. Let us begin by habitual imparting. Let me feel that I am to be a lover. I am to see to it that the world is the better for me, and to find my reward in the act.

A. J. Davis,—Teachings.

—Be contented with the Past, and with all it has brought you.

Be thankful for the Present, and for all you have.

Be patient and hopeful for the Future, and for all it promises to bring you.

It may cause many conflicts and efforts, but *resolve that from this moment you will live harmoniously.* Every day will strengthen your resolution. Live thus and every morning the spirit will feel new and pure as an infant.

—The science, the chemistry and mechanism of Divine Creation are represented in the human form; and the holy elements and attributes of God are incarnated in every human spirit. To be like heaven let us aspire to heaven; to be like God let us aspire to God. Harmony must begin with the individual; it will thence spread over families, societies and nations; and then the whole will represent the individual, and the individual the whole; and God will be ALL IN ALL.

—Disease is a want of equilibrium in the circulation of the spiritual principle through the physical organization. In plainer language, disease is discord; and this discord or derangement must exist *primarily* in the spiritual forces by which the organization is actuated and governed.

—Popular theology or education are insufficient to supply the spirit with its proper nourishment or encouragement to an easy and natural progression. Theology is inadequate to the reconstruction of society; and popular education, which is saturated with this theology, is inadequate to the proper direction and education of the spirit. It requires but little time to learn what is *useful*, what is *just*, and *what is pure*;—and Beauty, Aspiration and Harmony are familiarly explained in the fields of universal Nature and Humanity. To understand what harmony is, the spirit must become harmonious. A harmonious individual is a revelation of the Divine Mind.

—The philosophy of death is the philosophy of change; not of change in the personality of the individual, but of change in the *situation* of the human Spiritual Principle; which, instead of being situated in an earthly body, is placed in a spiritual organization; and instead of living among the objects and personalities of the planet on which the spirit was born, its situation is so altered as to fit it to live amidst more beauteous forms and in higher societies. * * Believe not that what is called death is a final termination of human existence, nor that the *change* is so thorough and entire as to alter or destroy the constitutional peculiarities of the individual; but believe righteously that death causes as much *alteration* in the condition of the individual as the *bursting* of a rose-bud causes in the situation and condition of the flower. Death is therefore only an *event, a circumstance,* in the eternal life and experience of the human soul. As the death of the *germ* is necessary to the birth and development of the *flower*, so is the *death* of man's physical body an indispensable precedent and indication of his spiritual *birth* or resurrection. * * Night and sleep correspond to physical death; but the brilliant day and human wakefulness correspond to spiritual birth and individual elevation.

—If the soul is faithful to Nature and her principles, there can and will be no limits to its health, happiness, and power to work the sublimest miracles. The faithful spirit is God-like in its every manifestation. Such a mind is capable of interpreting the multifarious phenomena of Nature; and through the instrumentality of eternal principles, its attributes can be unfolded even to the perception of gorgeous spheres, radiant with purity, beauty and peacefulness. If one is true to Nature (which is being true to himself and to the Divine Mind) he can improve the condition of his neighbor, and heal persons of many apparently incurable maladies. Let us all aspire to this glorious state of spiritual exaltation! The remedial agents of Nature are: Dress, Food, Water, Air, Light, Electricity and Magnetism.

—A child is the repository of infinite possibilities. Enfolded in the human infant is the beautiful "image" of the imperishable and perfect human being. In the baby constitution we recognize the holy plans of Divine Goodness—the immortal impartations of Divine Wisdom—the image and likeness of the Supreme Spirit—the possibilities of the greatest manhood, womanhood and angelhood. The human mind is the most richly endowed. Its sphere of influence and action is the broadest. It is empowered to hold dominion over time, events, things, and circumstances. It draws its life unceasingly from the divine life of Nature. It feeds on the phenomena of truth. It aspires intuitively after perfection. It rises to the sphere of individuality and freedom. It includes all the laws and conditions of growth, variety, genius, renewal, progress, and completeness.

—"Man is the measure of all things," said Protagoras, one of the Greek sophists; "and as men differ there can be no absolute truth." "Man *is* the measure of all things," replied Socrates, the true philosopher; "but descend deeper into his personality, and you will find that underneath all varieties there is a ground of *steady truth.* Men differ, but men also agree; they differ as to what is fleeting; they agree as to what is eternal. Agreement is the region of truth; let us endeavor to penetrate that region."

—Harmonial spirit-culture is the noblest work of the sciences. The divine image is *within.* It is the end of true education to develop that image, and so truly too that the child's individuality and constitutional type of mind shall not be impaired, but revealed in its fulness and personal perfection. "Be ye perfect even as your Father in Heaven is perfect," is an injunction of sublimest import. Every faculty and function of the individual is amenable to that heavenly principle. Everything has a glory of *its own.* The highest aim of education is to reveal the life and *form* of that individual perfection which Divine Wisdom has implanted in the human spirit, and different minds demand different methods.

—What do you believe? I believe that all mankind are the children of God and Nature; that discord is the cause of all unhappiness; that harmony is heaven; that there is no death to the soul and spirit; that sins are not forgiven, but outgrown through repentance and a righteous life.

Who are nearest heaven?

They who have healthy bodies and harmonious minds.

What is the light of world?

Eternal Truth which cannot be destroyed, or hidden.

What are the most beautiful forms of Truth?

Good works.

Who shall be called great, in the Summer Land?

He who loves truth in his deepest heart, and exemplifies it in his relations to the world.

To whom shall the temple of Harmony be opened?

To those who lovingly knock at the door of Wisdom.

What is sin?

Sin is a name for excess—the blunder of man in his development, a ditch into which, when blinded by ignorance or passion, we stumble for a season.

What are man's highest attractions?

His best and highest attractions take their rise in the superior parts of the brain—the wisdom-region—from the organs of benevolence, veneration, conscientiousness, firmness, hope, and ideality and marvelousness.

What is forbidden by the law of beauty?

All physical habits which impair the most agreeable proportions of form or feature; and especially, mental dispositions that deface the richer beauty with which the Father hath adorned the inner life.

What is true religion?

True religion is universal Justice—which begins at the center of the individual and widens outwardly, wave-like as the ocean swells—predicating thus the happiness of all upon the harmony of each.

What are the sacraments of this religion?

First, personal cleanliness and chastity; second, a heart full of warm devotional love to man and Deity; third, a head full of serene, strong, steady wisdom; fourth, reverence for the marriage relation; fifth, the regeneration of the world as far as possible through little children; sixth, and every humanitary institution.

What are the sacraments of the New Dispensation?

First, the immortality of the spirits of all men; second, the immediate resurrection of the soul (retaining the shape of the body) at death into a purer progressive world; third, the enjoyment of intercourse with the departed through several mediations.

What is prayer?

The spontaneous act of filial love; the soul's involuntary yearning for perpetual aid; an intuitive acknowledgment to the Supernal for the fact of existence; a desire for additional benefits and continued happiness.

What is the legitimate effect or prayer?

The effect of too much reliance on the invisible for aid is to beget weak-mindedness and unfitness for any great work; no man can accomplish much who doubts his personal capabilities and shrinks individual responsibility.

But the normal effect of prayer is two-fold—first, to open and prepare the soul for spiritual influx and illumination,—second, to attract a portion of the angel-world into harmony with our interior necessities.

True spirit-prayer, like the glory of the morning dew, ascends noiselessly. The answer, *that* comes, welcome as the fall of rain, when the soul most needs nutrition.

What is fidelity?

The integrity of your soul to itself, obedience to the angel of God within.

What is infidelity?

The wilful violation of that within you, which you believe to be Truth, Justice, and Righteousness.

Who is the most successful man?

He who seeth the secret victory that ever dwelleth within any defeat of an honest effort.

Who is the mightiest man?

He who can, at all times and amid all circumstances, control the impulses of Love by the voice of Wisdom.

Who is the greatest philanthropist?

He who does good to some and harm to none.

Who is the most holy man?

He who never acts contrary to his highest perceptions of right.

Who is the best husband?

He who, when you examine him by your highest attractions, hath the purest spirit and the cleanest body.

Who is the best wife?

She who, when you examine her by the intuitions of your highest temperament, is the sweetest girl, the truest friend, the gentlest sister, the most attractive woman.

What is man?

A product of all the universe. Physiologically—of all orders and properties of matter; psychologically—of all essences and properties of mind.

What shall be done with a system of sectarian religion which promulgates despotic doctrines or dogmas?

The declarations of Science must be denounced; Reason must be silenced; Experience, on its bended knees, must confess to lies; Truth must conform; Virtue be vilified; Justice denied; and man's whole nature must bow in obedience to the dictates of arbitrary authority. The authority of opinion must be imposed on the plastic mind of youth; pressed, regardless of all healthy resistance, into its very substance! He grows to manhood shackled in bondage. He cannot think. He worships, not the Truth, but *the Authority;* he is therefore a bigot and a slave.

Should a man guard his individualism against the authority of Institutions?

Certainly: Does it profit to sell the soul for popularity? What is there in the world more valuable than manhood or womanhood? The world answers, "Nothing!" And yet behold the universal distrusting and crucifying of the individual! Before the gods man bows, yielding adoration to mythological idols—to his own dishonor and degradation.

—Association, progression, development, are everywhere the processes by which matter is moulded into all forms, from the granite rock to the wondrous body of man.

—Everything is designed to subserve the vast and boundless laboratory of the All-wise and great Positive Mind; and immutable laws operate upon a divine and universal system of cause, effect, and end.

God said, "Let us make man:"

And then USE, the first attribute of wisdom, said: Man shall be a culmination of universal Nature; so organized in his body as to receive and elaborate the animating elements of nature into an eternal soul; and his soul, being constituted of those principles which are pure, everlasting, and infinite, shall possess and obey the tendency to unfold and progress forever.

And Justice, the second attribute of wisdom, said: Man shall occupy such position in the universe as will secure to all things, organized or unorganized, visible or invisible, a permanent equilibrium of power, possessions and demands.

And Power, the third attribute of wisdom, said: Man shall be created through the mediums and instrumentalities of countless suns and planets, and through the regular development of minerals, animals and vegetables; each of which shall correspond to, represent, and embody some particular portion of his organism.

And Beauty, the fourth attribute of wisdom, said: Man shall represent and embrace all suns and planets, all minerals and vegetables; and the energy, strength, symmetry, and structural beauty of all animals, in his form, organs, and functions.

And Aspiration, the fifth attribute of wisdom, said: Man shall know himself to be immortal, he shall be the king, the crown, the coronation of Nature; he shall aspire to be an Angel, a Seraph, a God.

And Harmony, sixth and highest attribute of wisdom, said: Man shall be an embodiment of the Great Spirit who creates him; he shall represent, in a finite degree, the elements and attributes of the Infinite; he shall desire, and be capable of, and shall enjoy the most ineffable blessedness; he shall aspire after harmony, shall unfold it, and shall give his eternal existence to its maintenance; he shall be an embodiment of Nature, a revelation of Harmony, and an image of God.

Such is deeply impressed on my spirit as the far shadow of the Divine plans.

—The intention of Nature, everywhere manifest, is the perfection of Man.

—All the processes of nature combined to produce Man as an ultimate; all were essential for this intent and result.

—The central idea and inspiration of the Harmonial Philosophy is PERFECT LOVE OF ALL WISDOM. Wisdom is the highest comprehension and embodiment of all scientific, philosophical, spiritual and celestial principles or ideas, which are eternal and universal; knowledge pertains to facts, things, events and external experiences.

—Ideas being universal, the Fraternity of Ideas runs like a golden thread, through all religions, and therein they agree. Thoughts and prejudices being personal, local, and limited, make the clash of conflicting creeds, and feed the passions of bigots.

TEACHINGS AND INSPIRATIONS FROM MANY SOURCES.

The law of marriage is universal.—BRAHM.
The end of human life is righteousness.—BUDDHA.
The character of God is a unit.—MOSES.
All evil will be overcome by good.—ZOROASTER.
Charity is fraternal justice.—CONFUCIUS.
The origin of harmony is Divinity.—PYTHAGORAS.
Goodness is the only happiness.—SOCRATES.
All things have a spiritual origin.—PLATO.
Health is temperance in all things.—EPICURUS.
Internal purity is the cause of Charity.—JESUS.
All truth is consistent and harmonious.—ORIGEN.
Every man's faith is a sovereign power.—LUTHER.
God is Almighty and will prevail.—CALVIN.
God is present in every human spirit.—FOX.
The law of correspondence is universal.—SWEDENBORG.
All men are missionaries.—WESLEY.

God is both Father and Mother.—ANN LEE.

The love of God is impartial.—JOHN MURRAY.

Man is capable of eternal improvement.—CHANNING.

Human nature is relatively perfect.—PARKER.

Self-reliance is obedience to God.—EMERSON.

The right to liberty is inherent and universal.—GARRISON.

Every person is naturally immortal.—SPIRITUALISM.

The love of all wisdom is man's integral aspiration.—HARMONIAL PHILOSOPHY.—*A. J. Davis.*

LOVE AND GOOD WORKS THE LIFE OF HEAVEN.

But the crowning excellence of this celestial sphere, and which distinguishes the souls of the just from the dark spirits below—and marks the difference between our visions of the heavens and all revelations hitherto—is the high, paramount prominence which is awarded to the great love-element of universal charity. Here we find no loud eternity of idle harping and perpetual song; no cruel transports of unpitying delight over the ever-ascending smoke of a brother's torment; no dreamless slumber of an everlasting repose; no drowsy revelings in the lotus-dreams of an eternal voluptuousness; no heaven of beatific sensualism, where, bright and beautiful, ten thousand houris minister to the royal pleasure of a single hero—hero no longer in his luxurious abode; no airy Valhalla, where the ghosts of warriors drink the foaming mead, and clash their resounding arms in day-long wassailing and the fabled tales of heroes; though all these images are humanely acceptable, as types of the ever-acknowledged fact that souls in heaven are intrinsically and essentially what they are on earth, only perfecting there the ideal of all excellence here.

Moreover, our new heaven infringes not on the domain of any other heaven. Ours is that vast unclaimed—the heart's unexplored realm of generous work—of work that blesses others and delights the doer. The inhabitants of that beautiful domain are souls that keep their warm love and the blessed sympathies which made them so beautiful on earth—higher, and deeper, and broader there, making them still more beautiful. No heart could retain its best and loveliest element in a home of delight from which it knew a fellow-heart was excluded; and to be ignorant of a brother's fate were a loss, and to souls of a higher order, an impossibility. I pray that I may not forget erring and wandering souls in the brightest hour that ever dawns upon my spirit.

The revelations of these last years show us how to reconcile the beatified soul's completeness with the fact of souls in gloom and misery. In bringing the wanderer back to light, in breathing hope and cheer into hearts yet repining in their clay, in pouring promise down the dark abysses of despair and pain—in this work the souls of the redeemed find their best delight, and deeds of mercy *make* the heaven they people with all renovated lives.

Have you not seen how a most beautiful face grows more intensely beautiful with deep thought? How even conquered suffering, and the soul's hard-earned victory over loss, desolation, and woe, can make the calm eye like a spirit's, and the pale cheek radiant with more than earthly physical beauty? With a far more prevailing power, the soul in light shapes the obedient features of its vesture, the spirit-body which encumbers it not. Every sweet thought is a line of beauty to the form. Every noble impulse shapes the dilated figure to a grander expression of its strength, beauty, and grace.

This beautiful life speaks no fear, no crouching vassalage of soul, but a deep, natural, filial love, that so involves and permeates all the being, that existence with them can be nothing less than "worship"—an expression meaning naught else but high aspiration and unceasing praise to the all-loving Father. They do his work on earth, and in the nether spheres; and this is joy, this is life; this is the immortal heaven of souls who have gone up from suffering to delight. And in the joy of their great ransom, knowing how grateful is unexpected kindness, how inexpressibly dear is guardian love, they can never forget from whence they came, nor the pained struggling souls that lift their eyes to the blank heaven with such hushed agony of mute beseeching, where, thanks to the new light, they find the heavens no longer brass over their heads. They come ! the beautiful ones, the shining angels, in their love and light !

Oh ! beautiful upon the mountains are their feet, as they come laden with glad tidings. The mourner, though he sees not their transparent glory, hears not the mellow music of their love-breathing voices, nor even feels the quiet presence hallowing the spot, and the tender touch that smooths the throbbing head, yet feels that the hot tear has been swept away—the heart's strained pulses softened to a gentler flow—and blessed glimpses of a clearer faith come in upon the night of his grief. O look to these realms of light and love, when care, and pain, and doubt, make life a weariness. Let not dark unbelief put away the promise of "the light" which comes only to bless.—*Charlotte B. Wilbour.*

Birth to the Higher Life—as seen Clairvoyantly.

Death is but a door which opens into a new and more perfect existence, and there is really nothing more painful or repulsive in the *natural* process of dying (that not induced by disease or accident) than in passing into a quiet, dreamless slumber. The truthfulness of this is illustrated and confirmed by the observation and investigation into the physiological and psychological phenomena of death, which my spirit was qualified to make at the moment of the physical dissolution of a personal friend.

She was a woman about sixty years of age, who had consulted me as a physician eight months before her death. When the hour arrived, being an inmate of her house, I was fortunately in a proper state of mind and body to induce the Superior Condition, and previously sought a position where I might make my observations unnoticed and undisturbed. They were these :

I saw that the physical organization could no longer subserve the many purposes and requirements of the Spiritual Principle. But the various internal organs of the body appeared to *resist* the withdrawal of the animating soul. The muscular system struggled to retain the element of Motion; the vascular system strove to retain the element of Life; the nervous system put forth all its power to retain the element of Sensation; and the cerebral system labored to retain the principle of Intelligence. The body and soul, like two friends, resisted the circumstances which made their eternal separation imperative. These internal conflicts gave rise to manifestations of what seemed, to the material senses, to be most painful and thrilling sensations; but I was unspeakably thankful when I perceived and realized the fact that those physical manifestations were indications, *not of pain or unhappiness*, but simply that the Spirit was dissolving its partnership with the material organism.

Now the head of the dying person became suddenly enveloped in a fine, soft, mellow, luminous atmosphere; and as instantly, I saw the cerebrum and cerebellum expand their most interior portions; I saw them discontinue their appropriate galvanic functions; and then I saw that they became highly charged with the vital electricity and vital magnetism which permeate subordinate structures and systems. That is to say, the brain, as a whole, suddenly declared itself to be tenfold more positive over the lesser portions of the body than it ever was in health. This invariably precedes physical dissolution.

Now the process of dying, or the spirit's departure from the body, was fully commenced. The brain began to attract the elements of electricity, magnetism, motion, life, and sensation, into its various and numerous departments. The head became intensely brilliant; and I remarked that just in proportion as the extremities of the body grew dark and cold, the brain appeared light and glowing.

Now I saw, in the mellow spiritual atmosphere, which emanated from and encircled her head, the indistinct outlines of the *formation* of another head! *The reader should remem-*

ber that these super-sensuous processes are not visible to any one, except the spiritual perceptions be unfolded; for material eyes can only behold material things, and spiritual eyes can only behold spiritual things. This is a law of Nature. This new head unfolded more and more distinctly; and so indescribably compact and intensely brilliant did it become, that I could neither see through it, nor gaze upon it as steadily as I desired. While this spiritual head was being eliminated and organized from out of and above the material head, I saw that the surrounding aromal atmosphere, which had emanated from the material head, was in great commotion; but, as the new head became more distinct and perfect, this brilliant atmosphere gradually disappeared. This taught me that those aromal elements, which were, in the beginning of the metamorphosis, attracted from the system into the brain, and thence eliminated in the form of an atmosphere, were indissolubly united, in accordance with the divine principle of affinity in the universe, which pervades and destinates every particle of matter, and that they developed the spiritual head which I beheld.

With inexpressible wonder, and a heavenly reverence, I gazed on these holy processes. In the same manner in which the spiritual head was eliminated and unchangeably organized, I saw unfolding in their natural progressive order, the harmonious development of the neck, the shoulders, and the entire spiritual organization. It appeared from this that the innumerable particles of what might be called unparticled matter, which constitute a man's spiritual principle, are constitutionally endowed with certain elective affinities, analogous to an immortal friendship. The innate tendencies which the elements and essences of her soul manifested, by uniting and organizing themselves, were the efficient and imminent causes which unfolded and perfected her spiritual organization. The defects and deformities of the physical body were almost removed in this spiritual body. In other words, it seemed that those hereditary obstructions and influences, which had arrested the full and proper development of her physical constitution, were now removed; and therefore, that her spiritual constitution, being elevated above those obstructions, was enabled to unfold and perfect itself, in accordance with the universal tendencies of all created things.

While this spiritual formation was going on, perfectly visible to my spiritual perceptions, the material body manifested, to the outer vision of her friends around her bed, many symptoms of uneasiness and pain; but they were wholly caused by the departure of vital or spiritual forces from the extremities and the viscera into the brain, and thence into the ascending organism.

The spirit rose at right angles over the head of the deserted body. But immediately previous to the final dissolution of the relationship which had so long existed between the two, I saw, playing between the feet of the elevated spiritual body and the head of the prostrate physical form, a bright stream or current of vital electricity. This taught me that what is termed *Death* is but a *Birth* of the spirit from a lower to a higher state; that an inferior body and mode of existence are exchanged for a superior body and corresponding endowments and capabilities of happiness. I learned that the correspondence between the birth of a child into this world, and the birth of a spirit into the higher world, is absolute and complete, even to the *umbilical cord*, represented by the thread of vital electricity, which, for a few minutes, subsisted between and connected the two organisms. And here I saw that a small portion of this vital electrical element returned to the deserted body, just before the separation of this thread, and instantly diffused itself through the entire structure, to prevent an immediate decomposition.

As soon as the spirit, whose departing hour I thus watched, was disengaged from the tenacious physical body, I directed my attention to the movements and emotions of the former; and I saw her begin to breathe the most interior or spiritual portions of the surrounding terrestrial atmosphere, which at first was done with difficulty, but soon with ease and delight.

And I now saw that she was beautified, yet in every particular with those proportions which characterized her earthly organism; so that had her friends beheld her (as I did) they would have exclaimed, "How well you look!"

I did not particularly notice the emotions of her fast unfolding spirit, except to remark her philosophic tranquility, and her non-participation with the members of her family present, in their bewailing of her departure, to unfold in Love and Wisdom. She understood at a glance that they could only look upon the cold and lifeless form which she had just deserted; and she comprehended the fact that it was owing to want of true knowledge, that they thus vehemently regretted her physical death.

The period of this change was about two hours or more, but this varies in different cases. Becoming accustomed to her new situation, she descended from her position over the body, and, by an effort of her will-power, passed out of the open door of the bedroom. It being summer the open doors offered no obstruction, and I saw her pass out from the house into the atmosphere! To my delight and surprise I saw her walk in the atmosphere, as we tread the earth, which all spiritual organizations can do.

Immediately she was joined by two friendly spirits from the spiritual country; and after tender recognition, the three gracefully ascended obliquely through the air. I gazed upon them until distance shut them from my view, and returned to my external and ordinary condition.—*A. J. Davis.*

APPENDIX.

APPENDIX A.

The word Veda means knowing or knowledge in the original Sanscrit, the sacred language of the Hindoos. Max Muller, with others, considers the Rig-Veda as the oldest, and indeed the original from whence the others were chiefly derived. The Yagur-Veda, the Sama-Veda, and the Atharva-Veda, are mostly liturgies or hymns for sacrificial occasions. Rig, or Rich, is from a Sanscrit root meaning to celebrate, and the ten books of the Rig-Veda contain about a thousand hymns, and for at least 2,500 years their verses and words have been carefully counted and memorized in the schools of the Brahmins, and countless commentaries have been written upon them.

The first Ashtaka, or book, of the Rig-Veda has been translated by H. H. Wilson, F. R. S., &c, an eminent English scholar and resident in India, and his work is published in London, under the patronage of the Directors of the East India Company. Max Muller, Professor in Oxford University, and eminent in character and learning, has published a part of his translation. Rev. J. Stevenson, D. D., of London, has published, under the auspices of the Oriental Translation Fund, his translation of a part of the Sama-Veda, made after a residence in India. From these sources, and from the Progress of Religious Ideas by Mrs. L. M. Child, I have made my extracts. The hymn to Agni, page 9, and the two following, are from Wilson; for the rest from the Rig Veda, I have used Muller, except as parts thereof may be with other Vedas, from Mrs. Child's valuable work. Harug, Rosen, Burnouf, and others, have rendered valuable aid by research and translation, and the work of Muller now in progress will give us the fullest translation of these ancient books.

Dr. Harug, an eminent authority, dates the Vedic period in which these books were composed and collected, at from 1,200 to 2,400 B. C., and the oldest hymns of the Rig Veda at 2,400 B. C. Muller says we cannot well assign a later date than from 1,200 to 1500 B. C., supposes that writing was unknown at the date of the oldest hymns, and calls the Rig Veda "most venerable of Books."

Brahmins trace back the Vedas 4,000 years, and Sir William Jones dates them about 1,580 B. C., or more than a century before Moses.

The Code or Institutes of Menu, or Manu, dates probably from 900 to 1,200 B. C.

Of course, there can be no exactness in such remote dates, but the opinion of the best authorities leaves little doubt that the Rig Veda is the oldest of all Sacred Books. It is the Bible of Brahminism, and Muller says that India "is saturated with the idea of revelation;" although there is a wide departure from the simple purity of these old Vedic teachings.

The Vedas know no idols, and teach a consciousness of sin which the divine powers can remove, if repentance be real, and prayer and sacrifice be observed. Personal immortality is taught in some of the hymns. The transmigration of souls would seem a later idea of Brahminism. The great sacrifice of the juice of the Soma, or moon-plant, is the occasion for many of the Vedic hymns. The idea of One God is taught. Rig Veda, hymn 164, says: "They call Him Indra, Mithra, Varuna, Agni; that which is One the wise call it in divers names."

Sometimes each of these is called the God. The thought of a Great Soul and Cause seems present, yet mingled with a personification of Nature's attributes and powers; Indra is sunlight; Agni fire, and messenger; Varuna is day; Ushas dawn; Murats Storms, &c. Rakshakas are evil spirits, Rishis saints, and sometimes spirits of the departed. Of later date are

Shasters, Puranas, Brahmanas, and many other works, in which are gradually brought out the strange mythology mingled with the great truths of Brahminism; such for instance as the following from the *Ramayana:* "The sacrifice of a thousand horses has been put in the balance with the true word, and that one true word weighed down the balance. No virtue surpasses veracity. It is by truth alone that men attain to the highest realms of bliss. There are two roads that conduct to perfect virtue; to be true, and to do no evil to any creature."

Father Bouchet, a Catholic missionary in Hindostan, found the Trinity and the incarnation of the second person thereof taught there. Brahm, the Infinite, was manifest through Brahma and Vishnu, the preserving powers, and Siva the destroyer, in Brahminical teachings, and Whittier has well interpreted their idea:

"For wisely taught the Hindoo seer,
Destroying Siva, forming Brahm,
Who woke by turns earth's love and fear,
Were one, the same."

Incarnations of Vishnu were a part of their belief.

The BHAGVAT GEETA, or Dialogues between Kreeshna, or Chrishna, an incarnation of Deity, and his disciple Arjoun, is dated by Sir William Jones at 3,000 B. C.

This is probably too ancient a date, but the fact that only the three oldest books of the Vedas are mentioned in it would indicate a high antiquity.

I have used the translation of Charles Wilkins, A. D. 1785. He was an Englishman in the employ of the East India Company, and a letter of endorsement of his ability and character, and of the excellence of his work, from the well-known Governor of India, Warren Hastings, is in the preface of the volume before me.

J. C. Gangooly, an educated Hindoo, a convert to Unitarianism, who visited this country some years ago, giving the Hindoo belief as to signs and wonders that attended the birth of Chrishna, said that he was born in prison, and that: "In the presence of the heavenly babe the fetters that bound the prison broke; the cell began to dazzle, and joy overwhelmed the parents. A heavenly voice whispered to the father to fly with the child beyond the Jumna, which was done. The tyrant who sought to destroy the child sent messengers to kill the children in neighboring places." The similarity between this and other like traditions, and the New Testament narrative of Christ's lowly birth, and Herod's slaughter of the innocents, is noteworthy.

The remarkable extracts from the Bhagvat Geeta need no comment or illustration.

APPENDIX B.

Buddha is a title, meaning "The Enlightened." Buddhists teach that there have been several Buddhas, and may be more; men who become such by pure and true lives and high effort and endowment. Buddha, the great reformer, from whose influence Buddhism grew, was the son of a Prince, and was born at Kapilwarta, capital of his father's kingdom, at the foot of the Nepaul mountains, near the end of the Seventh Century before Christ.

A Siamese Life of Buddha says: "The Great, the Holy Lord, the Being who was about to become Buddha, passed the first twenty-nine years of his life as a layman by the name of Prince Sidharta (one who has attained his aim). He then became a religious mendicant, and for six years subjected himself to self-denials of a nature that other men could not endure. Thereafter he became the Lord Buddha, and gave to men and angels the draught of Immortality, which is the savor of the True Law. Forty-five years after this he entered the Holy Nirwana." He was also called Gautama, from the clan or tribe to which the family belonged. M. Barthelemy St. Hilaire gives 543 B. C. as the date of his death, and he lived about eighty years. Renouncing his princely station and wealth, he went out as a preacher of The Word for more than forty years, and by his singular beauty and purity of life, and his spiritual insight and large abilities, wrought a vast change amidst the great power of Brahminism. Buddhism to-day counts some 300,000,000 disciples (or more than Christianity), spread over Hindostan, Ceylon, Thibet, Burmah and China, and it is a proof of the power of this form of religion that it abolished caste wherever it spread in Brahminical countries.

With the Brahmins the Infinite was everything, and man, and this life, nothing in comparison. Buddhism reacted against this, and elevates righteousness in this life, and makes much of man and Nature.

Buddha reached to Atheism in his purely metaphysical statements, and sometimes towards nihilism or extinction of soul and being; yet in some of his writings, immortality, reward and punishment therein, and of course, eternal law, were clearly taught.

Nirwana, or Nirvana, of which frequent mention is made in Buddhist works, strictly translated, means annihilation, yet he did not teach that, and as Max Muller says: "If we consider that Buddha himself, after he had already seen Nirwana, still remains on earth and is a prey to death, that in the legends Buddha appears to his disciples after his death, it seems to me that all these circumstances are hardly reconcilable with the orthodox metaphysical doctrine of Nirwana."

Nirwana would seem an elevated state, only possible to the pure and true, above all perturbation of passion or fear or anxiety.

The extracts from the "Dammaphada," said to be the teachings of Buddha himself, and certainly full of spiritual insight and power, must speak for themselves. This work was recognized by the great Council of Asoka, 243 B. C., as being by Buddha. We have made use of three works for information and quotation: "A Catena of Buddhist Scriptures, from the Chinese," by S. Beal; "The Wheel of the Law," by Henry

Alabaster; "Buddhagosha's Parables," by Capt. T. Rogers, with a translation of the Dammaphada therein by Max Muller. The original language from which these ancient Buddhist writings are translated is called the Pali.

All these works are by English gentlemen, officers of the Government, and residents in Asia, and are published by Trubner & Co., London, England.

"The Modern Buddhist," I find in "The Wheel of the Law," and also a Life of Buddha translated from the Siamese. To give some idea of the narrations of wonderful events connected with his appearance on earth, I extract the incidents of his birth. The story of the marriage of his mother, Queen Maia, to the Prince Suddhodana, is told in glowing and beautiful Oriental language. The Queen, in a dream, was told of the *immaculate conception* of her child, and informed her husband, when, the Life continues:

"The king rejoiced exceedingly, and gave orders that all care might be taken of his queen; that wherever she might be, sleeping or waking, she might be surrounded by that which was pure, melodious, harmonious, refined, elegant, and simple.

"And the forty thousand guardian angels of the ten thousand worlds watched around her with perfect delicacy. Never were they seen when she desired privacy, but at all other times she saw them guarding her day and night, and she saw them without fear.

"From this time no sensual desire ever disturbed her thoughts. She steadfastly obeyed, as she had done from her youth up, the Five Great Commandments, and abstained from all impurity, as the mothers of Buddhas ever have done. * * Going to visit her parents, the king had the road cleared and levelled, and made gay with flags and flowers, and jars of water were placed along it. A golden litter was provided for the queen, and an escort of a thousand noble ladies attended her.

"Between the cities of Kapila and Dewadaha, there was a forest of most beautiful trees, named Simwaliwana. Interlacing branches sheltered the traveler, as if with a canopy. The sun's scorching rays could not penetrate the delicious shade. From the trunks to the very tops of the trees flowers budded, bloomed, and shed their fragrant leaves, ever again budding and blooming. Attracted by their sweet pollen, flights of shining beetles buzzed around them, filling the air with melodious humming like the music of the heavens. Lotuses of all colors grew in the pools, their sweet scent wafted by gentle breezes. When the Queen Maia entered this forest the trees bowed before her, as if they would say, 'Enjoy yourself, O, Queen among us, ere you proceed on your journey!' And the queen, looking on the forest lovely as the garden of the angels, ordered her litter to be stayed, that she might descend and walk.

"Then, standing under one of the majestic trees, she desired to pluck a twig from the branches, and they bent themselves down that she might reach what she desired; and at that moment her labor came upon her. Her attendants held curtains around her; the angels brought garments of the most exquisite softness; and standing there, holding the branch, she brought forth her son, without pain or any of the circumstances which usually attend that event."

This gives a glimpse of the wonderful stories told of Buddha, which he never sanctioned or authorized, but which have clustered around his memory.

In the Notes to this Life is the Pali narration of his death, at the close of forty-five years of meditation, penance, travel and preaching.

"Hastening, as much as his malady permitted, to the city of Kusinagaru, attended by Anunda and his disciples, he gave some further instruction on various points, including the ceremonials of cremation. Reclining between two lofty sala trees, in the garden of the Malla Princes, close to Kusinagaru, he spoke his last words: 'Transitory things are perishable; qualify yourselves (for the imperishable)!' Absorbed in ecstatic meditation (Dhyana) he remained until the third watch of the night and then expired.

"Then was there a great earthquake, and the pious who had

not yet the perfection of saints wept aloud with uplifted arms; they sunk on the earth, they reeled about, exclaiming: 'Too soon has the blessed one expired, too soon has the eye closed on the world.' But those more advanced in religion calmly submitted themselves, saying: 'Transitory things are perishable; in this world there is no permanence.'"

APPENDIX C.

Confucius was born 551 B. C., at Shang-ping, near the town of Tseuse, in the little kingdom of Lu. His name was Kong, called Kong-fu-tse by his disciples, which the Jesuits Latinized into Confucius. Kong is master or teacher. His father died when he was three years old, and he was carefully brought up by his mother, Yan she, at whose death he passed three years in mourning and solitary study, thereby no doubt prepared for his great work. He taught pure ethics, was a Theist, believed in immortality, and his aim in life was *perfect* virtue. His "Seven Steps" are simple: the investigation of things; the completion of knowledge; the sincerity of thought; the rectifying of the heart; the cultivation of the person; the regulation of the family; the government of the State. His system of education was superior to that of any nation in his day. He held important public offices, and had many followers among the thoughtful and influential, but his eminent purity was too far above the realm of public life, and his last days were passed in retirement and comparative poverty.

He passed away at the age of seventy-three years, and his ideas bear sway to-day among a large number of the more cultivated Chinese.

Mencius was born 371 B. C. He was learned, noble, and pure in life, was the child of a mother of remarkable character, who is held up to-day as a model of motherhood, and his education was under her care, owing to the early death of his father.

I follow the translation of Rev. James Legge, D. D., of the London Missionary Society, in my extracts from both.

APPENDIX D.

Zoroaster, it is supposed, lived between 560 and 700 B. C., yet Dollinger fixes an earlier date, and with Rupp gives 1200 to 1300 B. C.

Some suppose two Zoroasters. He was a prince, or of high birth. The Zendavesta is probably made up of fragments of different works, partly by Zoroaster, and the Gathas, or songs, are its oldest parts, considered by Dr. Haug as dating back to Moses' time, or 1480 B. C. It is the sacred and infallible book of the Persians. The Zend language is probably a dialect of the Sanscrit, yet scholars are not agreed on this.

I use Mrs. Child's work, an article in the *Radical*, by C. D. B. Mills, of Syracuse, and Ross Winans' "One Religion, Many Creeds," for my authorities.

APPENDIX E.

The author of the Divine Pymander, or Poemander, is spoken of by Lord Bacon as of kingly power, priestly illumination, and profound wisdom—"*Potestate regis, illuminatione sacerdotis, eruditione philosophiae!*" I use Dr. Everard's translation, made in England, A. D. 1650. The preface says the work has been published in Arabic, Greek, Latin, French and Dutch. Hermes Mercurius Trismegistus was a king of Egypt. Probabilities put him with the Pharaohs before Moses, yet this is disputed by some. This remarkable work is held authentic by eminent authorities.

APPENDIX F.

Marcus Aurelius Antonius was Emperor of Rome, A. D. 121.

Epictetus was a native of Hieropolis, a city of Phrygia, and was a slave in Rome to Epaphroditus, a courtier of Nero, about A. D. 65. He was made free and died old and poor, ever cheerful and kind to all.

Seneca was of Spanish birth, came to Rome with his father in the reign of Augustus Cæsar, and rose to eminence, but suffered for his liberal opinions.

All three, especially the two last, were of the Stoic Philosophers.

I use the translations in Bohn's Classical Library.

www.ingramcontent.com/pod-product-compliance
Lightning Source LLC
LaVergne TN
LVHW020108110826
845151LV00001B/96

* 9 7 8 1 4 2 5 5 4 3 8 1 5 *